THE ANCIENT SOUTH ASIAN == WORLD ==

TEACHING GUIDE

OXFORD
UNIVERSITY PRESS

Oxford University Press, Inc., publishes works that
further Oxford University's objective of excellence
in research, scholarship, and education.

Oxford   New York
Auckland   Cape Town   Dar es Salaam   Hong Kong   Karachi
Kuala Lumpur   Madrid   Melbourne   Mexico City   Nairobi
New Delhi   Shanghai   Taipei   Toronto

With offices in
Argentina   Austria   Brazil   Chile   Czech Republic   France   Greece
Guatemala   Hungary   Italy   Japan   Poland   Portugal   Singapore
South Korea   Switzerland   Thailand   Turkey   Ukraine   Vietnam

Copyright © 2005 by Oxford University Press, Inc.

Published by Oxford University Press, Inc.
198 Madison Avenue, New York, NY, 10016
www.oup.com

Oxford is a registered trademark of Oxford University Press
All rights reserved. No part of this publication may be reproduced,
stored in a retrieval system, or transmitted in any form or by any means,
electronic, mechanical, photocopying, recording, or otherwise,
without the prior permission of Oxford University Press.

Writer: Kimberley Heuston
Editor: Robert Weisser
Project Editor: Lelia Mander
Project Director: Jacqueline A. Ball
Education Consultant: Diane L. Brooks, Ed.D.
Design: designlabnyc

Casper Grathwohl, Publisher

ISBN-13: 978-0-19-522288-3 (California Edition)   ISBN-13: 978-0-19-517901-9

Printed in the United States
on acid-free paper

CONTENTS

Note to the Teacher   5

The World in Ancient Times Program   6
    Using the Teaching Guide and Student Study Guide

Improving Literacy with *The World in Ancient Times*   16

Teaching Strategies for *The Ancient South Asian World*

    Unit 1   Origins of South Asian Civilization
                (Introduction, Chapters 1–3)   20

    Unit 2   The Cities of the Indus (Chapters 4–7)   36

    Unit 3   Expansion and Decline (Chapters 8–10)   56

    Unit 4   The Vedic Era (Chapters 11–14)   72

    Unit 5   War and Empire (Chapters 15–18)   92

    Unit 6   The Andean World (Chapters 14–16)   112

    Unit 7   Life in Ancient South Asia (Chapters 19–21)   128

Wrap-Up Test   140

Graphic Organizers   141

Rubrics   149

Answer Key   153

HISTORY FROM OXFORD UNIVERSITY PRESS

"A thoroughly researched political and cultural history... makes for a solid resource for any collection."
— School Library Journal

THE WORLD IN ANCIENT TIMES
RONALD MELLOR AND AMANDA H. PODANY, EDS.
THE EARLY HUMAN WORLD
THE ANCIENT NEAR EASTERN WORLD
THE ANCIENT EGYPTIAN WORLD
THE ANCIENT SOUTH ASIAN WORLD
THE ANCIENT CHINESE WORLD
THE ANCIENT GREEK WORLD
THE ANCIENT ROMAN WORLD
THE ANCIENT AMERICAN WORLD

"Bringing history out of the Dark Ages!"

THE MEDIEVAL AND EARLY MODERN WORLD
BONNIE G. SMITH, ED.
THE EUROPEAN WORLD, 400-1450
THE AFRICAN AND MIDDLE EASTERN WORLD, 600-1500
THE ASIAN WORLD, 600-1500
AN AGE OF EMPIRES, 1200-1750
AN AGE OF VOYAGES, 1350-1600
AN AGE OF SCIENCE AND REVOLUTIONS, 1600-1800

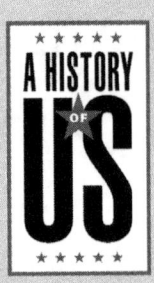

"The liveliest, most realistic, most well-received American history series ever written for children."
— Los Angeles Times

A HISTORY OF US
JOY HAKIM
THE FIRST AMERICANS
MAKING THIRTEEEN COLONIES
FROM COLONIES TO COUNTRY
THE NEW NATION
LIBERTY FOR ALL?
WAR, TERRIBLE WAR
RECONSTRUCTING AMERICA
AN AGE OF EXTREMES
WAR, PEACE, AND ALL THAT JAZZ
ALL THE PEOPLE

FOR MORE INFORMATION, VISIT US AT WWW.OUP.COM

New from Oxford University Press
Reading History, by Janet Allen
ISBN 0-19-516595-0 hc 0-19-516596-9 pb

"*Reading History* is a great idea. I highly recommend this book."
–Dennis Denenberg, *Professor of Elementary and Early Childhood Education, Millersville University*

NOTE TO THE TEACHER

Dear Educator

You probably love history. You read historical novels, watch documentaries, and enjoy (and, as a history teacher, no doubt criticize) Hollywood's attempts to recreate the past. So why don't most kids love history too? We think it might be because of the tone of the history books they are assigned. Many textbook authors seem to assume that the sole goal of teaching history is to make sure the students memorize innumerable facts. So, innumerable facts are crammed onto the pages, facts without context, as thrilling to read as names in a phone book.

Real history, however, is not just facts; it's the story of real people who cared deeply about the events and controversies of their times. And learning real history is essential. It helps children to understand the events that brought the world to where they find it now. It helps them distrust stereotypes of other cultures. It helps them read critically. (It also helps them succeed in standardized assessments of their reading skills.) We, like you, find history positively addictive. Students can feel the same way. (Can you imagine a child reading a history book with a flashlight after lights out, just because it is so interesting?)

The World in Ancient Times books reveal ancient history to be a great story—a whole bunch of great stories—some of which have been known for centuries, but some of which are just being discovered. Each book in the series is written by a team of two writers: a scholar who is working in the field of ancient history and knows what is new and exciting, and a well-known children's book author who knows how to communicate these ideas to kids. The teams have come up with books that are historically accurate and up to date as well as beautifully written. They also feature magnificent illustrations of real artifacts, archaeological sites, and works of art, along with maps and timelines to allow readers to get a sense of where events are set in place and time. Etymologies from the *Oxford English Dictionary,* noted in the margins, help to expand students' vocabulary by identifying the ancient roots, along with the meanings, of English words.

The authors of our books use vivid language to describe what we know and to present the evidence for *how* we know what we know. We let the readers puzzle right along with the historians and archaeologists. The evidence comes in the form of primary sources, not only in the illustrations but especially in the documents written in ancient times, which are quoted extensively.

You can integrate these primary sources into lessons with your students. When they read a document or look at an artifact or building in the illustrations they can pose questions and make hypotheses about the culture it came from. Why was a king shown as much larger than his attendants in an Egyptian relief sculpture? Why was Pliny unsure about what to do with accused Christians in his letter to the emperor? In this way, students can think like historians.

The series provides a complete narrative for a yearlong course on ancient history. You might choose to have your students read all eight narrative books as they learn about each of the civilizations in turn (or fewer than eight, depending on the ancient civilizations covered in your school's curriculum). Or you might choose to highlight certain chapters in each of the books, and use the others for extended activities or research projects. Since each chapter is written to stand on its own, the students will not be confused if you don't assign all of them. The *Primary Sources and Reference Volume* provides longer primary sources than are available in the other books, allowing students to make their own interpretations and comparisons across cultures.

The ancient world was the stage on which many institutions that we think of as modern were first played out: law, cities, legitimate government, technology, and so on. The major world religions all had their origins long ago, before 600 CE, as did many of the great cities of the world. *The World in Ancient Times* presents this ancient past in a new way—new not just to young adults, but to any audience. The scholarship is top-notch and the telling will catch you up in the thrill of exploration and discovery.

Amanda H. Podany and Ronald Mellor
General Editors, *The World in Ancient Times*

THE WORLD IN ANCIENT TIMES PROGRAM

I. STUDENT EDITION

- Engaging, friendly narrative
- A wide range of primary sources in every chapter
- The authority of Oxford scholarship
- Period illustrations and specially commissioned maps

II. TEACHING GUIDE

- Wide range of activities and classroom approaches
- Strategies for universal access and improving literacy (ELL, struggling readers, advanced learners)
- Multiple assessment tools

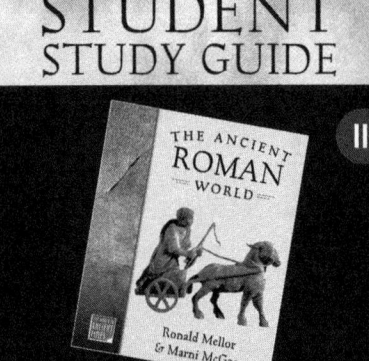

III. STUDENT STUDY GUIDE

- Exercises correlated to Student Edition and Teaching Guide
- Portfolio approach
- Activities for every level of learning
- Literacy through reading and writing

PRIMARY SOURCES AND REFERENCE VOLUME

- Broad selection of primary sources in each subject area
- Ideal resource for in-class exercises and unit projects

TEACHING GUIDE: **KEY FEATURES**

The Teaching Guides organize each *The World in Ancient Times* book into units, usually of three or four chapters each. The chapters in each unit cover a key span of time or have a common theme, such as a civilization's origins, government, religion, economy, and daily life.

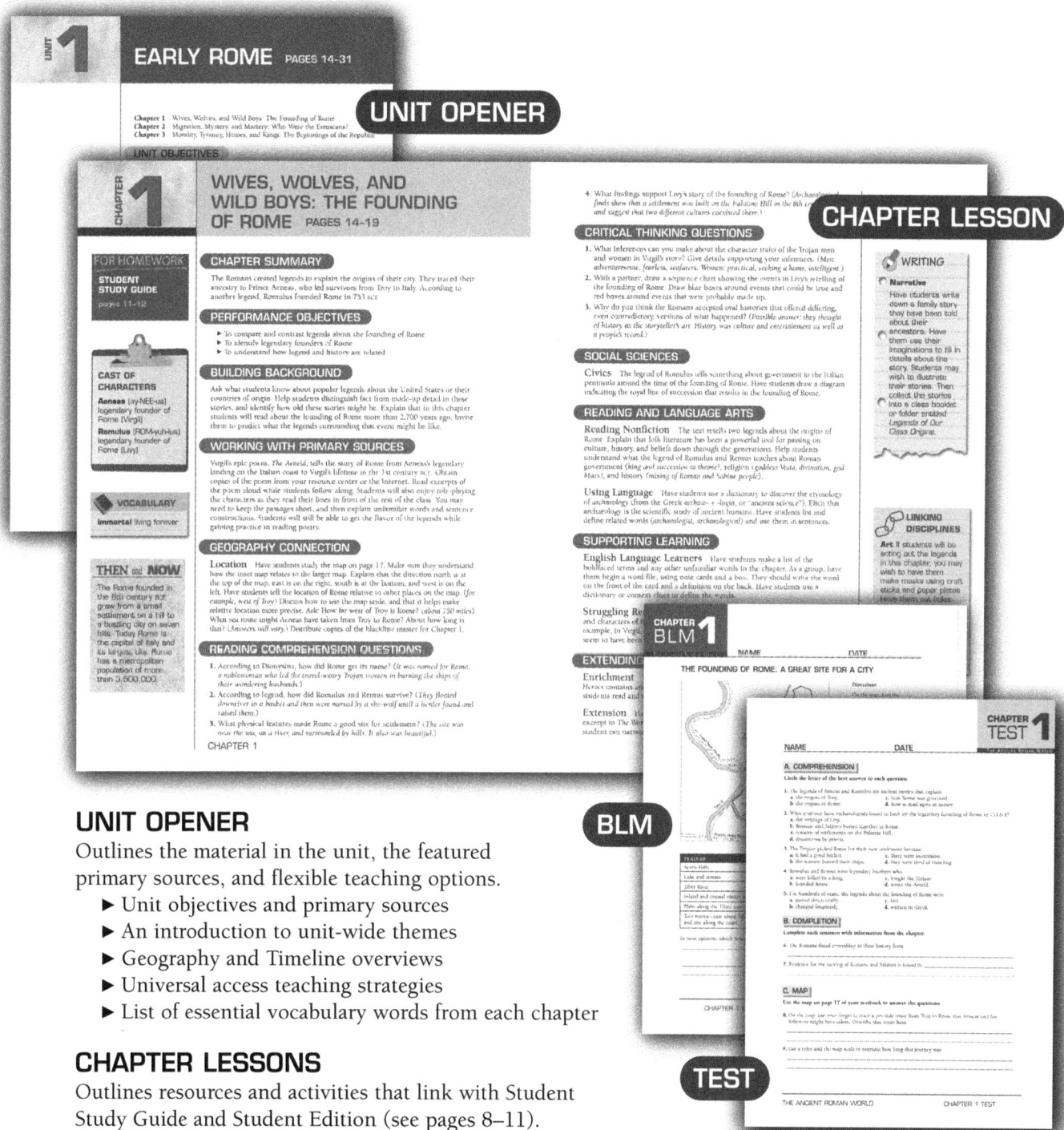

UNIT OPENER
Outlines the material in the unit, the featured primary sources, and flexible teaching options.
- Unit objectives and primary sources
- An introduction to unit-wide themes
- Geography and Timeline overviews
- Universal access teaching strategies
- List of essential vocabulary words from each chapter

CHAPTER LESSONS
Outlines resources and activities that link with Student Study Guide and Student Edition (see pages 8–11).

TESTS AND BLACKLINE MASTERS (BLMS)
Reproducible tests and exercises for assessment, homework, or classroom projects

7

TEACHING GUIDE: CHAPTER LESSONS

Organized so that you can easily find the information you need.

CHAPTER SUMMARY AND PERFORMANCE OBJECTIVES
The Chapter Summary gives an overview of the information in the chapter. The Performance Objectives are the three or four important goals students should achieve in the chapter. Accomplishing these goals will help students master the information in the book.

BUILDING BACKGROUND
This section connects students to the chapter they are about to read. Students may be asked to use what they know to make predictions about the text, preview the images in the chapter, or connect modern life with the ancient subject matter.

WORKING WITH PRIMARY SOURCES
A major feature of *The World in Ancient Times* is having students read about history through the words and images of the people who lived it. Each book includes excerpts from the best sources from these ancient civilizations, giving the narrative an immediacy that is difficult to match in secondary sources. Students can read further in these sources on their own or in small groups using the accompanying *The World in Ancient Times Primary Sources and Reference Volume*. The Teaching Guide recommends activities so students of all skill levels can appreciate the ways people from the past saw themselves, their ideas and values, and their fears and dreams.

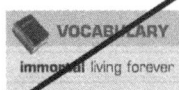

GEOGRAPHY CONNECTION
Each chapter has a Geography Connection to strengthen students' map skills as well as their understanding of how geography affects human civilization. One of the five themes of geography (Location, Interaction, Movement, Place, and Regions) is highlighted in each chapter. Map skills such as reading physical, political, and historical maps; using latitude and longitude to find locations; and using the features of a map (mileage scale, legend) are taught throughout the book and reinforced in blackline masters.

8

READING COMPREHENSION AND CRITICAL THINKING QUESTIONS

The reading comprehension questions are general enough to allow free-flowing class or small group discussion, yet specific enough to be used for oral or written assessment of students' grasp of the important information. The critical thinking questions are intended to engage students in a deeper analysis of the text and can also be used for oral or written assessment.

SOCIAL SCIENCES ACTIVITIES

Students can use these activities to connect the subject matter in the Student Edition with other areas in the social sciences: economics, civics, and science, technology, and society.

READING AND LANGUAGE ARTS

These activities serve a twofold purpose: Some are designed to facilitate the development of nonfiction reading strategies. Others can be used to help students' appreciation of fiction and poetry, as well as nonfiction, by dealing with concepts such as word choice, description, and figurative language.

SUPPORTING LEARNING AND EXTENDING LEARNING

Each chapter gives suggestions for students of varying abilities and learning styles; for example, advanced learners, below-level readers, auditory/visual/tactile learners, and English language learners. These may be individual, partner, or group activities, and may or may not require your ongoing supervision.
(For more on Supporting or Extending Learning sections, see pages 16–19.)

---

4. What findings support Livy's story of the founding of Rome? (*Archaeological finds show that a settlement was built on the Palatine Hill in the 8th century BCE and suggest that two different cultures coexisted there.*)

CRITICAL THINKING QUESTIONS

1. What inferences can you make about the character traits of the Trojan men and women in Virgil's story? Give details supporting your inferences. (*Men: adventuresome, fearless, seafarers. Women: practical, seeking a home, intelligent.*)
2. With a partner, draw a sequence chart showing the events in Livy's retelling of the founding of Rome. Draw blue boxes around events that could be true and red boxes around events that were probably made up.
3. Why do you think the Romans accepted oral histories that offered differing, even contradictory, versions of what happened? (*Possible answer: they thought of history as the storyteller's art. History was culture and entertainment as well as a people's record.*)

SOCIAL SCIENCES

Civics The legend of Romulus tells something about government in the Italian peninsula around the time of the founding of Rome. Have students draw a diagram indicating the royal line of succession that results in the founding of Rome.

READING AND LANGUAGE ARTS

Reading Nonfiction The text retells two legends about the origins of Rome. Explain that folk literature has been a powerful tool for passing on culture, history, and beliefs down through the generations. Help students understand what the legend of Romulus and Remus teaches about Roman government (*king and succession to throne*), religion (*goddess Vesta, divination, god Mars*), and history (*mixing of Roman and Sabine people*).

Using Language Have students use a dictionary to discover the etymology of *archaeology* (from the Greek *archaio-* + *-logia*, or "ancient science"). Elicit that archaeology is the scientific study of ancient humans. Have students list and define related words (*archaeologist, archaeological*) and use them in sentences.

SUPPORTING LEARNING

English Language Learners Have students make a list of the boldfaced terms and any other unfamiliar words in the chapter. As a group, have them begin a word file, using note cards and a box. They should write the word on the front of the card and a definition on the back. Have students use a dictionary or context clues to define the words.

Struggling Readers Have students make a chart comparing the events and characters of the two legends. Then help students draw conclusions: for example, in Virgil, the founders of Rome came from Troy; in Livy, the founders seem to have been living in Italy already.

EXTENDING LEARNING

Enrichment Edith Hamilton's book *Mythology: Timeless Tales of Gods and Heroes* contains another myth about the founding of Rome by Aeneas. Have students read and summarize this myth for the class.

Extension Have student groups act out scenes from *The Aeneid*, from the excerpt in *The World in Ancient Times Primary Sources and Reference Volume*. One student can narrate while the others take the parts of the characters involved.

THE ANCIENT ROMAN WORLD

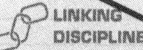

WRITING

Narrative Have students write down a family story they have been told about their ancestors. Have them use their imaginations to fill in details about the story. Students may wish to illustrate their stories. Then collect the stories into a class booklet or folder entitled *Legends of Our Class Origins*.

LINKING DISCIPLINES

Art If students will be acting out the legends in this chapter, you may wish to have them make masks using craft sticks and paper plates. Have them cut holes for eyes and mouth. They can model their characters' features after the pictures of Roman men and women in Chapters 1–3.

TEACHING GUIDE: CHAPTER SIDEBARS

Icons quickly help to identify key concepts, facts, activities, and assessment activities in the sidebars.

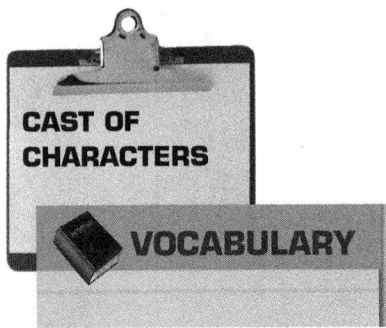

▶ Cast of Characters/Vocabulary
These sidebars point out and identify bolded, curriculum-specific vocabulary words and significant personalities in the chapter. Pronunciation guides are included where necessary. Additional important vocabulary words are listed in each unit opener.

▶ Writing
Each chapter has a suggestion for a specific writing assignment. You can make these assignments as you see fit—to help students meet state requirements in writing as well as to help individual students improve their skills. Areas of writing covered include the following:

Description	Personal writing (journal/diary)
Narration	News article (print and electronic)
Explanation	Dialogue
Persuasion	Interview
Composition	Poetry

▶ Then and Now
This feature provides interesting facts and ideas about the ancient civilization and relates it to the modern world. This may be an aspect of government that we still use today, word origins of common modern expressions, physical reminders of the past that are still evident, and other features. You can use this item simply to promote interest in the subject matter or as a springboard to other research.

▶ Linking Disciplines
This feature offers opportunities to investigate other subject areas that relate to the material in the Student Edition: math, science, arts, and health. Specific areas of these subjects are emphasized: **Math** (arithmetic, algebra, geometry, data, statistics); **Science** (life science, earth science, physical science); **Arts** (music, arts, dance, drama, architecture); **Health** (personal health, world health).

▶ For Homework
A quick glance links you to additional activities in the Student Study Guide that can be assigned as homework.

ASSESSMENT

The World in Ancient Times program intentionally omits from the Student Edition the kinds of section, chapter, and unit questions that are used to review and assess learning in standard textbooks. It is the purpose of the series to engage readers in learning—and loving—history written as good literature. Rather than interrupting student reading, and enjoyment, all assessment instruments for the series have been placed in the Teaching Guides.

▶ **CHAPTER TESTS**
A reproducible chapter test follows each chapter in this Teaching Guide. These tests will help you assess students' mastery of the content standards addressed in each chapter. These tests measure a variety of cognitive and analytical skills, particularly comprehension, critical thinking, and expository writing, through multiple choice, short answer, and essay questions.
An answer key for the chapter tests is provided at the end of the Teaching Guide.

▶ **WRAP-UP TEST**
After the last chapter test you will find a wrap-up test consisting of 10 essay questions that evaluate students' ability to synthesize and express what they've learned about the ancient civilization under study.

▶ **RUBRICS**
The rubrics at the back of this Teaching Guide will help you assess students' written work, oral presentations, and group projects. They include a Scoring Rubric, based on the California State Public School standards for good writing and effective cooperative learning. In addition, a simplified hand-out is provided, plus a form for evaluating group projects and a Library/Media Center Research Log to help students focus and evaluate their research. Students can also evaluate their own work using these rubrics.

▶ **BLACKLINE MASTERS (BLMs)**
A blackline master follows each chapter in the Teaching Guide. These BLMs are reproducible pages for you to use as in-class activities or homework exercises. They can also be used for assessment as needed.

▶ **ADDITIONAL ASSESSMENT ACTIVITIES**
Each unit opener includes suggestions for using one or more unit projects for assessment. These points, and the rubrics provided, will help you evaluate how your students are progressing towards meeting the unit objectives.

USING THE STUDENT STUDY GUIDE FOR ASSESSMENT

▶ Study Guide Activities
Assignments in the Student Study Guide correspond with those in the Teaching Guide. If needed, these Student Study Guide activities can be used for assessment.

▶ Portfolio Approach
Student Study Guide pages can be removed from the workbook and turned in for grading. When the pages are returned, they can be part of the students' individual history journals. Have students keep a 3-ring binder portfolio of Study Guide pages, alongside writing projects and other activities.

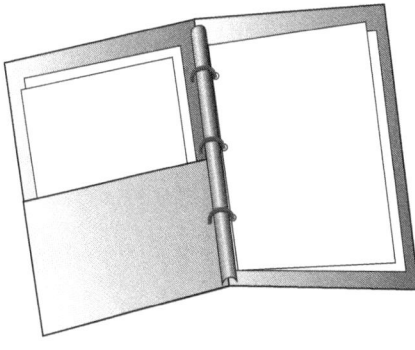

STUDENT STUDY GUIDE: KEY FEATURES

The Student Study Guide works as both standalone instructional material and as a support to the Student Edition and this Teaching Guide. Certain activities encourage informal small-group or family participation. These features make it an effective teaching tool:

Flexibility

You can use the Study Guide in the classroom, with individuals or small groups, or send it home for homework. You can distribute the entire guide to students; however, the pages are perforated so you can remove and distribute only the pertinent lessons.

A page on reports and special projects in the front of the Study Guide directs students to the Further Reading resource in the student edition. This feature gives students general guidance on doing research and devising independent study projects of their own.

FACSIMILE SPREAD
The Study Guide begins with a facsimile spread from the Student Edition. This spread gives reading strategies and highlights key features: captions, primary sources, sidebars, headings, etymologies. The spread supplies the contextualization students need to fully understand the material.

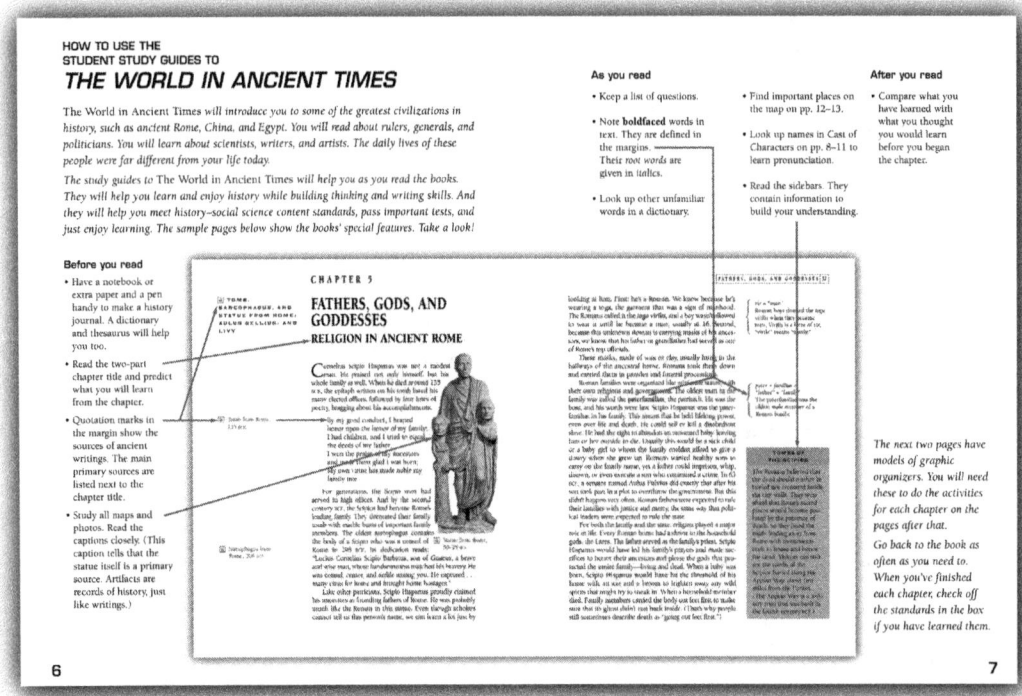

Portfolio Approach

The Study Guide pages are three-hole-punched so they can be integrated with notebook paper in a looseleaf binder. This history journal or portfolio can become both a record of content mastery and an outlet for each student's unique creative expression. Responding to prompts, students can write poetry or songs, plays and character sketches, create storyboards or cartoons, or construct multi-layered timelines.

The portfolio approach gives students unlimited opportunities for practice in areas that need strengthening. Students cam share their journals and compare their work. And the Study Guide pages in the portfolio make a valuable assessment tool for you. It is an ongoing record of performance that can be reviewed and graded periodically.

> **GRAPHIC ORGANIZERS**
> This feature contains reduced models of seven graphic organizers referenced frequently in the guide. Using these devices will help students organize the material so it is meaningful to them. (Full-size reproducibles of each graphic organizer are provided at the back of this Teaching Guide.) These graphic organizers include: outline, main idea map, K-W-L chart (What I Know, What I Want to Know, What I Learned), Venn diagram, timeline, sequence of events chart, and T-chart.

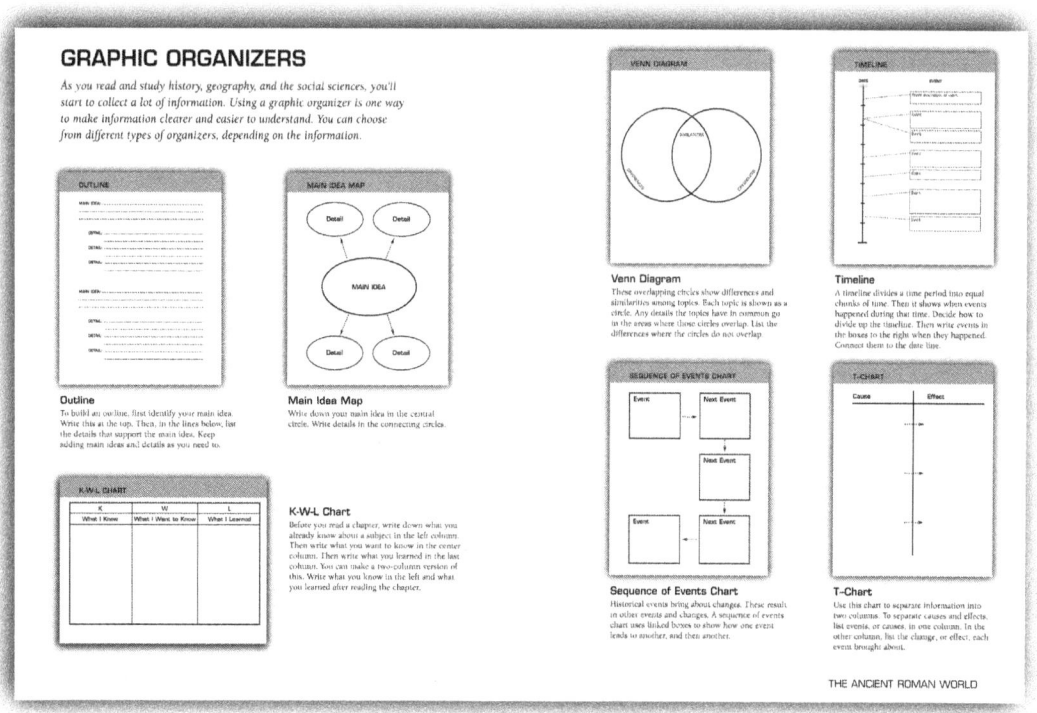

STUDENT STUDY GUIDE: **CHAPTER LESSONS**

Each chapter lesson is designed to draw students into the subject matter. Recurring features and exercises challenge their knowledge and allow them to practice valuable analysis skills. Activities in the Teaching Guide and Student Study Guide complement but do not duplicate each other. Together they offer a wide range of class work, group projects, and opportunities for further study and assessment that can be tailored to all ability levels.

CHAPTER SUMMARY briefly reviews big ideas from the chapter.

ACCESS invites students into the content by building background, tapping prior knowledge, or visual note-taking.

ADDITIONAL VOCABULARY Additional vocabulary words important to accessing student book content are listed on page 10 of every Student Study Guide.

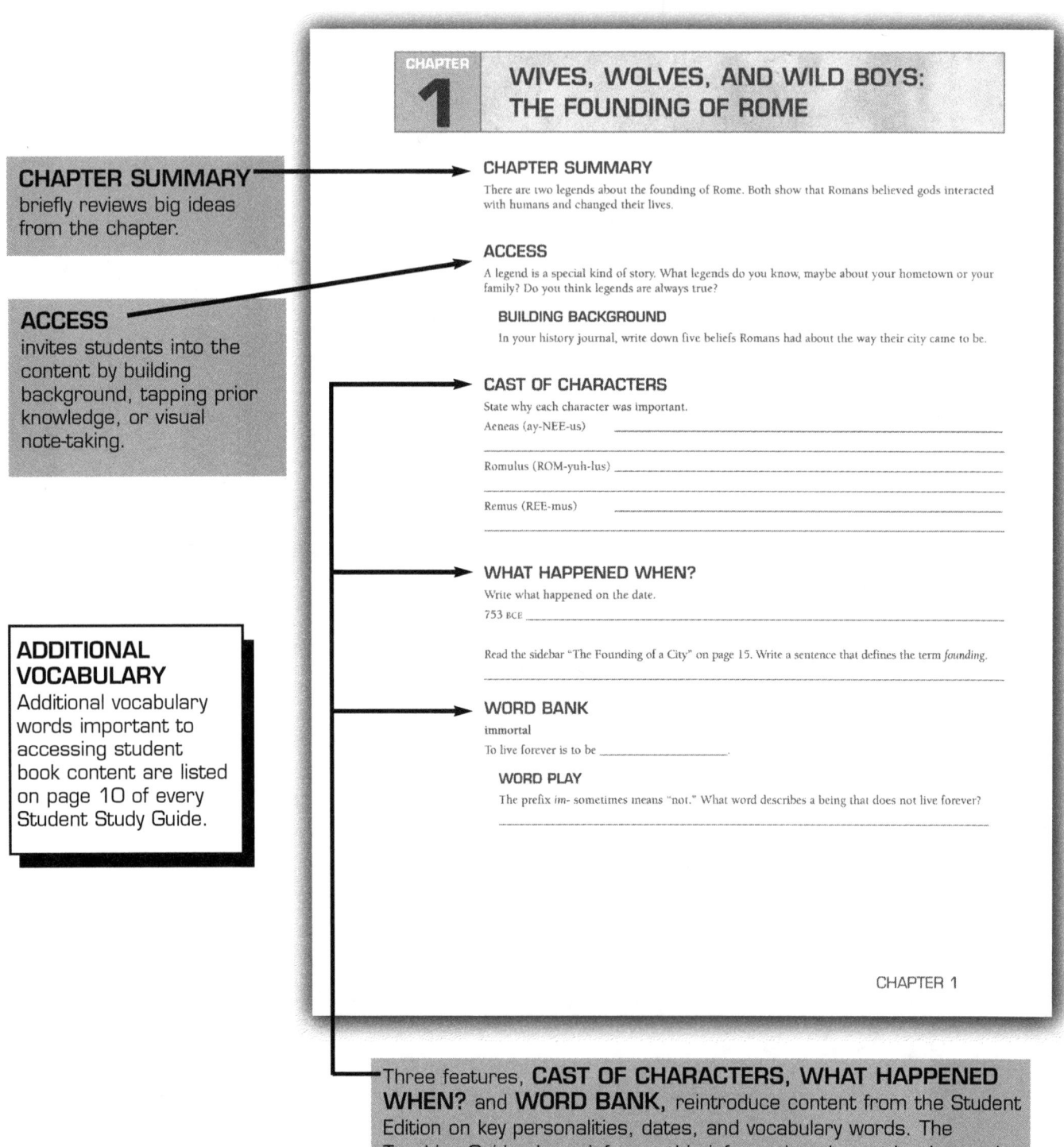

CHAPTER 1: WIVES, WOLVES, AND WILD BOYS: THE FOUNDING OF ROME

CHAPTER SUMMARY
There are two legends about the founding of Rome. Both show that Romans believed gods interacted with humans and changed their lives.

ACCESS
A legend is a special kind of story. What legends do you know, maybe about your hometown or your family? Do you think legends are always true?

BUILDING BACKGROUND
In your history journal, write down five beliefs Romans had about the way their city came to be.

CAST OF CHARACTERS
State why each character was important.
Aeneas (ay-NEE-us) _____
Romulus (ROM-yuh-lus) _____
Remus (REE-mus) _____

WHAT HAPPENED WHEN?
Write what happened on the date.
753 BCE _____

Read the sidebar "The Founding of a City" on page 15. Write a sentence that defines the term *founding*.

WORD BANK
immortal
To live forever is to be _____.

WORD PLAY
The prefix *im-* sometimes means "not." What word describes a being that does not live forever?

CHAPTER 1

Three features, **CAST OF CHARACTERS**, **WHAT HAPPENED WHEN?** and **WORD BANK**, reintroduce content from the Student Edition on key personalities, dates, and vocabulary words. The Teaching Guide also reinforces this information chapter-by-chapter in the VOCABULARY and CAST OF CHARACTERS sidebars.

CRITICAL THINKING
CAUSE AND EFFECT
Draw a line from each cause and connect it to the result, or effect. (There is one extra effect.)

CAUSE	EFFECT
1. Amulius feared he would be overthrown,	a. they floated down the river and were saved by a she-wolf.
2. Rhea Silvia broke her vows,	
3. A servant couldn't kill the babies,	b. the Romans and Sabines went to war.
4. Remus made fun of Romulus,	c. Romulus killed Remus.
5. Romulus's men kidnapped Sabine women,	d. Romans and Sabines called a truce.
6. The Sabine women ran onto the battlefield,	e. Romulus and Remus were born.
	f. he forced Rhea Silvia to join the Vestal Virgins.
	g. Remus killed Romulus.

WITH A PARENT OR PARTNER
When you have completed the chart, read aloud each cause-and-effect pairing to a parent or partner. Use the word "so" to connect each cause with each effect.

WRITE ABOUT IT
The Trojan women were *appalled* that Aeneas and the Trojan men were planning another journey after they reached the mouth of the Tiber River. To be *appalled* means to be

a) happy.
b) excited.
c) shocked.

Circle your answer.

In your history journal, write a short dialogue or a descriptive scene between the Trojan men and women about making this second journey. Why were the women appalled? How did the men respond?

WORKING WITH PRIMARY SOURCES
The image at left is an ancient Roman coin. It shows an image of a Roman god. Think about what we can learn about ancient cultures through artifacts like this one. Answer the following questions in your history journal.

1. Why do you think the figure is wearing an olive wreath?
2. Why would the Romans put a god on their coins?
3. What famous people do we use on coins today? (It's okay to take a peek at your pocket change!)
4. If people found your coins hundreds of years from now, what conclusions might they draw about your culture?
5. Think up a design for your own coin and draw it in your history journal.

THE ANCIENT ROMAN WORLD

CRITICAL THINKING exercises draw on such thinking skills as establishing cause and effect, making inferences, drawing conclusions, determining sequence of events, comparing and contrasting, identifying main ideas and details, and other analytical process.

WRITE ABOUT IT gives students writing suggestions drawn from the material. A writing assignment may stem from a vocabulary word, a historical event, or a reading of a primary source. The assignment can take any number of forms: newspaper article, letter, short essay, a scene with dialogue, a diary entry.

WORKING WITH PRIMARY SOURCES invites students to read primary sources closely. Exercises include answering comprehension questions, evaluating point of view, and writing and other forms of creative expression, including music, art, and design. "In Your Own Words" writing activities ask students to paraphrase a primary source.

IMPROVING LITERACY WITH THE WORLD IN ANCIENT TIMES

The books in this series are written in a lively, narrative style to inspire a love of reading history–social science. English language learners and struggling readers are given special consideration within the program's exercises and activities. And students who love to read and learn will also benefit from the program's rich and varied material. Following are strategies to make sure each and every student gets the most out of the subjects you will teach through *The World in Ancient Times*.

ENGLISH LANGUAGE LEARNERS

For English learners to achieve academic success, the instructional considerations for teachers include two mandates:

- Help them attain grade level, content area knowledge, and academic language.
- Provide for the development of English language proficiency.

To accomplish these goals, you should plan lessons that reflect the student's level of English proficiency. Students progress through five developmental levels as they increase in language proficiency:

Beginning and Early Intermediate *(grade level material will be mostly incomprehensible, students need a great deal of teacher support)*

Intermediate *(grade level work will be a challenge)*

Early Advanced and Advanced *(close to grade level reading and writing, students continue to need support)*

The books in this program are written at the intermediate level. However, you can still use the lesson plans for students of different levels by using the strategies below:

Tap Prior Knowledge
What students know about the topic will help determine your next steps for instruction. Using K-W-L charts, brainstorming, and making lists are ways to find out what they know. English learners bring a rich cultural diversity into the classroom. By sharing what they know, students can connect their knowledge and experiences to the course.

Set the Context
Use different tools to make new information understandable. These can be images, artifacts, maps, timelines, illustrations, charts, videos, or graphic organizers. Techniques such as role-playing and story-boarding can also be helpful. Speak in shorter sentences, with careful enunciation, expanded explanations, repetitions, and paraphrasing. Use fewer idiomatic expressions.

Show—Don't Just Tell
English learners often get lost as they listen to directions, explanations, lectures, and discussions. By showing students what is expected, you can help them participate more fully in classroom activities. Students need to be shown how to use the graphic organizers in this guide and the mini versions in the student study guide, as well as other blackline masters for note-taking and practice. An overhead transparency with whole or small groups is also effective.

Use the Text
Because of unfamiliar words, students will need help. Teach them to preview the chapter using text features (headings, bold print, sidebars, italics). See the suggestions in the facsimile of the Student Edition, shown on pages 6–7 of the Student Study Guide. Show students organizing structures such as cause and effect or comparing and contrasting. Have students read to each other in pairs. Encourage them to share their history journals with each other. Use Read Aloud/Think Aloud, perhaps with an overhead transparency. Help them create word banks, charts, and graphic organizers. Discuss the main idea after reading.

Check for Understanding
Rather than simply ask students if they understand, stop frequently and ask them to paraphrase or expand on what you just said. Such techniques will give you a much clearer assessment of their understanding.

Provide for Interaction
As students interact with the information and speak their thoughts, their content knowledge and academic language skills improve. Increase interaction in the classroom through cooperative learning, small group work, and partner share. By working and talking with others, students can practice asking and answering questions.

Use Appropriate Assessment
When modifying the instruction, you will also need to modify the assessment. Multiple choice, true and false, and other criterion reference tests are suitable, but consider changing test format and structure. English learners are constantly improving their language proficiency in their oral and written responses, but they are often grammatically incorrect. Remember to be thoughtful and fair about giving students credit for their content knowledge and use of academic language, even if their English isn't perfect.

STRUGGLING READERS

Some students struggle to understand the information presented in a textbook. The following strategies for content-area reading can help students improve their ability to make comparisons, sequence events, determine importance, summarize, evaluate, synthesize, analyze, and solve problems.

Build Knowledge of Genre
Both the fiction and narrative nonfiction genres are incorporated into *The World in Ancient Times*. This combination of genres makes the text interesting and engaging. But teachers must be sure students can identify and use the organizational structures of both genres.

Fiction	Nonfiction
Each chapter is a story	Content: historical information
Setting: historical time and place	Organizational structure: cause/effect, sequence of events, problem/solution
Characters: historical figures	Other features: maps, timelines, sidebars, photographs, primary sources
Plot: problems, roadblocks, and resolutions	

In addition, the textbook has a wealth of the text features of nonfiction: bold and italic print, sidebars, headings and subheadings, labels, captions, and "signal words" such as *first*, *next*, and *finally*. Teaching these organizational structures and text features is essential for struggling readers.

Build Background

Having background information about a topic makes reading about it so much easier. When students lack background information, teachers can preteach or "front load" concepts and vocabulary, using a variety of instructional techniques. Conduct a chapter or book walk, looking at titles, headings, and other text features to develop a big picture of the content. Focus on new vocabulary words during the "walk" and create a word bank with illustrations for future reference. Read aloud key passages and discuss the meaning. Focus on the timeline and maps to help students develop a sense of time and place. Show a video, go to a website, and have trade books and magazines on the topic available for student exploration.

Comprehension Strategies

While reading, successful readers are predicting, making connections, monitoring, visualizing, questioning, inferring, and summarizing. Struggling readers have a harder time with these "in the head" processes. The following strategies will help these students construct meaning from the text until they are able to do it on their own.

> **PREDICT:** Before reading, conduct a picture and text feature "tour" of the chapter to make predictions. Ask students if they remember if this has ever happened before, to predict what might happen this time.
>
> **MAKE CONNECTIONS:** Help students relate content to their background (text to text, text to self, and text to the world).
>
> **MONITOR AND CONFIRM:** Encourage students to stop reading when they come across an unknown word, phrase, or concept. In their notebooks, have them make a note of text they don't understand and ask for clarification or figure it out. While this activity slows down reading at first, it is effective in improving skills over time.
>
> **VISUALIZE:** Students benefit from imagining the events described in a story. Sketching scenes, story-boarding, role-playing, and looking for sensory details all help students with this strategy.
>
> **INFER:** Help students look beyond the literal meaning of a text to understand deeper meanings. Graphic organizers and discussions provide opportunities to broaden their understanding. Looking closely at the "why" of historical events helps students infer.
>
> **QUESTION AND DISCUSS:** Have students jot down their questions as they read, and then share them during discussions. Or have students come up with the type of questions they think a teacher would ask. Over time students will develop more complex inferential questions, which lead to group discussions. Questioning and discussing also helps students see ideas from multiple perspectives and draw conclusions, both critical skills for understanding history.

DETERMINE IMPORTANCE: Teach students how to decide what is most important from all the facts and details in nonfiction. After reading for an overall understanding, they can go back to highlight important ideas, words, and phrases. Clues for determining importance include bold or italic print, signal words, and other text features. A graphic organizer such as a main idea map also helps.

Teach and Practice Decoding Strategies

Rather than simply defining an unfamiliar word, teach struggling readers decoding strategies:

- Have them look at the prefix, suffix, and root to help figure out the new word.
- Look for words they know within the word.
- Use the context for clues, and read further or reread.

ADVANCED LEARNERS

Every classroom has students who finish the required assignments and then want additional challenges. Fortunately, the very nature of history and social science offers a wide range of opportunities for students to explore topics in greater depth. Encourage them to come up with their own ideas for an additional assignment. Determine the final product, its presentation, and a timeline for completion.

▶ **Research**

Students can develop in-depth understanding through seeking information, exploring ideas, asking and answering questions, making judgments, considering points of view, and evaluating actions and events. They will need access to a wide range of resource materials: the Internet, maps, encyclopedias, trade books, magazines, dictionaries, artifacts, newspapers, museum catalogues, brochures, and the library. See the Further Reading section at the end of the Student Edition for good jumping-off points.

▶ **Projects**

You can encourage students to capitalize on their strengths as learners (visual, verbal, kinesthetic, or musical) or to try a new way of responding. Students can prepare a debate or write a persuasive paper, play, skit, poem, song, dance, game, puzzle, or biography. They can create an alphabet book on the topic, film a video, do a book talk, or illustrate a book. They can render charts, graphs, or other visual representations. Allow for creativity and support students' thinking.

Cheryl A. Caldera, M.A.
Literacy Coach

ORIGINS OF SOUTH ASIAN CIVILIZATION

PAGES 14–34

Introduction	Beads in the Backyard
Chapter 1	Mountains and Monsoons: The Geography of South Asia
Chapter 2	Stone Serpents: Early Humans and Stone Age Cultures
Chapter 3	Farmers and Herders: Neolithic Times

UNIT OBJECTIVES

Unit 1 introduces students to the geography and prehistory of ancient South Asia to about 3300 BCE. In this unit your students will learn

- the geography and climate of the South Asian subcontinent, including the significance of the monsoon.
- the origins of the people we call South Asians.
- the archaeology of prehistoric South Asia.
- the characteristics of both Paleolithic and Neolithic life in South Asia.

PRIMARY SOURCES

Unit 1 includes excerpts from the following primary sources:

- Valmiki, *Ramayana*
- *Nilmata Purana*

Unit 1 also includes pictures of the following artifacts from earliest South Asian times, which can be analyzed as primary sources:

- Beads, Shorkot
- Bead pot
- Chalcedony and carnelian, Khambhat
- Bead-grinding stone, Chanhu Daro
- Beads, Chanhu Daro
- Hand axe, Kashmir
- Stone tool, Riwat, Pakistan
- Petroglyphs
- Stone sculpture of Naga serpent deity
- Bitumen-coated basket, Pakistan
- Sickle, Pakistan

BIG IDEAS IN UNIT 1

Ancient South Asia's **geography** and **archaeological record** are the big ideas presented in Unit 1. The unit presents the geologic processes that have resulted in the South Asian subcontinent, the rhythm of its seasons, and its considerable mineral wealth. It also introduces South Asia's earliest archaeological record and the theories archaeologists have constructed to explain it.

One way to introduce the special opportunities and challenges of prehistory is to ask students to reproduce what they did yesterday, a week ago, and three years ago. When students get to the limits of their knowledge, brainstorm strategies for reconstructing what happened. Ask: What if there were no records or people to consult? What if the society was nomadic, with no means of accumulating or storing goods? What evidence would you have to work with?

GEOGRAPHY CONNECTION

Introduce the notion of the South Asian subcontinent by considering its northern boundary, the Himalaya Mountains. Discuss the effects such a geographical boundary might have on South Asia's climate and people. One great source on the origin of the Himalayas can be found at *www.pbs.org/wgbh/nova/everest/earth/birth.html*.

TIMELINE

7000 BCE	Neolithic era; agriculture begins in the Indus Valley; people make stone beads and shell bangles in Mehrgarh
5500 BCE	Artisans make pottery and copper and bronze tools in Mehrgarh
3900 BCE	Stone beads and shell bangles used in Harappa
2600–1900 BCE	Heavy trade of beads, grain, wool, and animals in South Asia
1500–800 BCE	Large communities grow in north of region; black and deep-red glass beads created
600–500 BCE	Painted carnelian beads and prayer beads become popular
550–326 BCE	Glass beads from Mediterranean reach South Asia
550 BCE–200 CE	Crystal and amethyst beads traded to Greeks and Romans
1100 CE	Epic of *Nilmata Purana* written

UNIT PROJECTS

Drama

A group of students can create a skit of the summer trip to Mehrgarh and then the return in the fall. Have students practice their skit and present it to the rest of the class.

Chronology

Students can create a class timeline to show the sequence of events in this unit. The concentration should not necessarily be on dates, but rather on the cause-and-effect chain of events that makes up history. You may want to draw the timeline itself on poster board, then have students write specific dates and events on note cards and attach them in the appropriate places. Students can then copy the timelines into their notebooks for later review.

Artwork

Have students analyze and interpret some of the artwork they see in the unit, or artwork they find in other resources. Ask them to do additional research into petroglyphs, for example: how were these images made? What do archaeologists think the images mean? As part of their projects, students could draw their own petroglyphs, reflecting aspects of their lives. Suggest they add modern aspects to their artwork, such as a skateboard or BMX bike. Ask them to explain what they want the petroglyph to express about themselves.

Writing Myths

Discuss the characteristics of a myth. Read the myth about Satisaras and the Nagas in Chapter 2. Have students choose partners and write their own myths about some aspect of South Asia's physical geography. The partners may read their myths to the class or create an illustrated book of the myth to display in class. For assessment, require the students to explain the meanings behind their myths. What aspect of life in prehistoric South Asia does the myth attempt to explain? What fears and hopes did the people have about daily life, and how did these feed the local mythology?

Research Report

Divide the class into small groups to investigate subjects of their choice to bring more information back to the rest of the class. Possible subjects include Mount Everest and the Himalayas, monsoons, and individuals in the text. Suggest sources from the school resource center that students can use. Groups can create a panel discussion or a visual display to explain the information to the class.

ADDITIONAL ASSESSMENT

Use any of these unit projects for additional assessment. For Unit 1, divide the class into groups and have them all undertake the Research Report or Writing Myths. To assess their work, note how the reports show students' grasp of the significance of the geography and climate of South Asia, and how these factors shaped the culture of the people living there in prehistoric times. Use the scoring rubric at the back of this guide to assess group projects, and have students rate their own work with the self-assessment rubric. For the Research Report, be sure to distribute the library/media center research log (see rubric at the back of this guide) to help students evaluate their sources as they conduct their research.

LITERATURE CONNECTION

Legends and hymns, such as the *Nilmata Purana*, written down in ancient Sanskrit, have been passed down for generations and are still exchanged in South Asia today. Various modern retellings of The Ramayana are available on-line and in print, including books that illustrate the Sanskrit epic with ancient Mughal and Rajput miniature paintings. As a classroom activity, have students illustrate one of these ancient legends, through drawings or skits performed for the class.

UNIVERSAL ACCESS STRATEGIES

The exciting narrative of *The Ancient South Asian World* will hold students' interest and encourage them to enjoy learning about ancient South Asia. The following strategies are designed to cover a range of learning styles and reading, language, and skill levels. This section includes suggestions to help differentiate instruction to meet the needs of a diverse student population, and you may find that any of your students will benefit from the various strategies presented. Select the most appropriate activities for the needs of the students in your class.

Reading Strategies

- ▶ To facilitate reading, point out text features such as side-column notes, captions, definitions, and other graphic aids that students will encounter as they read. Help students understand that these features relate to the main text and help them more fully understand the material. As you read chapters with students, call on volunteers to read these special features.
- ▶ There will be many unfamiliar names of people and places in these chapters. Make students aware of the Cast of Characters in the front of their book. If a name doesn't appear there, you may be able to find it in an encyclopedia or biographical dictionary. Say each name several times and then write it on the board. Help students associate the spoken word with the written word.
- ▶ Have partners read the text together. Suggest that one student read a section aloud, and then the other paraphrase the reading.

Writing Strategies

▶ Have students make a K-W-L chart for chapters as they read (see graphic organizer at the back of this guide). After you preview the chapter, have them fill in the first column with what they *know* about the subject, and the second column with what they *want to learn* from the text. When they have finished reading, have them fill in the third column with what they *learned*.

▶ Chapters 1 and 3 introduce students to hypothetical characters. Their stories are told from the third-person point of view. Suggest that students choose one of the stories and rewrite it from the first-person point of view. Students might also rewrite one of the legends in the form of a skit to be read aloud by classmates.

Listening and Speaking Strategies

▶ To spark students' interest, read aloud the title and first paragraph of each chapter. Use the reading as a springboard for predicting what the chapter is about. Record and review students' predictions. When students have finished reading the chapter, ask whether their predictions were correct.

▶ Encourage a group of students to prepare a dramatic reading of a section of a chapter. They might choose to be gods and goddesses looking down on the humans, commenting on their follies, and deciding to take a hand in their lives. The group can present their dramatization to the class.

UNIT VOCABULARY LIST

The following words that appear in Unit 1 are important for your students' understanding of the social studies content as well as for development of literacy. Use these words for vocabulary study or to reinforce language arts skills (e.g., synonyms, compound words, prefixes and suffixes, and related words). The words are listed below in the order in which they appear in the chapters.

Introduction	Chapter 1	Chapter 2	Chapter 3
figurine	mine	glacial deposit	bitumen
carnelian	chalcedony	climate	harvest
lapis lazuli	symbolize	fertile	sickle
precious	mass	memorize	bullock
manufacturer	cultivate	equivalent	nomad
monk	earthquake	unfortunately	experiment
tribute	concrete	emerge	kernel
import	peninsula	atomic analysis	channel
	tectonic plate	invincible	irrigation
	molten		intruder
	landmass		bandit
	barter		humankind
	tropical		agriculture
	plateau		

MOUNTAINS AND MONSOONS: THE GEOGRAPHY OF SOUTH ASIA

PAGES 19–25

FOR HOMEWORK
STUDENT STUDY GUIDE
pages 11–12

monsoon a seasonal wind that blows across South Asia, bringing rain in the summer and dry air in the winter

Paleolithic having to do with the Old Stone Age, the era when people used stone tools and had not yet discovered agriculture

basalt a dark-colored volcanic rock

- **Narrative** Using the excerpt from Arrian as a model, have students write a legend that explains some aspect of India's environment.

CHAPTER SUMMARY

A good part of South Asian life is determined by its geography. The creation of the Himalayas exposed precious stones and metals that have been the basis of South Asian trade for thousands of years. The monsoon, a changing pattern of winds that brings summer storms in its wake, is the basis for South Asia's agriculture.

PERFORMANCE OBJECTIVES

▶ To understand the formation of the Himalaya Mountains and their significance to South Asian life
▶ To describe the monsoon and its effects on South Asia
▶ To identify traditional patterns of regional land use in South Asia

BUILDING BACKGROUND

Obtain a video from your school or public library that shows footage of K2 or Mount Everest so that students get an accurate idea of the scale of the Himalayas. Useful videos or DVDs include *After the Climb: Expedition on Everest* (Discovery Channel; see their website: *http://dsc.discovery.com/ convergence/everest/everest.html*) and *Lost on Everest* and *Everest: The Death Zone*, two NOVA films originally broadcast in 1998 (*www.pbs.org/wgbh/nova/ everest/*).

WORKING WITH PRIMARY SOURCES

Ask a student to read aloud the excerpt from Arrian on page 22. As a class, discuss the way myths emerge.

GEOGRAPHY CONNECTION

Place Distribute copies of the blackline master for Chapter 1 and have students complete them to gain a better understanding of the significance of the monsoon in South Asian life.

READING COMPREHENSION QUESTIONS

1. What caused the Himalaya Mountains to form? (*The Indian landmass crashed into the Eurasian plate, crumpling the earth's crust and pushing up the mountains. The Himalayas are still growing.*)
2. How do you make carnelian? (*by baking chalcedony that contains iron until it turns orange-red*)
3. Describe the annual monsoon cycle. (*Winds blow inland, bringing rain in the late summer and early fall; in the late fall and winter, dry winds blow from the land toward the water.*)
4. Why is South Asia prone to earthquakes? (*The region sits where two major tectonic plates meet. The rubbing of the plates together causes the earthquakes.*)

CRITICAL THINKING QUESTIONS

1. If monsoons can be so destructive, why do they bring such joy to the people of South Asia? *(They are the chief source of water for most of the subcontinent. Without the rains, crops can't grow.)*
2. Why do archaeologists think that prehistoric peoples believed beads were powerful? *(because they buried them with their dead, perhaps to protect them)*
3. Why was it easier for people to travel by boat than overland? *(It was safer from robbers and also faster and more predictable because there were no major road systems at this time.)*

SOCIAL SCIENCES

Economics Have students use a two-column chart to keep track of all the economic activities described in this chapter. In the first column they should describe the activity. In the second they should record where in South Asia that activity takes place.

READING AND LANGUAGE ARTS

Reading Nonfiction Assign a paragraph from the chapter to each student. Have the student pick out the main idea and list the details used to support it. Then have students read their topic sentences and examples aloud in order.

Using Language Point out that elephants are used as metaphors both in the quotation from Valmiki on page 21 and in the legend that ends the chapter. Have students use the main idea map graphic organizer (see graphic organizers at the back of this book) to analyze the different aspects of elephants that are used as figures of speech.

SUPPORTING LEARNING

English Language Learners Have students create cards using the vocabulary list for Chapter 1 (see page 27 of this guide). They should write the word on the front of the card and a definition on the back. Have them use a dictionary or context clues to define the words.

Struggling Readers Have students use the main idea map graphic organizer (see graphic organizers at the back of this book) to create a web describing the ways in which the environment impacts Mani's life.

EXTENDING LEARNING

Enrichment To sensitize students to the impact of monsoon floods, conduct this activity. Using an outline map of Bangladesh, have students label the Ganga, the Meghna, and the Brahmaputra Rivers and the Bay of Bengal. Point out that half of the country is less than 15 feet above sea level and that storms in the Bay of Bengal sometimes create waves 20–30 feet high. Discuss the reasons for flooding in Bangladesh.

Extension During the first six weeks of the 2004 monsoon season, flooding damaged about 5.7 million acres of cropland in Bangladesh, causing losses estimated at $282 million. Have students research statistics for the current monsoon season in Bangladesh.

LINKING DISCIPLINES

Earth Science Have students explore the PBS online site about Mount Everest. It can be found at *www.pbs.org/wgbh/nova/everest/*. Ask students to draw conclusions based on the information to explain how the Himalayas formed and what makes them unique.

THEN and NOW

On December 8, 2004 a deadly tsunami struck the shores of Indonesia, Sri Lanka, Thailand, and other coastal areas of the Indian Ocean. The wave was caused by an undersea earthquake with a magnitude of 9.0. The final death toll may never be known, but estimates range from 8000 to as many as 30,000 people. Have students research the state of the devastated communities since the disaster.

THE ANCIENT SOUTH ASIAN WORLD

THE MONSOON: WIND, NOT RAIN

Directions
Use the information from the map and Chapter 1 to answer the questions.

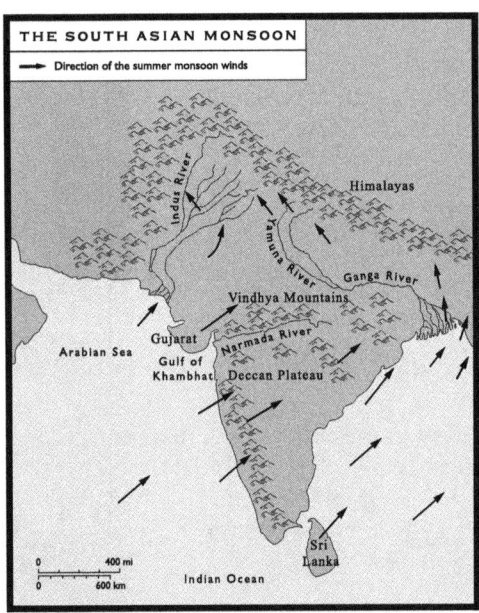

Although most people think that the word monsoon refers to huge rainstorms, it is actually the annual change in the direction of wind patterns over South Asia. The winds come inland from the Indian Ocean in the late summer and early fall, dumping huge amounts of rain over the subcontinent. Later, the winds change direction and blow from the northeast out to sea, until they change again the next summer and the rains begin again.

Without the monsoon, many regions of South Asia would receive no rain at all. The monsoon can be a curse as well as a blessing, however; flooding is a serious and sometimes deadly problem during monsoon season.

The South Asian year can be divided into three seasons. *Garmi*, which means "hot," runs from March to June. *Barsat*, which means "rainy" or "wet," runs from July to October. Finally, *sardi*, which means "cold," runs from November to February.

1. Describe the kinds of clothing you would bring on a trip to South Asia in August, January, and April. Explain your choices.

_____

_____

_____

2. Write a short paragraph explaining the risks and benefits that the monsoon introduces to life in South Asia.

_____

_____

_____

_____

CHAPTER TEST 1

THE ANCIENT SOUTH ASIAN WORLD

NAME _____ DATE _____

A. MULTIPLE CHOICE

Circle the letter of the best answer for each question.

1. Ancient South Asian beads may have been used for all of the following **except**
   a. money.
   b. good luck.
   c. a form of writing.
   d. decoration.

2. Gujarat is famous for
   a. fertile volcanic soil.
   b. high mountains.
   c. being the gateway to South Asia.
   d. production of beads.

3. An important economic activity in Paleolithic South Asia was
   a. farming.
   b. trading.
   c. hunting.
   d. pottery making.

4. All of the following are a direct result of the collision between Asia and South Asia **except**
   a. earthquakes.
   b. the Himalaya Mountains.
   c. the monsoon.
   d. India's hot summer.

5. The Deccan plateau
   a. includes some of South Asia's highest mountains.
   b. is the site of many of India's jungles.
   c. is a good place to grow things, even though it receives relatively little rainfall.
   d. was crumpled during the collision between Eurasia and South Asia.

B. SHORT ANSWER

Write a sentence or two to answer each question.

6. Explain the geological process that formed the Himalaya Mountains.

_____

_____

7. How has the formation of the Himalaya Mountains had an impact on the people of South Asia?

_____

_____

C. ESSAY

On a separate sheet of paper, write an essay explaining what a monsoon is and the effect it has on the people of South Asia.

STONE SERPENTS: EARLY HUMANS AND STONE AGE CULTURES

PAGES 26–29

FOR HOMEWORK

STUDENT STUDY GUIDE
pages 13–14

CAST OF CHARACTERS

Kashyapa (kuh-SHYUH-pah) mythical sage who saved the Nagas from the demons of Satisaras Lake

- **Comic Book** Comic book versions of South Asian myths and legends are very popular in South Asia. Have students write and illustrate a comic book version of the myth of the Nagas and Satisaras Lake.

CHAPTER SUMMARY

During the second half of the 20th century, scientists discovered stone tools in Kashmir in northern Pakistan that suggest that people have been living in South Asia for as long as 2 million years. Oddly enough, a foundation myth about the Nagas near Satisaras Lake seems to mirror geologic events that took place over millions of years.

PERFORMANCE OBJECTIVES

▶ To understand the relationship of archaeology and history
▶ To use primary sources to ascertain information about a civilization
▶ To discern fact from fiction using historical artifacts and oral tradition
▶ To understand the significance of the geology of Kashmir and its relation to the early humans who settled there

BUILDING BACKGROUND

Write *archaeologist* on the board. Ask students what words they associate with archaeologists. Read the first few paragraphs of Chapter 2 and discuss which of the students' expectations fit the story of Dr. Hasmukh Sankalia's discovery of the stone tool.

WORKING WITH PRIMARY SOURCES

Show students pictures of the lovely vale of Kashmir, either online at such sources as *www.koausa.org/VParimoo/* or *www.euronet.nl/users/ e_wesker/jpg/ pakind.html,* or from a reference or travel book.

GEOGRAPHY CONNECTION

Regions   Kashmir is a mountainous region at the intersection of Pakistan, China, and India that is famous for its beauty, its wool, and its fertile soil. All three countries claim portions of the region. Show students a map of the region, such as the one found at *www.lib.utexas.edu/maps/kashmir.html.*

READING COMPREHENSION QUESTIONS

1. Who is Dr. Hasmukh Sankalia? *(A great Indian archaeologist who as a young man stumbled across what was then the earliest known evidence of a human presence in South Asia.)*
2. How and when was Kashmir formed? *(It was a huge lake formed 4 million years ago when the South Asian peninsula crashed into Asia.)*
3. What happened to the lake 200,000 years ago? *(Earthquakes created a river through the mountains surrounding the lake. The lake began to drain.)*
4. What happened in Kashmir 10,000 years ago? *(The climate warmed, making the area around Nagin Lake fit for year-round habitation.)*

CRITICAL THINKING QUESTIONS

1. What mistake did Dr. Sankalia's more experienced colleagues make? (*They assumed that there was nothing to learn from the site and left before examining it fully.*)
2. What mistake did Dr. Sankalia make when he excavated the stone tool? (*He removed it from the earth before photographing it.*)
3. Which version of the story is easier for you to remember? Why? (*Answers will vary.*)

SOCIAL SCIENCES

Science, Technology, and Society Remind students that this chapter is about South Asia's Paleolithic era, or Old Stone Age. Ask: Why is it called the "stone age"? Was everything the people used made of stone? (*The people may well have used wood or other natural materials, but it has not survived. The people had not yet learned to work with metal.*)

READING AND LANGUAGE ARTS

Reading Nonfiction Point out the timeline on page 27. Pass out cards and have students copy each of the entries onto a separate card without including the dates. Divide the class into pairs, and have one partner shuffle the cards and the other put them in correct order.

Using Language Have students break down the first three sentences into simple sentences. Read the resulting paragraph, and ask them to compare the effect of lots of short, choppy sentences and the effect of longer sentences.

SUPPORTING LEARNING

English Language Learners Ask students to compare the legend of the Nagas to legends from their own countries of origin. They can ask members of their families for information. Have them prepare a short oral report comparing the legends, to be presented to the class or a small group.

Struggling Readers Have students paraphrase Dr. Sankalia's description of finding the stone tool on the first page of the chapter.

EXTENDING LEARNING

Enrichment Have students fill out a sequence of events chart (see graphic organizers at the back of this guide) to explain the geological events that led to the creation of Nagin Lake and the other small lakes in Kashmir.

Extension Ask students to make a two-column chart. On the left they should list the elements of the myth of the Nagas. On the right they should write in the corresponding history of the area.

LINKING DISCIPLINES

Art Have students bring in a bar of soap and use plastic knives to carve their own Nagas or water demons.

THEN and NOW

Today Kashmir covers an area of 880 square miles and has a population of over 10 million. Products of Kashmir include corn, wheat, rice, saffron, pears, apples, walnuts, and, of course, cashmere wool. Both India and Pakistan continue to claim jurisdiction over portions of Kashmir. Have students research the most recent news using the Internet or resources in your media center.

VOCABULARY

Nagas mythological serpent-like beings that lived near springs and lakes

THE ANCIENT SOUTH ASIAN WORLD

CHAPTER 2 BLM
THE ANCIENT SOUTH ASIAN WORLD

NAME   **DATE**

HOW OLD IS IT?

Directions
Scientists have four major ways of finding out the age of artifacts. Use the information in this chart on dating techniques to answer the questions.

Technique	How It Works	What It Can Date
Carbon Dating	All living things contain the element carbon, which decays at a constant rate. By measuring how much carbon has decayed, scientists can estimate the age of an object.	Anything that was once alive: wood, cloth, human remains
Thermoluminescence Dating	When a stone or clay object is heated, some of its electrons move out of their usual places. By reheating the object and taking certain measurements, scientists can estimate when the object was last heated.	Clay or stone objects heated to more than 350°C, like hearthstones or clay objects fired in a kiln
Written or Pictorial Records	If an object is mentioned or illustrated in a text or piece of art, we know that it is at least as old as the record.	Something for which a datable record exists
Comparative Dating	Something that is buried with objects that can be dated is at least as old as those objects. Likewise, two objects made of similar materials and with a similar design were probably made at roughly the same time.	Similar artifacts from a wide area. If one cooking pot is dated to 3000 BCE, pots with similar technology and construction found in another settlement can be dated to about that time.

1. What techniques could you use to date a wooden statue? Why?

   _____

2. How would you date a length of thread?

   _____

3. How would you date a clay pot found in a hearth
   a. if it had food in it?

   _____

   b. if it were empty?

   _____

4. Name two possible ways to date a stone sickle whose wooden handle has rotted away.

   _____

CHAPTER TEST 2

THE ANCIENT SOUTH ASIAN WORLD

NAME _____ DATE _____

A. MULTIPLE CHOICE

Circle the letter of the best answer for each question.

1. South Asia's oldest stone tools have been dated to about
   a. 10,000 years ago.
   b. 200,000 years ago.
   c. 400,000 years ago.
   d. 2 million years ago.

2. No one lived in the land around Nagin Lake year-round until about 10,000 years ago because
   a. the water demons of Satisaras Lake wouldn't let them.
   b. there was no river access through the mountains.
   c. the winters were too hard for humans to survive.
   d. melting glaciers caused too many floods.

3. Kashmir was initially
   a. one of the tall mountains formed when South Asia crashed into Asia.
   b. a huge lake dammed by surrounding mountains.
   c. a large meadow well suited to cashmere sheep.
   d. a land of many rivers near the Bay of Bengal.

4. The *Nilmata Purana* is the name of
   a. a Sanskrit legend.
   b. a technique of dating artifacts.
   c. the chief water demon.
   d. the river that drained Nagin Lake.

5. Archaeologists believe the stone tool that Dr. Hasmukh Sankalia found is 400,000 years old because
   a. of carbon dating.
   b. of an inscription on its side.
   c. that is when stone tools of this kind were being used.
   d. the rocks and fossils that were around it are all about that old.

B. SHORT ANSWER

Write a sentence or two to answer each question.

6. What was the significance of the hand axe that Dr. Sankalia found in Kashmir, and how was it related to another discovery?

   _____

   _____

7. Explain who the Nagas were.

   _____

   _____

C. ESSAY

Write an essay on a separate piece of paper giving a possible explanation of the similarities between the legend of the Nagas and what really happened geologically. Use details from the chapter to support your explanation.

FARMERS AND HERDERS: NEOLITHIC TIMES

PAGES 30–34

FOR HOMEWORK
STUDENT STUDY GUIDE
pages 15–16

VOCABULARY

domesticate to accustom animals to living close to humans

Neolithic having to do with the New Stone Age, a time when the first farmers used stone tools

analogy a way of understanding something by comparing it to something else with similar characteristics

WRITING

- **Essay** According to the chapter, Neolithic peoples "change[d] their world to better serve their needs." Instruct students to write an essay on this topic. The essay should begin with an introduction and end with a conclusion. Each body paragraph should explain one way in which Neolithic peoples changed their world and give specific examples.

CHAPTER SUMMARY

In about 7000 BCE the peoples of South Asia began to make the transition from the hunting/gathering of Paleolithic times to the settled agriculture of Neolithic times. This chapter examines this transition in the Pakistani village of Mehrgarh.

PERFORMANCE OBJECTIVES

- To describe characteristics of Neolithic societies in South Asia
- To compare patterns of life of early and later Neolithic societies
- To understand how archaeologists make inferences from artifacts

BUILDING BACKGROUND

Instruct students to list three items that tell a lot about themselves. Have students share their lists in small groups and make inferences about each other. Elicit that these inferences may be correct but can't reveal everything about a person. Explain that this is the challenge for archaeologists when dealing with Neolithic times in South Asia.

WORKING WITH PRIMARY SOURCES

Distribute copies of the blackline master for Chapter 3. Have students fill out the table to help clarify their understanding of the inferences archaeologists have made from physical evidence of Neolithic times.

GEOGRAPHY CONNECTION

Location Provide contemporary atlases or maps of South Asia, showing modern political borders and cities. Explain that Mehrgarh is close to the modern city of Quetta, Pakistan (30°15′N 67°E). Have students identify Quetta's relative location *(just south of the border with Afghanistan)*. Ask students to use the mileage scale to estimate Quetta's distance from other cities in the region, such as Lahore and Islamabad, Pakistan; and Kabul, Afghanistan.

READING COMPREHENSION QUESTIONS

1. How could Neolithic people settle in one place when Paleolithic people had to travel? *(Neolithic people used agriculture—farming and herding—and so could stay in one place instead of following their food.)*
2. What is Mehrgarh? *(Mehrgarh is a Neolithic site in Pakistan.)*
3. Why did some Neolithic peoples leave their homes each summer? *(They took their herds into the mountains to eat wild grasses, which they themselves harvested at the end of each summer before returning home.)*
4. Why didn't they just stay in the mountains? *(The winters were too cold for their animals, and it was difficult to find grazing land.)*

CRITICAL THINKING QUESTIONS

1. Why do we know so much more about Neolithic peoples than Paleolithic peoples? (*The sedentary Neolithic lifestyle meant they could make and collect more objects, which means more archaeological evidence has survived for them than for the wandering Paleolithic peoples.*)
2. Summarize the advantages and disadvantages of planting new domesticated grains. (*Advantages: They had bigger kernels with thinner husks, and so were easier to grind; the bread was less chewy. Disadvantages: They required more water and so had to be irrigated; the fields had to be protected from wild animals, which could be tedious and sometimes dangerous.*)

SOCIAL SCIENCES

Economics As a class, discuss the enormous ramifications of the switch from a nomadic hunting/gathering society to a settled agricultural one. You may want to consider changes in diet, population, community size, tools, and work. Have students take notes in the form of a two-column cause and effect chart.

READING AND LANGUAGE ARTS

Reading Nonfiction Have students find inferences that the chapter makes about the Neolithic peoples based on what people of the region do today. Using the examples, elicit how archaeologists can make valid inferences this way.

Using Language Have students find as many "maybe" expressions as they can in the chapter—words or phrases like *probably*, *may have*, and *Let's say*. Elicit why a writer would use such expressions. Ask: Is it possible to know exactly what happened thousands of years ago without written records?

SUPPORTING LEARNING

English Language Learners Use the text to have students practice reading and writing regular and irregular past-tense verbs. Have them choose sentences, identify the verb or verbs, and write the present and past tenses of the verb. (For example, see *spun* on page 31.)

Struggling Readers Have a volunteer read aloud the Neolithic Cuisine sidebar on page 33. Have the class make up the table of contents for a Mehrgarh cookbook based on the kinds of food described.

EXTENDING LEARNING

Enrichment Some Neolithic families in Central India practiced slash-and-burn agriculture. Have students research this practice and report back to the class on the problems it solves and the problems it creates.

Extension Have students compose and perform a skit based on Neolithic life in Mehrgarh.

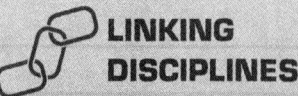

LINKING DISCIPLINES

Science Have students choose an animal that interests them and research whether it would make a good domestic animal. (They will learn that domesticated animals have four characteristics: They are not afraid of humans; they live in herds; they are willing to follow a leader; they can have babies in captivity.)

CHAPTER 3 BLM

NAME **DATE**

USING EVIDENCE TO LEARN ABOUT THE PAST

Directions
Complete the chart to evaluate how archaeologists make inferences about ancient peoples from the evidence they find. Read the evidence in the first column. In the second column, write "P" if the evidence is physical, "G" if the evidence is geographical, and "A" if the evidence is by analogy. In the third column, summarize the inferences archaeologists have made from the evidence.

Evidence	Kind of Evidence	Inference
Bones of animals with small horns near settlement; hoof prints in corrals		
Mountain climate too cold in winter for domesticated animals		
Mountain camps with stone tools similar to village tools		
Deposits of bitumen tar in mountain passes		
Modern males take herds to high mountains while females stay in camp and weave bags and baskets		
Spinning tools made of shells		
Woven baskets with bitumen tar		
Mud bricks with impressions of wild wheat and barley		
Chert blades in a row with bits of bitumen tar stuck to them		
Modern people loading sheep, goats, and bullocks with grain in saddlebags		

CHAPTER TEST 3

THE ANCIENT SOUTH ASIAN WORLD

NAME _____ **DATE** _____

A. MULTIPLE CHOICE

Circle the letter of the correct answer for each question.

1. When people practice agriculture, they
    a. only plant crops.
    b. plant crops and herd animals.
    c. herd animals and gather plants.
    d. hunt animals and gather plants.

2. Mehrgarh is
    a. a domesticated wheat.
    b. the name of a Neolithic girl.
    c. a game played by Neolithic children.
    d. a Neolithic village in Pakistan.

3. Jana's chores probably included all of the following **except**
    a. weaving bags and making willow baskets.
    b. taking the animals to high mountain pastures.
    c. planting and irrigating crops.
    d. guarding new crops from deer and antelope.

4. Neolithic peoples mostly ate
    a. cheese and yogurt.
    b. beef, goat meat, and lamb.
    c. dates and jujube relishes.
    d. barley and wheat.

5. According to the information in the chapter, Neolithic houses included
    a. food storage areas.
    b. hearths and chimneys.
    c. drains.
    d. a courtyard and sacred tree.

B. SHORT ANSWER

On the lines, write a possible explanation for how the Agricultural Revolution led to each innovation. Use complete sentences.

6. Walled towns

_____

7. Development of such crafts as pottery and bead making

_____

8. Larger communities

_____

C. ESSAY

On a separate sheet of paper, write an essay describing the artifacts that are presented in the chapter, particularly the bitumen-coated basket and the ancient sickle. Explain how archaeologists have used artifacts such as these to draw conclusions about the lives of the people in South Asia in Neolithic times.

THE CITIES OF THE INDUS

PAGES 35–57

Chapter 4	Gadgets Galore: The Beginnings of Technologies and Trade
Chapter 5	Walls and Wells: The First Cities of the Indus
Chapter 6	Scratches, Seals, and Symbols: The Birth of Writing
Chapter 7	Trash and Toilets: The Cities of the Indus

UNIT OBJECTIVES

Unit 2 introduces students to the Indus River culture, a trade-based culture that, like Minoan Crete, left written records that remain undeciphered. In this unit your students will learn about

- the crafts that were an important part of Indus life and culture.
- early cities in the Indus Valley.
- the significance of seals and written records to the Indus Valley people.
- the rise of large, interdependent urban centers in the Indus River Valley.

PRIMARY SOURCES

Unit 2 includes pictures of the following artifacts from ancient South Asia:

- Figurines, Nausharo
- Painted terracotta bowl, Baluchistan
- Ram toys, Harappa
- Shell bangles, Harappa
- Bead grinder replica
- Bead necklace, Mehrgarh
- Carved stone seal, Harappa
- Public well and bathing platforms, Harappa
- Pottery shards, Harappa
- Elephant seal, Mohenjo Daro
- Glazed tablet, Harappa
- Copper tablet, Mohenjo Daro
- Clay impression of a seal
- Unicorn figurine, Pakistan
- Streets, Mohenjo Dara
- Toilet, Harappa
- Stone head, Mohenjo Daro
- Great Bath, Mohenjo Daro

BIG IDEAS IN UNIT 2

The emergence of **specialization, trade,** and growing **urbanization** are the big ideas presented in Unit 2. The unit opens with the first settlements in the valley of the Indus River, surveys the development of the region's characteristic arts and crafts, and ends with the emergence of an extraordinarily wealthy and stable society during the third millennium BCE.

A good way to introduce these ideas is to ask students to imagine that they must complete the following tasks in a day: cook a large meal, clean three rooms, mow a lawn, coach a soccer game, plan a budget, make a speech to 500 people, sew a skirt, and fix a car. Reflect that it probably doesn't matter who does what.

Assuming that each task takes an hour and a half and that each person has time to perform eight tasks, tell students that they can try to swap tasks with those around them to better suit their own interests and abilities. Give them a few minutes to trade. When the time is up, discuss the advantages of a trading society, where each person can specialize in those activities they are uniquely qualified to perform.

GEOGRAPHY CONNECTION

Point out that specialization depends on more than personal ability and preference. Probably the most significant determinant of ancient trade, for example, was access to resources. Direct students' attention to the resource map on page 39 and have them examine the location of natural resources. Discuss why each of the resources named in the map would be valuable to others.

TIMELINE

4500 BCE	Potters use marks on pottery
3900 BCE	Stone beads and shell bangles used in Harappa
3500 BCE	Potter's wheels used at Mehrgarh
3300 BCE	Potter's wheels used at Harappa; earliest writing on pottery; early village culture
2800–2600 BCE	Early Harappan period; first mud-brick city walls built; early Indus Script
2600–1900 BCE	Indus Valley civilization develops; Harappan period; large, planned cities emerge throughout the Indus region
2600 BCE	City dwellers of Harappa and Mohenjo Daro build drains and baked-brick houses

UNIT PROJECTS

Exploring www.harappa.com

The website www.harappa.com is a wonderful introduction to the history and culture of the Indus Valley, written and maintained by many of the archaeologists who currently work there. Allow students to explore the site. Have them keep a record of questions their investigations uncover.

Chronology

Although it is impossible to know exactly what happened at what time in the Indus Valley without written records, it is possible to reconstruct a rough chronology of technological advances. Small groups can create sequence charts indicating the steps in these progressions. Display the charts for the rest of the class to review.

Artwork

Have students design and make their own seals, perhaps by carving potatoes. Have them do a sample stamp on a piece of paper and then annotate the seal, explaining the significance of each of its symbols. You may want to allow them to sign all their written work during this unit with their seal.

Research Report

Have students choose partners to investigate topics related to the traditional arts and crafts of the Indus Valley, including sculpture, seals, the progress being made on deciphering its mysterious script, and so on. They should write a short report on their subject and illustrate it with appropriate pictures or diagrams.

ADDITIONAL ASSESSMENT

Use any of these unit projects for additional assessment. For Unit 2, divide the class into groups and have them all undertake the Chronology project. To assess their work, note how the timelines show students' understanding of how crafts developed among the people of the Indus and the rise of written records, and how both of these developments affected life in the urban centers of the Indus River Valley. Use the scoring rubric at the back of this guide to assess group projects, and have students rate their own work with the self-assessment rubric. For the Research Report, be sure to distribute the library/media center research log (see rubric at the back of this guide) to help students evaluate their sources as they conduct their research.

LITERATURE CONNECTION

In South Asia, the concept of entertaining and instructing children through literature is ancient. The birth of writing did not disrupt this tradition; oral storytelling continues today. Many modern books written for children and young adults incorporate stories of animals and gods, such as:

- Narayan, R. K. *A Tiger for Malgudi*. Penguin Books; Reissue edition, 1994. With a tiger as a protagonist, this story runs back to the ancient times, to uncover the wisdom of the first people of the Indus Valley.

- Rushdie, Salman. *Haroun and the Sea of Stories*. New York: Viking and Granta, 1990. This advanced young adult fantasy tells the story of a man and his son's journey to rediscover the father's lost storytelling gift.

- Mukerji, Dhan Gopal. *Kari, the Elephant* (Penguin Group, 1922). Mukerji tells the story of the elephant Kari with direct sincerity as one who knows and appreciates the innate intelligence and the personality of an educated elephant. Mukerji, a writer from India's Bengal province, won the coveted Newbery Medal for the most distinguished contribution to American literature for children in 1928.

UNIVERSAL ACCESS

The following strategies are designed to cover a range of learning styles and reading, language, and skill levels. You may find that any of your students will benefit from the various strategies presented.

Reading Strategies

- To facilitate reading, review the reason for the punctuation elements students will encounter as they read. For Chapter 4, for example, explain that commas, dashes, and parentheses can all be used to set off parenthetical information.
- Remind students not to ignore unfamiliar words. Students can have their journals open as they read so they can jot down unfamiliar words and then look them up in a dictionary when they have finished the section.
- Have partners read the text silently together and then review the main ideas and details when they are both finished reading.

Writing Strategies

- These chapters explain a variety of technological processes. This might be a good time to talk about composing clear and effective explanations. Have students work in small groups, with each student writing his or her own explanation of the activity of the group's choice. (You may want to establish

some guidelines about which activities are acceptable and which are inappropriate.) When everyone has finished, group members can compare their work and write one final draft that uses the best of all the explanations.
▶ Students may enjoy writing about their activities or environment from the point of view of an archaeologist of the future.

Listening and Speaking Strategies

▶ To set the stage for reading a chapter, tell students three or four questions they can use to organize their reading. The questions can be keyed to sections of the chapter or to the main topics discussed. Students can write down the questions and take notes under each.
▶ If reading a chapter aloud, have volunteers practice reading the excerpts from primary sources with expression. Then, when you reach each excerpt, have the volunteer stand and read it. Or divide the whole class into groups and have them practice reading excerpts to each other.

UNIT VOCABULARY LIST

The following words that appear in Unit 2 are important for your students' understanding of the social studies content as well as for development of literacy. Use these words for vocabulary study or to reinforce language arts skills (e.g., synonyms, compound words, prefixes and suffixes, and related words). The words are listed below in the order in which they appear in the chapters.

Chapter 4	Chapter 5	Chapter 6	Chapter 7
vessel	abandoned	hesitate	decoded
silty	littered	identified	ruined
knead	evidence	mint	tragic
socket	failure	inscriptions	repaved
artisan	legacy	syllable	divided
bonfire	ordinary	consonant	specializing
kiln	mortar	bleached	alabaster
figurine	maintain		grandeur
deposit	impressions		
deforest	dissolve		
terracotta	cinders		
	furnaces		
	afford		
	tributaries		

CHAPTER 4

GADGETS GALORE: THE BEGINNINGS OF TECHNOLOGIES AND TRADE

PAGES 35–40

FOR HOMEWORK
STUDENT STUDY GUIDE
pages 17–18

bangle a round bracelet in the shape of a ring

ore a rock that contains metal

- **Poetry** Ask students to write a poem about one of the crafts described in the chapter. Encourage them to use descriptive verbs, nouns, and adjectives to convey the physical nature of the activity.

CHAPTER SUMMARY

The discovery and refinement of clay pottery was a watershed in South Asian history. For the first time, people could store liquids, keep grains safe from rodents, and cook in vessels directly over the fire. But this was only the first in a series of technological breakthroughs—including harvesting and working metals, marine shell, and precious stones—that led to the beginnings of a market economy.

PERFORMANCE OBJECTIVES

▶ To understand the significance of clay pottery to ancient peoples
▶ To explore the way that scattered natural resources work to inspire trade networks
▶ To describe the ingenuity and sophistication of South Asia's traditional crafts

BUILDING BACKGROUND

Have students read the title of the chapter. As a class, define *gadget* (a small tool) and *galore* (lots). In other words, this is a chapter about lots of nifty little tools. Why is that a new idea in Neolithic South Asia? (*Paleolithic peoples had neither the time, the resources, nor the storage space to produce many gadgets.*)

WORKING WITH PRIMARY SOURCES

Ask students if any of them have ever thrown a pot. If so, have them describe how the wheel worked. Now direct their attention to the illustration of the potter on page 37. Ask them to compare the evidence of the photograph with the description. How can they explain the differences?

GEOGRAPHY CONNECTION

Interaction Find pictures of Baluchistan, one of Pakistan's southern states, on the Internet or in a library book or journal. Display to students. How does their book explain the barren landscape? (*It was deforested long ago for fuel to smelt metal ore.*)

READING COMPREHENSION QUESTIONS

1. How did South Asians solve the problem of water storage and cooking over fires? (*through the invention of baked clay vessels*)
2. What are two possible explanations for the many clay figurines historians have found? (*They may have been toys or offerings to the gods.*)
3. Why do historians believe that women were the first potters? (*They were the ones who cooked and carried water; the earliest designs look like basket and fabric designs, which women made, maybe because they saw the clay as they were washing clothes in the river.*)
4. What resources did the South Asians discover in Baluchistan and the Aravalli hills? (*copper*)

CRITICAL THINKING QUESTIONS

1. Ask students to consider the shell drilling kit on page 40 and try to figure out how it worked. *(The string of the bow drill wraps around the pencil-shaped drill. The drill operator pulls the wooden part of the bow back and forth so that it spins around and turns the drill.)*
2. Have students determine the distance between Rajasthan, Baluchistan, Gujarat, and Afghanistan with the aid of an atlas. Remembering that people traveled these distances without the aid of roads, police, or fast-food restaurants, what does that suggest about the value of the trade items to those who bought them? *(obviously very valuable, perhaps because there was so little variety in local life)*

SOCIAL SCIENCES

Science, Technology, and Society Distribute copies of the Chapter 4 blackline master to have students investigate how cooking vessels correspond to societal changes in the lifetimes of their relatives.

READING AND LANGUAGE ARTS

Reading Nonfiction Direct students' attention to the And We Do Mean Tiny sidebar on page 36. Ask a volunteer to read it aloud. What difference does knowing a little bit more about clay make? Sometimes more information makes things more complicated. Other times more information makes things easier to understand. Discuss whether this sidebar helps or hinders understanding of the chapter.

Using Language Point out that the title of the chapter includes two examples of *alliteration*, or the repetition of initial consonant sounds. Discuss the effect of alliteration. Ask: Why might an author use alliteration in a title? *(perhaps to focus attention on the words, which will be important guides to the story to follow)*

SUPPORTING LEARNING

English Language Learners Cut construction paper into pot shapes. Have each student find an unfamiliar word in the chapter and use a thesaurus to find a synonym. Have students write the word, its synonym, and a context sentence on a paper pot. Hang the pots in a prominent spot.

Struggling Readers When students have finished reading the chapter, have each of them write five short-answer questions. Have students form small groups and take turns reading questions aloud for others to answer.

EXTENDING LEARNING

Enrichment Divide the class into small groups and have each group research one of the regions named in the chapter. Have them compose a travel brochure that encourages tourists to visit the place they have researched.

Extension Have students make an illustrated booklet explaining the steps in making a pot, from gathering the clay to applying the glaze.

THEN and NOW

South Asian women still offer figurines to the gods in the hopes of receiving a blessing. For example, women leave horse figurines at the shrine of one saint in Pakistan in the hopes that he will send them healthy sons.

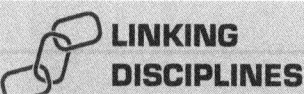
LINKING DISCIPLINES

Health Scientists estimate that about half of the grain and cereals harvested worldwide is lost to rodents. Discuss the impact that the invention of rodent-proof fired clay vessels might have had on South Asian health.

NAME _____ DATE _____

WHY DO WE KEEP TALKING ABOUT POTTERY?

Directions
Read the information about how archaeologists use pottery shards to learn about the lives of ancient peoples. Then answer the questions below.

> The most common artifacts that archaeologists find are pottery shards. These bits of broken pots and dishes may seem unimportant, but they can tell us a lot about the people who used them.
> - ▶ Many societies that didn't keep written records did make pottery. And they made a lot of pots, because they used them every day for many different purposes.
> - ▶ Since pottery does not decay like organic materials, there's a lot of it around for archaeologists to study.
> - ▶ Pots that are important for archaeologists are ones that show changes in a people's culture. Cooking and religion are very conservative aspects of culture: They don't change unless there is some outside influence. When the styles of cooking pots or ritual containers change, it usually corresponds to an important change in cultural traditions—an influx of new peoples, or a change in technology. Such culture changes can then be assigned an approximate date by dating the pottery.
> - ▶ Pottery can be dated by thermoluminescence (THUR-moh-loo-muh-NESS-enns) dating, by carbon dating of charcoal found with it, and by relative dating with other pottery shards.

Containers used for cooking can tell us a lot about what people had to eat and how they prepared it. What cooking containers are used at your house? How have these changed over time in your family? Interview older relatives about the way they cooked and the foods they ate many years ago. Match changes in cooking and diet with technological advances that your family members recall. Take notes on your interviews. Use the notes to write a short essay about the changes in society shown by cooking techniques in the lifetime of your relatives.

NAME _____ **DATE** _____

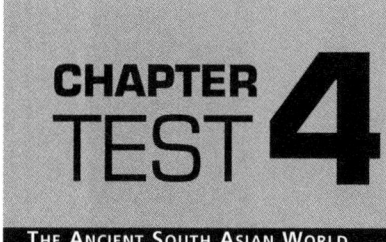

A. MULTIPLE CHOICE

Circle the letter of the best answer for each question.

1. Before 5500 BCE, South Asians probably used all of the following in cooking **except**
   a. clay pots.
   b. baskets.
   c. leather sacks.
   d. fire and hot rocks.

2. Clay is made of
   a. sand and pebbles.
   b. slip and river mud.
   c. silica and alumina.
   d. mud mixed with chaff and straw.

3. At first, clay pots were hardened by
   a. adding sand and straw to the clay.
   b. baking in special kilns.
   c. burning them in bonfires covered with burning brush.
   d. painting them with slip.

4. The clay rams pictured in the text were probably
   a. offerings to the gods.
   b. toys.
   c. household ornaments.
   d. earrings.

5. Chert is
   a. a hard, easy-to-split stone.
   b. a gray stone that turns orange-red when it is baked.
   c. a precious green stone from Baluchistan.
   d. a precious blue stone from Afghanistan.

B. SHORT ANSWER

Write a sentence or two to answer each question.

6. Why were beads important to people in South Asia?

_____

_____

7. Why did craftspeople come to live in large walled villages and towns?

_____

_____

C. ESSAY

Write an essay on a separate piece of paper explaining the connection between the scattered natural resources of South Asia (copper, clay, shells) and the growth of trade.

CHAPTER 5

WALLS AND WELLS: THE FIRST CITIES OF THE INDUS

PAGES 41–46

FOR HOMEWORK

STUDENT STUDY GUIDE pages 19–0

 **WRITING**

- **Persuasion** Have students write a letter from Alexander Cunningham to the British railway office asking officials to stop using bricks from Harappa. Remember that neither Cunningham nor anyone else knew that the Harappan civilization ever existed.

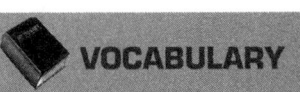 **VOCABULARY**

caravanserai a combination inn and warehouse outside city walls for the use of traveling merchants

CHAPTER SUMMARY

A British archaeologist, Alexander Cunningham, stumbled onto the ruins of Harappa more than 150 years ago, but its significance was not recognized until it was excavated in the 1920s. At that time, archaeologists were stunned to discover evidence of a wealthy, sophisticated, literate society that no one had known existed.

PERFORMANCE OBJECTIVES

▶ To examine the discovery of Harappan civilization
▶ To understand the significance of carved steatite seals
▶ To explore the importance of trade to the Harappan civilization

BUILDING BACKGROUND

Ask students if any of them are interested in unicorns. Ask if they know where the unicorn came from. Explain that this chapter will reveal the origins of that mythical animal.

WORKING WITH PRIMARY SOURCES

Direct students' attention to the carved stone seal on page 42. Tell students what it is: the Indus unicorn. Some archaeologists believe that the object depicted in the lower left-hand corner of the seal is a ritual offering stand. Ask: What would you put in an offering stand to a unicorn?

GEOGRAPHY CONNECTION

Location   Harappa was built in a good location for a city. Have students use the main idea map graphic organizer (see graphic organizers at the back of this book) to analyze Harappa's location. Have them write "Harappa's Location" in the center circle, then have them fill in the other circles with details from the book.

READING COMPREHENSION QUESTIONS

1. What lies under the mysterious mounds in the Punjab? (*ruins of Indus Valley cities like Harappa*)
2. Why did Alexander Cunningham think he was a failure? (*Because he couldn't find any evidence of a Buddhist-era civilization in these mounds; in fact, he had stumbled across a previously unknown civilization as old as those of Egypt and Mesopotamia.*)
3. Why were the cities of the Indus Valley surrounded by walls? (*probably to control the movement of traders so they could be taxed*)
4. In what ways was the Indus Valley civilization easy to overlook? (*no great temples, tradition of warfare, royal burials, or a script that is deciphered*)

CRITICAL THINKING QUESTIONS

1. Why might the city have been divided into walled neighborhoods? *(Perhaps it was to separate its people by family or village of origin or, more probably, by profession.)*
2. What does the fact that houses were built with courtyards and flat roofs have to do with the climate of northern India? *(The courtyards were outdoor shaded spaces for working or sleeping when the inside of the house was too hot.)*
3. What ended the Indus Valley civilization? *(Scholars aren't sure; over-expansion and breakdown of trade and changes in the rivers may have had something to do with it.)*

SOCIAL SCIENCES

Civics   The growth of trade and cities would have changed the political life of the people. Informal traditions and village councils would no longer work in a complicated urban society. Ask students what difference this would make to the way people governed themselves.

READING AND LANGUAGE ARTS

Reading Nonfiction   Help students understand that some of the statements in this chapter are not facts but conclusions drawn from scattered historical sources and the writers' knowledge and assumptions about the South Asians. Have students find examples of these conclusions and assumptions.

Using Language   On page 44 the seals, broken clay impressions, and stone weights are called "the ancient world's version of pens, stamps, and weight registers." Discuss how accurate this analogy is.

SUPPORTING LEARNING

English Language Learners   *Caravanserai* (page 44) is a compound word that means "inn/warehouse for merchants." Have students find and define other examples of compound words in the chapter.

Struggling Readers   Distribute copies of the main idea map graphic organizer. Ask three or more volunteers to read aloud the three paragraphs starting with "As it happens . . ." on page 43. Have students write "Harappa's mysterious walls" in the central circle, then write the questions archaeologists have about the walls in each of the surrounding circles.

EXTENDING LEARNING

Enrichment   Have students research the life of Alexander Cunningham. Encourage them to report their findings in a creative way, in the form of an obituary, comic book, résumé, or interview.

Extension   Distribute copies of the blackline master for Chapter 5, a blank page from an archaeologist's field journal. Have students imagine they are archaeologists who have discovered one of the clay garbage pots used in Harappa. Have them sketch the contents of their discoveries using the information from Chapters 4 and 5 as a guideline. They should label each item.

THEN and NOW

Now, as then, most people in the Indus River valley are farmers. Important crops of the Indus River cultures were wheat, barley, rice, sesame (for oil), and cotton. Have students research the agriculture of northern India and Pakistan to discover which of these products are still important. The website *www.nationmaster.com* is a good online source.

LINKING DISCIPLINES

Art Have small groups of students construct a model of Harappa according to its description in the book. They should include a caravanserai outside the gates.

THE ANCIENT SOUTH ASIAN WORLD

ARCHAEOLOGICAL FIELD NOTES FROM HARAPPA

Directions

Imagine you are an archaeologist working at Harappa. You have uncovered one of the garbage pots that Harappans used. Using the information in Chapters 4 and 5 as your guide, sketch the items that you find in the pot. Label each item, and add a short comment on how it was used. Finally, write a conclusion you can draw about the Harappans from the contents of the pot.

Pot and contents as originally arranged:

Individual items:

Comments: _____

_____

Conclusions: _____

_____

NAME DATE

CHAPTER TEST 5
THE ANCIENT SOUTH ASIAN WORLD

A. MULTIPLE CHOICE

Circle the letter of the best answer for each question.

1. Harappa was accidentally discovered when British engineers were
   a. clearing land for a football field.
   b. burning wood to keep warm.
   c. sent on an archaeological expedition.
   d. building a railroad.

2. By 2600 BCE, Harappa had all of the following **except**
   a. baked-brick houses.
   b. drains and sewers.
   c. steeply pitched roofs so that heavy snow would just slide off.
   d. two-story houses with courtyards and kitchens.

3. At its peak, the largest cities of the Indus civilization had a population of
   a. 500.
   b. 2,000.
   c. 80,000.
   d. 400,000.

4. Harappa was in a good location for all of the following reasons **except that**
   a. it had an ample water supply.
   b. there were nearby forests.
   c. it was above the flood plain.
   d. it was near lapis and malachite mines.

5. Harappa's city walls
   a. were quickly thrown up.
   b. kept out greedy merchants.
   c. kept out attacking neighbors.
   d. helped the city collect taxes.

B. SHORT ANSWER

Write a sentence or two to answer each question.

6. Why do archaeologists know more about Harappa than Mohenjo Daro?

7. What was the purpose of the walls built around the city of Harappa?

C. ESSAY

On a separate piece of paper, write an essay explaining to Alexander Cunningham the importance of the small stone seal he found. Use details from the chapter to support your statements.

CHAPTER 6

SCRATCHES, SEALS, AND SYMBOLS: THE BIRTH OF WRITING

PAGES 47–50

STUDENT STUDY GUIDE

pages 2–2

CHAPTER SUMMARY

Beginning as early as 4000 BCE, South Asians began to experiment with potters' marks and graffiti, two early steps on the road to literacy. The expanded use of symbolic seals and eventually the adoption of a symbolic written language followed.

PERFORMANCE OBJECTIVES

▶ To trace the development of writing in South Asia
▶ To understand the utility of potters' marks and graffiti
▶ To analyze the uses of seals and faience and copper tablets
▶ To explore what it means to be a civilization

BUILDING BACKGROUND

Read the title of the chapter aloud, and tell students they have just heard the story of this chapter—the evolution of Indus Valley writing from scratches on a pot to pictures on seals to a symbolic written language. Encourage them to use the title as a way of organizing the information of the chapter.

WORKING WITH PRIMARY SOURCES

Direct students' attention to the clay impression of a seal on page 49. The technical term for an impression made by a seal is *sealing*. You may wish to demonstrate the utility of a sealing with either sealing wax or a lump of soft clay. Secure a package with twine, seal the twine with sealing wax or clay, and ask students to try to remove the packaging while leaving the sealing intact.

GEOGRAPHY CONNECTION

Place Many historians have pointed out that early civilizations all arose on the banks of a river. Ask students to provide reasons why rivers were important and to give examples of the benefits and challenges of living near a river. (*Benefits: water for people, animals, and crops; source of food (fish); transportation; challenges: flooding*) Explain that the need to forecast flooding; to plan and build irrigation and drainage projects pushed these societies into developing true civilization. Distribute copies of the Chapter 6 blackline master and have students complete it to help them make the connection between solving the challenges of living in a river valley and becoming civilized.

READING COMPREHENSION QUESTIONS

1. What is the difference between ancient graffiti and pottery marks? (*Pottery marks are scratched onto the pot before firing; graffiti comes after; pottery marks were probably used to distinguish which pot belonged to whom when craftsmen shared kilns.*)
2. Why did writing spread so rapidly? (*because it was so useful for keeping track of commercial transactions, and perhaps for recording religious rituals*)
3. Why do archaeologists believe that the Indus Valley script includes both symbol-pictures and sound-specific letters? (*If it were just symbol-pictures,*

WRITING

- **Narrative** Have students write a story set in the Indus Valley called "The Clue of the Unicorn Seal." To help students organize their writing, have them use a story map. Remind students that their stories should have a conflict or problem, a climax, and a resolution. Have students peer-edit and then publish their writing.

VOCABULARY

shards pieces of broken pottery

graffiti identifying scratches incised into pottery

steatite also called "soapstone"; very soft, white stone

48 CHAPTER 6

they would have found more symbols; if it were just letters, they would have found fewer individual symbols.)

4. Why did artisans apply a chemical solution to carved steatite seals and then bake them? (*to harden the soft steatite*)

CRITICAL THINKING QUESTIONS

1. How is literacy similar to pottery? (*It allows people to store things—in this case, knowledge.*)
2. Why do archaeologists believe that seals were probably used only by the wealthy and powerful? (*Possible answers include that they were expensive to purchase and that they would have been useful only to people who had reason to keep records or protect property.*)
3. How does the comparison to modern credit cards help you understand the importance of the ancient Indus Valley seals? (*Credit cards represent money to modern people; identity theft is a major concern nowadays, so people try to be careful with their credit cards and destroy them when they are no longer useful. Losing one's seal in the ancient Indus Valley would be like having your identity stolen—someone else could say that your property was theirs.*)

SOCIAL SCIENCES

Economics Demonstrate how necessary written records are to trade by asking students to imagine the challenges of running an international corporation without the benefit of e-mail, mail service, or any way of sending a long-distance message.

READING AND LANGUAGE ARTS

Reading Nonfiction Direct students' attention to the timeline of Indus Valley writing on page 50. Point out that the spread of writing corresponds to the rise of larger villages and towns. Ask students if the two are related.

Using Language The second-to-last sentence of the chapter says that "No matter how carefully we look at the puzzle pieces, some of them are still missing." Point out that this is a figurative expression. Ask students to brainstorm other figurative expressions that could communicate the same information.

SUPPORTING LEARNING

Struggling Readers Divide the class into groups, and assign each group one section of the chapter. Have each group summarize the information in their section. Ask a presenter from each group to paraphrase the information for the rest of the class.

EXTENDING LEARNING

Enrichment Ask students to create a poster for a presentation comparing the early writing systems of the Indus Valley with those of two or three other ancient cultures, such as Egypt, Mesopotamia, Minoan Crete, Phoenicia, or China. References include French and Collins, *Write Around the World* (Oxford, 2002) and Samoyault, *Alphabetical Order: How the Alphabet Began* (Viking, 1998).

Extension Have students create a semantic map of terms and information from the chapter. Ask them to share their information with a small group. Encourage them to continue the mapping practice and use it as a study guide.

LINKING DISCIPLINES

Art Have students make a seal of their own. One method is to make a drawing on a heavy index card, then cut it out and glue it onto another card. Roll printer's ink across the card, then press it firmly against a sheet of newsprint or other paper that accepts ink easily. Another method is to have students use plastic knives to carve seals from bars of soft soap.

THEN and NOW

The trend toward larger communities that began with the invention of writing continues in South Asia, which is one of the most densely populated places on earth. India's average population density is about 94 people per square mile, while that of Bangladesh is a whopping 200 people per square mile. The United States has about 8 people per square mile.

THE ANCIENT SOUTH ASIAN WORLD

MORE THAN GOOD MANNERS

Directions
Read the information below. Then use these statements and information from Chapter 6 to answer the questions.

According to scholar Gordon Childe, a civilization is a culture that has these 10 qualities:

1. It has a city.
2. Its people have specialized jobs.
3. It collects taxes.
4. It has public works projects.
5. It has an organized government.
6. It has laws.
7. It has a written language and standard weights and measures.
8. It has a calendar.
9. It tells stories about itself.
10. It trades with other communities.

1. Most early civilizations arose on the banks of a river that often flooded in the spring. How would that influence people to create a calendar?

   _____

2. Crops grown near rivers often need to be irrigated. How would planning, building, and maintaining an irrigation system influence the formation of an organized government?

   _____

3. How would workers on these large projects be paid?

   _____

4. How would people who had full-time jobs building and maintaining public works get food to feed themselves?

   _____

5. Why would people who traded goods need to learn how to keep records?

   _____

6. On a separate sheet of paper, write an essay summarizing why early civilizations began along the banks of river valleys.

CHAPTER TEST 6

THE ANCIENT SOUTH ASIAN WORLD

NAME _____ DATE _____

A. MULTIPLE CHOICE

Circle the letter of the best answer for each question.

1. The earliest known form of writing in South Asia
   - **a.** is an alphabet.
   - **b.** includes about 70 characters.
   - **c.** was graffiti marks on pots.
   - **d.** was steatite seals.

2. Seals were probably used by all of the following **except**
   - **a.** wealthy merchants.
   - **b.** priests.
   - **c.** poor farmers.
   - **d.** government officials.

3. The Indus script
   - **a.** was recently deciphered.
   - **b.** is based on Chinese characters.
   - **c.** is an alphabet.
   - **d.** combines letters and symbols.

4. All of the following are true about most examples of Indus script **except that**
   - **a.** they were written either right to left or "as the ox turns."
   - **b.** they were frequently passed from person to person, as a dollar bill is today.
   - **c.** they are found on inscriptions on seals.
   - **d.** they are only a few characters long.

5. Pottery shards are
   - **a.** marks on pots that distinguish the maker of each pot.
   - **b.** inscriptions scratched onto pots after they have been fired.
   - **c.** broken pieces of pottery.
   - **d.** a new kind of kiln.

B. SHORT ANSWER

Write a sentence or two to answer each question.

6. What do most historians believe to be the world's most important invention? Why?

_____

7. Explain why ancient Indus seals were like modern credit cards.

_____

C. ESSAY

Write an essay on a separate piece of paper explaining the statement, "the ability to read and write is power."

THE ANCIENT SOUTH ASIAN WORLD   CHAPTER 6 TEST   **51**

CHAPTER 7

TRASH AND TOILETS: THE CITIES OF THE INDUS

PAGES 51–57

FOR HOMEWORK

STUDENT STUDY GUIDE

pages 23–24

CHAPTER SUMMARY

This chapter focuses on three of the five large cities of the Indus Valley: Harappa, Mohenjo Daro, and Dholavira. Although the cities share striking similarities in design, organization, and technology, archaeologists have not yet found compelling evidence for a single powerful political, economic, or religious authority linking them. They were organized as independent city states.

PERFORMANCE OBJECTIVES

- To explain the design of Indus cities
- To understand the sophistication of their public sanitation
- To identify the differences and similarities between Harappa, Mohenjo Daro, and Dholavira

BUILDING BACKGROUND

Explain building zones (or "zoning") in your area. Tell students that modern governments control zoning so that factories aren't built next to homes, for example, or potential sources of pollution aren't built in conservation areas. The cities of the Indus were also "zoned."

WORKING WITH PRIMARY SOURCES

Direct students' attention to the photograph of the Great Bath, Mohenjo Daro, on page 55, while a volunteer reads aloud the first paragraph on page 54. Elicit questions archaeologists might have about the Great Bath. (*What ceremonies and rituals took place there? How deep was the water in the sacred pool? How many pilgrims usually bathed at one time? How was the Great Bath cleaned?*)

GEOGRAPHY CONNECTION

Place Have students make a Venn diagram comparing Dholavira to Harappa and Mohenjo Daro. Have students include Dholavira's unique geographical location and natural resources in the diagram.

READING COMPREHENSION QUESTIONS

1. Why are old cities often found underground? (*Sometimes they get buried by volcanoes. Mostly, though, they are buried bit by bit by new construction. New cities get built on top of them.*)
2. How many people lived in Harappa? (*There was room for 80,000 people, but some of them may have lived on their farms during the summer or come to the city only for religious festivals.*)
3. How did the cities of the Indus Valley compare with other cities their size in the ancient world? (*cleaner; more orderly; less grand; more private*)
4. What was unusual about the Great Hall in Harappa? (*It was very large and was made of wood with a brick foundation.*)

WRITING

- **Explanation** As Dr. Miller remarks in her interview, as a historian "you never find out the answer, because there are always more questions." Have students write a short essay explaining this comment. They should include examples and details from the chapter to support their points.

VOCABULARY

orient to familiarize oneself with one's surroundings

52 CHAPTER 7

CRITICAL THINKING QUESTIONS

1. Why do you think the streets of the Indus cities ran north-south and east-west? *(Answers will vary.)*
2. Although the Indus cities had many similarities, each one also had distinctive features. Using the blackline master for Chapter 7, tell how the cities were different. *(Harappa: disturbed archaeological site and wooden Great Hall. Mohenjo Daro: not currently being excavated because bricks are dissolving; more large buildings than Harappa; possible palace or temple with broken statues of Priest King; Great Bath. Dholavira: on an island; stone, not brick; fewer farmers, more fisherfolk; very well preserved; cisterns for rainwater; gates and sign.)*

SOCIAL SCIENCES

Science, Technology, and Society The people of the Indus Valley used wedge-shaped bricks to line their wells. Have students draw various four-sided, wedge-shaped forms and see which ones fit together best to form a circular well. Ask students to describe their conclusions.

READING AND LANGUAGE ARTS

Reading Nonfiction Direct students' attention to the Archaeologist at Work feature on page 56. Elicit that italics are used for two purposes here: to set off introductory remarks from the body of the text, and to differentiate questions from answers.

Using Language Discuss the use of the apostrophe in contractions. Have students identify contractions in the chapter. Point out that contractions are much more common in informal speech, as in the interview, than they are in written speech.

SUPPORTING LEARNING

English Language Learners Read aloud the following statements of main ideas from the chapter. Have students supply the missing words in each sentence. Walls, doorways, and bricks in Indus Valley towns and cities were the same _____ (*size*). Most streets had built-in ____bins (*garbage*). Waste flowed through small drains in side streets into huge covered _____ (*sewers*) in the main streets. In Mohenjo Daro a pilgrim could wash and then enter the sacred pool of the _____ _____ (*Great Bath*).

Struggling Readers Display key words from the chapter, such as *orientation, travelers, bricks, garbage, drainage,* and *sewer,* and have each student choose a word. Have students define the word, use it in a sentence, and illustrate it on a strip of construction paper. Mount their work on poster board, and use the display for vocabulary review.

EXTENDING LEARNING

Enrichment Encourage students to check out volunteer dig programs in your area by exploring the websites for the Archaeological Institute of America at *www.archaeological.org* and the Society for American Archaeology at *www.saa.org*. Have students research programs that are available locally or are of regional interest and prepare a brochure for their classmates.

Extension The cities of the Indus were organized into job-specific neighborhoods. Have students plan an Indus city with all the neighborhoods they think would be necessary for the city to function well.

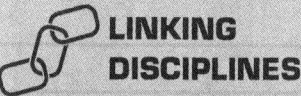

LINKING DISCIPLINES

Architecture Have small groups of students draw an architectural plan for the city of their choice according to the description found in the text and as researched online. Assign them the task of explaining the features of the city to their families.

CHAPTER 7 BLM

THE ANCIENT SOUTH ASIAN WORLD

NAME _____ **DATE** _____

ORGANIZING INFORMATION: THE CITIES OF THE INDUS

Directions For each city, place a checkmark in each box that applies to it. If you don't have information on something, leave the space blank.

Harappa	Mohenjo Daro	Dholavira
Standard-sized mud bricks		
Standard-sized streets, doors, and windows		
Streets laid out north-south and east-west		
Great Hall		
City walls		
Walled neighborhoods organized by profession		
Sacred tree		
Great Bath		
City gates with sign		
Nearby farms		
Nearby ports		
Water tanks that covered one-third of city		
Sandstone block buildings		

CHAPTER TEST 7

THE ANCIENT SOUTH ASIAN WORLD

A. MULTIPLE CHOICE

Circle the letter of the best answer for each question.

1. The Indus Valley cities shared all of the following **except**
   a. similar city plans.
   b. at least one large building.
   c. good drains.
   d. tanks for catching rain.

2. The Great Bath
   a. may have had a spiritual as well as a hygienic purpose.
   b. was for washing off the mud from the mud bricks.
   c. is in Dholavira.
   d. was probably used for doing laundry.

3. The cities of the Indus Valley smelled good for all of the following reasons **except that**
   a. people washed themselves after using the toilet.
   b. dirty water was carried outside the city by drains.
   c. every neighborhood had its own Great Bath.
   d. the covered sewers were probably cleaned out from time to time.

4. The people of ancient South Asia
   a. took special care to orient their houses and streets properly.
   b. loved to live in large, lavishly decorated palaces.
   c. were mostly city dwellers.
   d. were very loyal to their queen.

5. Most buildings and walls in the biggest Indus cities were made
   a. of wood.
   b. of sandstone.
   c. of fired brick.
   d. in the shape of a person.

B. SHORT ANSWER

Write a sentence or two to answer each question.

6. Describe the bricks used to make drainage pipes.

_____

_____

7. What was the purpose of the Great Bath at Mohenjo Daro?

_____

_____

C. ESSAY

On a separate piece of paper write an essay explaining the statement, "the cities of the Indus were very well organized."

EXPANSION AND DECLINE

PAGES 58–76

Chapter 8 Going Shopping: Arts and Crafts in the Indus Valley
Chapter 9 By Land and By Sea: Trade with the Near East
Chapter 10 Mystery in the City: Decline and Change in the Late Harappan Period

UNIT OBJECTIVES

Unit 3 discusses life in the Indus Valley during the third millennium BCE, when trade and city life were at their height. In this unit your students will learn

- more about the Harappan craft tradition.
- ideas about what it was like to grow up in ancient South Asia.
- about the restricted life led by most South Asian women.
- about the characteristics of South Asian society and government.

PRIMARY SOURCES

Unit 3 includes excerpts from the following primary sources:

- Sargon, tablet
- Valmiki, *Ramayana*
- *Rig Veda*

Pictures of South Asian artifacts from more than 2,500 years ago can also be analyzed as primary sources:

- Toy oxcart, Harappa
- Conch shell inlays, Mohenjo Daro
- Carnelian belt, Mohenjo Daro
- Deity seal
- Clay figurine
- Priest-King sculpture, Mohenjo Daro
- Deity and worshippers seal
- Queen Puabi's jewelry, Mesopotamia
- Bronze head of Akkadian king, Mesopotamia
- Boat tablet, Mohenjo Daro
- Clay boat model, Harappa
- Storage jar, Harappa
- Glass and faience beads, Harappa
- Pottery kiln, Harappa
- Cave painting, Ajanta, India
- Mass grave, Mohenjo Daro
- Cave paintings, Bhimbetka, India

BIG IDEAS IN UNIT 3

Markets, trade, and **decline** are the big ideas presented in Unit 3. The unit emphasizes the importance of markets and long-distance trade networks to the people of the Indus Valley and examines its puzzling decline after 700 prosperous years.

One helpful way to introduce these ideas is to make a two-column chart on the board on which students list the costs and benefits of international trade. The benefits might include a wider range of goods, more customers for the goods produced, and the influx of new ideas and technologies. Among the drawbacks might be the increased risk of conflict and vulnerability to changes in market conditions or the circumstances of your trading partners. Define *outsourcing* as the practice of companies saving money by hiring people in other countries to do work formerly done by people in their own country. Discuss outsourcing's pros (*lower prices for goods and services; employment for people in other countries*) and cons (*loss of employment for workers in home country; bad publicity for companies doing the outsourcing*).

GEOGRAPHY CONNECTION

Have students refer to the map of South Asia on pages 12–13. Point out that so far the class has learned about peoples living in what is now Pakistan and northern India. In this chapter they'll learn about those peoples' interactions with the wider geographic region.

TIMELINE

2600–1900 BCE   Indus Valley civilization develops; Harappan period; large, planned cities emerge throughout the Indus region
2600 BCE   Villagers of Harappa and Mohenjo Daro build drains and baked-brick houses
1900–1300 BCE   Indus cities decline
1700–1500 BCE   *Rig Veda*, the oldest part of the *Vedas*, compiled

UNIT PROJECTS

Market

Invite interested students to put together Mesopotamian and South Asian "markets," using paper cut-out replicas of the objects available in both economies. Have students go "shopping." Which goods are most popular? Which might command the highest prices?

Models

Interested students can create models of South Asian boats, using the description in the text and the illustrations on page 66 and 70 as their reference points. They should be prepared to point out the various features to their classmates.

Writing Dialogue

Have partners write dialogues between a Mesopotamian and a Harappan trader discussing what they find interesting and disturbing about each other's cultures and sympathizing with each other about the difficulties of the journey between their lands.

Research Report

Small groups can investigate subjects of their choice to bring more information back to the rest of the class. Possible subjects include legends associated with the Saraswati River, trade with Oman and Mesopotamia, and India's magnificent painted caves. Students can search for sources in the library/media center and on the Internet. Groups can create a panel discussion or a visual display to explain the information to the class.

ADDITIONAL ASSESSMENT

Use any of these unit projects for additional assessment. For Unit 3, divide the class into groups and have them all undertake the Writing Dialogue or Research Report projects. To assess their work, note how the dialogues show students' grasp of Mesopotamian and Harappan cultural differences and details of travel between their lands. Use the scoring rubric at the back of this guide to assess group projects, and have students rate their own work with the self-assessment rubric. For the Research Report, be sure to distribute the library/media center research log (see rubric at the back of this guide) to help students evaluate their sources as they conduct their research.

LITERATURE CONNECTION

Despite its deeply nested structure and potentially confusing narratives, "Arabian Nights" is perhaps one of the best known stories of South Asia. You might recommend this modern version of the tales:

▶ Alderson, Brian. *The Arabian Nights: Or, Tales Told by Sheherezade During a Thousand Nights and One Night.* Morrow Junior Books, 1995. An illustrated collection of stories from the "Arabian Nights," retold by the author, including those of Sinbad, Ali Baba, and Aladdin.

UNIVERSAL ACCESS

The following strategies are designed to cover a range of learning styles and reading, language, and skill levels. You may find that any of your students will benefit from the various strategies presented.

Reading Strategies

▶ To facilitate reading, preview the primary sources—photographs and/or text excerpts—in each chapter so that students will be aware of the subject of the chapter.
▶ Ask students to read their books aloud at home to family members. If oral reports are assigned, remind them to practice once or twice before an audience at home so they can do their best work in class.

Writing Strategies

▶ Have students put themselves in the place of the people studied in this unit. Ask them to write journal entries representing daily activities for these people.
▶ Have groups of students write skits involving people from several of the chapters in the unit. One such skit might involve a Harappan potter and his family. Another might involve a Harappan trader and his daughter visiting Mesopotamia for the first time. Groups can read their skits to the class.

Listening and Speaking

▶ To spark students' interest, state facts from the chapter that are diametrically opposed to their life experiences. Have them read to understand the context of such statements.
▶ Help teams of students prepare "debates" between types of people in these chapters. For instance, one student might be from Harappa and another from Mesopotamia. The two would debate which is the better place to live. Or one student might be a miner from the highlands and the other a jeweler in Mohenjo Daro.

UNIT VOCABULARY LISTS

The following words that appear in Unit 3 are important for your students' understanding of the social studies content as well as for development of literacy. Use these words for vocabulary study or to reinforce language arts skills (e.g., synonyms, compound words, prefixes and suffixes, and related words). The words are listed below in the order in which they appear in the chapters.

Chapter 8
bounty
emerged
overwhelmed
quarter
inlaid
soapstone
meditating
defaced
clan
solemn

Chapter 9
suddenly
extravagant
retreating
anxious
pipal tree
treacherous
interpret
convenient
textiles
frustratingly
strained
laden

Chapter 10
surpassing
desperate
agates
geometric
collapsed
occasionally
assumed
contagious

CHAPTER 8

GOING SHOPPING: ARTS AND CRAFTS IN THE INDUS VALLEY

PAGES 58–63

FOR HOMEWORK

STUDENT STUDY GUIDE
pages 25–26

VOCABULARY

inlay a decorative filling of a different color or material

yoga exercises that were initially designed to help people learn to concentrate during meditation

WRITING

- **Letter** Ask students to imagine that they are Sarang writing a letter home to his younger brother describing life in the city. What details would Sarang especially notice? What details might he include because he thought his little brother might be interested?

CHAPTER SUMMARY

Harappan craftsmen worked beads, ceramics, wood, and precious metals for both commercial and religious purposes. A few tantalizing clues seem to suggest that Harappan religious practices were strikingly similar to contemporary Hindu practices.

PERFORMANCE OBJECTIVES

▶ To describe the crafts of the Harappan period
▶ To analyze artifacts for clues about Harappan religious practices
▶ To explains the craftsmanship of Harappan artifacts

BUILDING BACKGROUND

Remind students of the bow drill they read about on page 40. Refer them to the carnelian belt pictured on page 60. Ask students to estimate how long it would take to drill one of those beads. (*Archaeologists estimate that it would take three working days to drill a single three-inch bead.*)

WORKING WITH PRIMARY SOURCES

Refer students to the yogi seal on page 61. Ask them to make observations about the figure. Archaeologists believe that the striped bands on his arms represent bangles. He is also wearing a horned, plumed headdress that seems to be associated with divinity. Some historians argue that this is one of the first depictions of the ancient Asian discipline of yoga. Invite students to share what they know about yoga.

GEOGRAPHY CONNECTION

Movement Point out that the interaction between nomad families and cities continues to this day in South Asia. Suzanne Staples Fisher's acclaimed young-adult novel, *Shabanu*, and its sequel, *Haveli*, are realistic portrayals of a young girl in a family of Pakistani nomads and her interaction with the city. Ask volunteers to read one of the novels and report back to the class about contemporary practices among nomad families.

READING COMPREHENSION QUESTIONS

1. What did Sarang's family bring to trade in the city? (*barley, wheat, cotton*)
2. What crafts were practiced in Harappan cities? (*bead drilling; ivory carving; inlay; goldsmithing and silversmithing; faience; carved stone seals; pottery; leatherwork; copperwork; textiles*)
3. What kinds of work did children do? (*Many apparently helped their parents; their fingerprints show up on pots.*)
4. What is the importance of the statues of the "priest-king"? (*All are broken, so the person or group they refer to probably lost favor; probably a ruling clan.*)

CRITICAL THINKING QUESTIONS

1. How do you think archaeologists have determined that the weeks after the spring and fall harvests were holidays for the people of the Indus Valley? *(perhaps by analogy with contemporary practice)*
2. What are some examples of centralized city planning? *(furnaces on the southern side of the city to avoid fire; smelly endeavors also placed so that prevailing winds would blow the smells away from the city)*
3. What evidence might be used to support the theory that holy men lived in sacred groves outside the city wall? *(Many seals show holy men sitting in or beneath trees. There is no evidence of groves within the city walls. Later, this is a common practice.)*

SOCIAL SCIENCES

Civics The fact that the priest-king statues are defaced suggests to archaeologists that the leaders or ruling clan they represent fell out of favor. Discuss what considerations could make a ruler fall from favor. *(natural disasters or military defeats that might have suggested that the leader's power was insufficient to protect the people; personal cruelty or incompetence)*

READING AND LANGUAGE ARTS

Reading Nonfiction Reread with students the You Can't Take It With You sidebar on page 63. Ask students which burial practices—Mesopotamian or Harappan—are better for the economy. *(Harappan, because precious goods remain in circulation.)*

Using Language This chapter uses vivid adverbs to describe city life, like *wildly*, *delicately*, and *intricately*. Remind students that adverbs are used to modify verbs, adverbs, and adjectives and that they often end in *-ly*. Have students find examples of adverbs in the chapter and tell how these words modify others.

SUPPORTING LEARNING

English Language Learners Have students talk to their families about special harvest traditions or festivals from their culture. Then have them meet and share their findings in small groups before delivering a presentation to the class.

Struggling Readers Have students use the main idea map graphic organizer (see graphic organizers at the back of this book) to identify and describe different reasons people came to the cities.

EXTENDING LEARNING

Enrichment According to the sidebar on page 62, some symbols holy to the Hindus date from the Indus Valley period. Have students research the original meaning of the symbols mentioned in the sidebar. Have them report their findings to the class.

Extension Distribute copies of the blackline master for Chapter 8 and have students complete it to better imagine wandering through ancient Harappa.

LINKING DISCIPLINES

Dance Direct students' attention to the carnelian belt on page 60. Tell them that today in South Asia, the sound of the beads the dancer is wearing is considered to be part of the beauty of the dance. Dancing is also a part of worship; many temples employ dancers. If possible, obtain a video of contemporary South Asian dance to illustrate the point.

THEN and NOW

Even today the agate mining regions of western India produce most of the carnelian used in the modern bead trade. Diamonds from South India and also from Africa are cut and polished in the many workshops of western India, and sold in the diamond markets of Mumbai (Bombay), a bustling city of 10 million people, just as they have been for thousands of years.

COMING TO HARAPPA

Use the chart to organize a description of the sights, smells, and sounds a young person from the country would experience on a visit to Harappa.

Landmark	Sights, Sounds, and Smells
Walking with oxcart	
Camping by road	
First sight of city	
Passing furnaces and leather-working areas	
Going through gates and having goods measured and weighed	
Wood-carver's shop	
Jeweler's shop	
Pottery shop	
Harvest Festival	

CHAPTER TEST 8

THE ANCIENT SOUTH ASIAN WORLD

NAME _____ DATE _____

A. MULTIPLE CHOICE

Circle the letter of the best answer for each question.

1. Many people visited Harappa
   a. during the monsoon, to escape flooding.
   b. during the winter, to be protected from cold and wind.
   c. after the spring and fall harvests, to trade and attend religious festivals.
   d. during the fall, to vote a new government into office.

2. Which of the following statements about Harappa is **not** true?
   a. Holy men probably lived outside the city gates.
   b. Leather dressers and furnaces were on the south side of the city, so that smells and sparks would be blown away from most people.
   c. The streets of the poor were as carefully cleaned as those of the wealthy.
   d. Potters made both practical and religious objects.

3. Harappan gods were commonly shown with all of the following **except**
   a. bangles.
   b. a thunderbolt.
   c. horned and plumed headdresses.
   d. a sacred tree.

4. Farmers went to the city for all of the following **except**
   a. food and clothing.
   b. religious worship.
   c. tools.
   d. pottery.

5. *Pipal* is another name for
   a. carnelian belts.
   b. the sacred fig tree.
   c. country folk.
   d. the Priest King.

B. SHORT ANSWER

On the lines, answer each question in one or two sentences.

6. Who do archaeologists believe the Priest King was? Why?
   _____
   _____

7. Describe the making of a carnelian belt, explaining why it was so valuable.
   _____
   _____

ESSAY

Write an essay on a separate piece of paper explaining why a family like the one described in the chapter would have traveled to Harappa and what they would have seen and done there.

CHAPTER 9

BY LAND AND BY SEA: TRADE WITH THE NEAR EAST

PAGES 64–71

STUDENT STUDY GUIDE
pages 27–28

CAST OF CHARACTERS

Puabi (poo-AH-bee) Queen of Ur who was buried with incredible wealth, including beads from the Indus region

- **News Article** Have students write a news article announcing the safe return of the sea captain from Dholavira. Tell them to include some quotations from the captain in their story.

CHAPTER SUMMARY

The cities of the Indus Valley were part of an international network of trading cities that included Mesopotamia, the Arabian peninsula, and even Africa, as well as inland sites such as the mines of Baluchistan and Afghanistan. Sea captains became adept at using the changing winds of the monsoon to sail north and west at the first of the year, returning when the winds changed in June.

PERFORMANCE OBJECTIVES

▶ To explain the risks and rewards of South Asia's trade networks
▶ To trace a sample voyage to Mesopotamia
▶ To describe inland trade routes

BUILDING BACKGROUND

Write *exports* and *imports* on the board and ask students what these words mean. Point out that successful economies export and import many goods. Brainstorm with students a list of products and raw materials that the United States exports and imports. Explain that the cities of the Indus Valley—like the United States—depended upon trade for their prosperity and stability.

WORKING WITH PRIMARY SOURCES

Have students study the tablet on page 66 while a volunteer reads aloud the last paragraph on page 65, the first one on page 66, and the caption. Have students analyze the tablet. How much information from the text is visible? How was the boat steered? (*possibly by rudder—like shapes at right of tablet*)

GEOGRAPHY CONNECTION

Regions Tell students that the physical danger of sailing in ancient times was considerable. You may wish to use the example of the tsunami created by an earthquake off the coast of Sumatra on the morning of December 26, 2004, when hundreds of thousands of people—some of them fishermen as far away as Kenya—were drowned with virtually no warning. (See Then and Now feature on page 24 of this guide.) Discuss the ways survivors coped with the 2004 tsunami and compare resources available today with those people had in ancient times. Students should understand that underwater earthquakes that cause tsunamis can now be detected and people alerted that a tsunami is coming.

READING COMPREHENSION QUESTIONS

1. What is Meluhha? (*The Akkadian name for the Indus Valley.*)
2. What danger did traders face soon after leaving Dholavira? (*a rocky coast and poisonous snakes*)
3. Why did the captain have to hire a guide as he approached Mesopotamia? (*because navigating the delta of the Tigris and the Euphrates was so treacherous*)
4. What goods did Magan (present-day Oman) offer for trade? (*copper and large marine shells for bangles and inlay*)

64 | CHAPTER 9

CRITICAL THINKING QUESTIONS

1. Lavish burials could be thought of as bad for the economy because they take precious resources out of circulation. What explanation can you give for such burials? *(Possible answers: They reinforce the power of the royal family; there was competition between kings for the grandest funeral; the people believed that the objects would be used in the afterlife)*
2. Harappan storage jars were pointed instead of flat at the bottom. What advantages did this shape offer? *(Not many surfaces were flat in the days before cement, so a flat bottom would not be all that helpful; pointed bottoms could be stuck into sand or embers; when their contents were heavy, the jars could be rolled instead of carried; they could be tipped for pouring and carried against the body more easily.)*
3. Why was navigating through the delta of the Tigris and the Euphrates so difficult that it required hiring local guides? *(because the rivers constantly deposited silt at the delta, so boats could easily run aground)*
4. How did sea-going ships and riverboats differ? *(Sea-going ships had a deep keel to keep them stable, rudders to steer with, and a cabin; riverboats were flat-bottomed and could be sailed or poled.)*

SOCIAL SCIENCES

Economics   Have students make a two-column chart and list the costs and benefits of long-distance trade to the cities of the Indus.

READING AND LANGUAGE ARTS

Reading Nonfiction   Explain that because there is so little direct information about South Asian trading networks, most of the statements in the chapter are generalizations about trading practices. Have students find examples of these generalizations.

Using Language   The chapter uses adjectives to describe South Asian trade, such as *sleek*, *tempting*, and *treacherous*. Have students identify these adjectives, use a dictionary or thesaurus to find synonyms, and then use the synonyms in sentences.

SUPPORTING LEARNING

English Language Learners   Direct partners to the pictures in the chapter. Ask them to determine what each picture shows. Have them find the text in the chapter that the pictures relate to. Ask students to state what these graphic aids add to their understanding.

Struggling Readers   Divide the class into small groups. Assign each group a section of the chapter to reread, and have each group identify the main idea and several details of the section. Then have the groups summarize their findings in an oral presentation.

EXTENDING LEARNING

Enrichment   Have students research the major products of Near East and South Asian countries like Afghanistan, Bahrain, Bangladesh, India, Iraq, Oman, and Pakistan and compare their economies today with what they were in the third millennium BCE. Have them present their discoveries to the class.

Extension   Distribute copies of the Chapter 9 blackline master to students and have them complete it to gain better understanding of South Asia's trade routes.

LINKING DISCIPLINES

Math   Obtain recent cotton-production figures like those found at *www.seedquest.com/statistics/asiapacific.htm* and have students construct either a pie chart or a bar graph to illustrate the information by country.

THEN and NOW

Cotton was first cultivated in South Asia. Taken collectively, South Asia is the largest producer of cotton in the world, slightly edging out China and the United States.

CHAPTER 9 BLM

THE ANCIENT SOUTH ASIAN WORLD

NAME   DATE

SOUTH ASIA'S TRADE NETWORKS

Directions
Label the locations of the following places on the map, using information from your book and the map on page 69 to help you. Below each label, list the items that each place offered for trade.

Bay of Bengal	Arabian Sea	Persian Gulf	Dilmun (Bahrain)
Magan (Oman)	Dholavira	Harappa	Mohenjo Daro
Kabul River	Ur	Tigris River	Euphrates River
Indus River	Afghanistan	Baluchistan	

West Asia, Central Asia, and South Asia

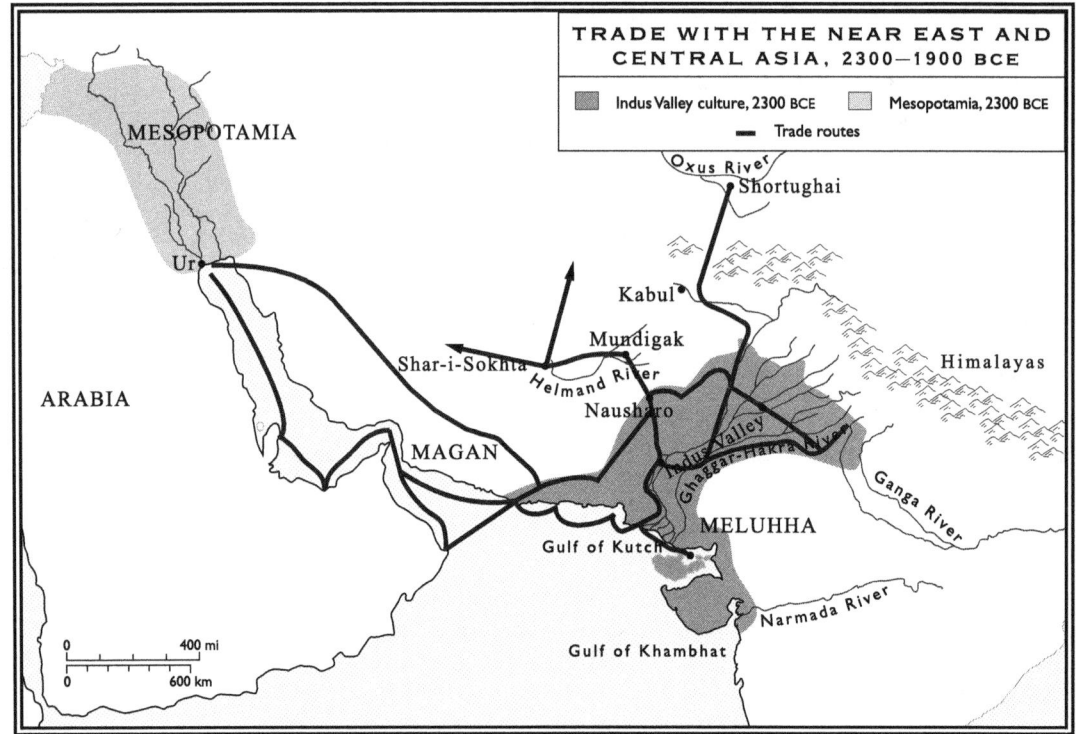

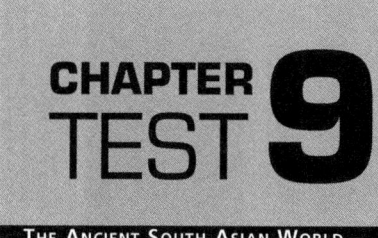

NAME _____ **DATE** _____

A. MULTIPLE CHOICE

Circle the letter of the best answer for each question.

1. The Indus Valley city that was best positioned for sea trade with Mesopotamia was
   a. Harappa.
   b. Dholavira.
   c. Mohenjo Daro.
   d. Dilmun.

2. All of the following are benefits of storage jars with pointed bottoms **except that**
   a. they could be rolled instead of carried.
   b. they were easier to pour from.
   c. it was easy to store them upright on flat-bottomed river boats.
   d. they were easier to hold against the body.

3. Mesopotamia imported all of the following from the Indus Valley **except**
   a. gold.
   b. long carnelian beads.
   c. exotic animals.
   d. cotton.

4. What were mountain colonies in the highlands eager to obtain from Indus Valley merchants?
   a. wood
   b. foodstuffs
   c. precious stones and metals
   d. exotic animals

5. Dilmun and Magan were the ancient names for
   a. Iraq and Iran.
   b. Kenya and Ethiopia.
   c. Bahrain and Oman.
   d. Afghanistan and northern Pakistan.

B. SHORT ANSWER

Write a sentence or two to answer each question.

6. What were some of the items brought by merchants from the Indus Valley to Mesopotamia?

_____

_____

7. Whom did Indus Valley merchants trade with in the high valleys of Badakshan?

_____

_____

C. ESSAY

Write an essay on a separate piece of paper explaining the costs and benefits of long-distance trade. Be sure to include specific details.

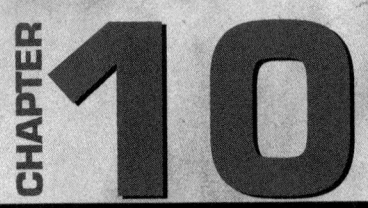

CHAPTER 10

MYSTERY IN THE CITY: DECLINE AND CHANGE IN THE LATE HARAPPAN PERIOD

PAGES 72–76

FOR HOMEWORK

STUDENT STUDY GUIDE
pages 29–30

VOCABULARY

intrepid without fear

arya "noble ones" in Sanskrit, it is the root word of *Ireland*, *Iran*, and *Aryans*

WRITING

○ **Persuasion** Have each student revise the paragraph they wrote as part of the blackline master exercise into a multi-paragraph essay.

CHAPTER SUMMARY

From about 1900 BCE, when the Saraswati River began to dry up, the cities of the Indus Valley entered into a long decline. A variety of technological and cultural changes followed, including the end of long-distance trade, the loss of the Indus script, new pottery techniques, new burial practices, and the introduction of horses and iron. Previously, historians ascribed these changes to an Aryan invasion. This interpretation is not supported by modern scholars who have looked carefully at the archaeology and literary evidence.

PERFORMANCE OBJECTIVES

▶ To trace the decline of the cities of the Indus Valley
▶ To catalog the cultural and technological changes that followed
▶ To construct a theory that explains these changes

BUILDING BACKGROUND

Read the title and subtitle aloud. Ask students what they think the "mystery in the city" might be. Ask them to state what they think this chapter is going to tell them about South Asian history. Record their statements and questions, and refer to them as you read.

WORKING WITH PRIMARY SOURCES

Direct students' attention to the photograph of the skeletons found at Mohenjo Daro on page 75. If they had excavated these skeletons, what conclusion would they have drawn at first? Review the more recent explanation of contagious disease. Discuss how likely that explanation is, given the overcrowded, disorganized conditions of city life during this period.

GEOGRAPHY CONNECTION

Movement   Consult the map at www.historyforkids.org/learn/maps/indoeuropean.htm. Ask: How could one small group of people spread their language so far and so fast? Point out that the Aryans had horses, a new and speedy technology that made it easy for them to move and conquer people rapidly.

READING COMPREHENSION QUESTIONS

1. What is the *Rig Veda*? (*It is the oldest South Asian scripture, a collection of hymns, stories, and prayers.*)
2. What is the significance of the Saraswati River? (*It is one of the great rivers of the Indus Valley, and its disappearance starting in about 1900 BCE may have sent the cities of the valley into an irreversible decline.*)
3. Why is the idea of an Aryan invasion no longer accepted? (*no evidence of battles or new people*)

CRITICAL THINKING QUESTIONS

1. According to archaeologists, pottery styles are very slow to change. Why might that be? (*Most pottery is used in the home and reflects one's identity and culture. People prefer to cook their traditional foods in their cultural styles of pots. Chinese cook in woks, Europeans cook in saucepans, tortillas are cooked on flat platters, etc.*)
2. In your opinion, what are the two most powerful innovations introduced during the Harappan decline? (*Answers will vary; iron and horses are good choices.*)
3. What was the most tragic loss? (*probably the loss of literacy, although a case could also be made for the decline of long-distance trade*)
4. Distribute copies of the Chapter 10 blackline master and have students complete it to solidify their understanding of changing conditions in South Asia at the beginning of the second millennium BCE.

SOCIAL SCIENCES

Science, Technology, and Society Ask students to identify ways in which the new leaders seem to have been less advanced than Harappan leadership during its golden age. (*Possible answers include the lack of a written culture and trade, or the fact that the cities were disorganized and dirty.*) In what ways were they more advanced? (*They had horses—faster transportation and communication—and iron—stronger weapons and tools.*) Discuss the influence of new technology on a society.

READING AND LANGUAGE ARTS

Reading Nonfiction Identify the excerpts in the chapter that are poetry and those that are prose. (Both quotations from the *Rig Veda*, on pages 72 and 75, are poetry.) Have students compare the two genres and draw conclusions about why a writer would use either one. Have students rewrite the poetry as prose, and vice versa.

Using Language Point out two closely related words in the chapter: *Aryan* and *Indo-Aryan*. Have students read the sidebar that explains the source of the word *Aryan* on page 75. Discuss what additional information the prefix *Indo-* provides. (*It identifies the Aryans who lived in what was broadly called India, the area that we now know as South Asia.*)

SUPPORTING LEARNING

Struggling Readers Write the following on note cards: *Rig Veda*, Saraswati River, faience, kiln, Indra, iron, Indo-Aryan language, cave paintings, Harappans. Have a volunteer come to the front of the room and hold up one of the cards without reading it. The rest of the class can offer clues about the term on the card until the volunteer guesses the word.

EXTENDING LEARNING

Enrichment Have students research more about the theory of the Aryan invasion at places like *www.wsu.edu:8080/~dee/ANCINDIA/ARYANS.HTM* and *www.historyforkids.org/learn/india/history/aryan.htm* and report their findings to the class.

Extension Ask students to act out certain scenes in the text. For example, a group can act out a scene of a Harappan inventor describing a new kiln design to a group of potters while one student narrates.

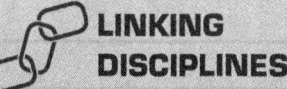

LINKING DISCIPLINES

Art Have students paint their own "caves at Ajanta." Have them make a drawing with a waterproof pen on watercolor paper. Remind them that the caves were quite intricate, with every space filled. Then have them go over their designs with watercolor.

THE ANCIENT SOUTH ASIAN WORLD

NAME   **DATE**

MYSTERY IN THE CITY: WHAT HAPPENED IN THE INDUS VALLEY (1900–1500 BCE)?

Directions
Read the following paragraphs. Then use the information on this page and in Chapter 10 to complete the cause and effect chart. When you have finished, write a paragraph explaining what *you* think happened in the Indus Valley. Was life there changed by armies, or by ideas?

For many years, historians believed that a lighter-skinned people called the Aryans invaded South Asia between 1900 and 1500 BCE. They believed that the Aryans conquered the people of the Indus Valley and introduced horses, camels, iron, and new ideas and tools.

Today, most archaeologists and historians disagree with this idea. They say there is no evidence that the Vedic people were lighter-skinned or that they invaded and conquered the Indus Valley. New leaders may have come to power, but that happened because the Indus Valley was facing new problems that the old ways couldn't solve.

Cause	Effect
	The Saraswati River dried up.
	Writing and long-distance trade stop.
	Jewelers begin to make imitation glass beads.
	Horses and camels are introduced to the Indus Valley.
	Iron tools and weapons appear.
	New pottery styles appear.
	People are buried differently.

In my opinion, life in South Asia changed between 1900 and 1500 BCE because

_____
_____
_____
_____

70   CHAPTER 10 BLM   THE ANCIENT SOUTH ASIAN WORLD

CHAPTER TEST 10

THE ANCIENT SOUTH ASIAN WORLD

A. MULTIPLE CHOICE

Circle the letter of the best answer for each question.

1. The Saraswati River is important to the history of South Asia for all of the following reasons **except** that it
   a. was one of the great rivers of the Indus Valley.
   b. began to dry up in about 1900 BCE.
   c. is mentioned in the *Rig Veda*.
   d. was the quickest route to Baluchistan.

2. After about 1900 BCE, people in the Indus Valley forgot how to
   a. bake pottery.
   b. live in cities.
   c. write.
   d. farm.

3. All of the following underwent important changes after 1900 BCE **except**
   a. cleanliness and orderliness of cities.
   b. jewelry.
   c. long-distance trade.
   d. farming.

4. Pottery changed after 1900 BCE in all of these ways **except that**
   a. new kilns burned hotter, so pottery became stronger and was made with thinner walls.
   b. potters painted new designs, like flowers, in new colors such as black and red.
   c. potters began to make flat-bottomed pots now that floors were more even.
   d. it began to hold the bones of the dead.

5. The Indo-Aryan speakers
   a. probably looked very different from the people of the Indus Valley.
   b. destroyed Harappan civilization.
   c. greatly expanded trade networks, since they could communicate with people as far away as Greece and Ireland.
   d. introduced horses, chariots, and iron weapons to South Asia.

B. SHORT ANSWER

Write a sentence or two to answer each question.

6. What were two effects of the Saraswati River drying up?

7. What do cave paintings from Central India tell us about Indo-Aryan speakers?

C. ESSAY

On a separate sheet of paper, write an essay stating what you think were the two most important innovations introduced in the Indus Valley after 1900 BCE. Be sure to back up your ideas with specific examples.

THE VEDIC ERA

PAGES 77–102

Chapter 11	Fire and Sacrifice: Living by the Vedas
Chapter 12	Two Great Adventures: Epic Traditions
Chapter 13	New Gods: From Brahmanism to Early Hinduism
Chapter 14	Two Gentle Religions: Buddhism and Jainism

UNIT OBJECTIVES

Unit 4 discusses life in South Asia during the Vedic era. The most important source of historians' knowledge of these years, roughly 1500–600 BCE, is the Vedas, a series of religious writings that were composed at about this time and got passed down orally. This is the period when people began to be divided into formal social groups based on their function in society, and when religious practices that would later become identified with Hinduism began. In this unit your students will learn

- the origins of South Asian ideas about *varna*, or social class.
- about religious practices during the Vedic era.
- the great epic poems *Ramayana* and *Bhagavad Gita*.
- about the beginnings of Buddhism and Jainism.

PRIMARY SOURCES

Unit 4 includes excerpts from the following primary sources:

- "Hymn to Agni," Vedas
- *Bhagavad Gita*
- Valmiki, *Ramayana*
- *Brahmavaivarta Purana*
- *Upanishads*
- Mahavira, *Discourses of Mahavira*
- Buddha, The Four Noble Truths
- Buddha, *Admonition to Singala*
- Ashokan Rock Edict

Pictures of South Asian artifacts can also be analyzed as primary sources. These include:

- Sanskrit inscription
- Carving of Agni, South India
- Illustration from *Mahabharata*
- Illustration from *Ramayana*
- Carving of Vishnu
- Statue of Brahma
- Statue of Ganesha
- Drawing of Shiva
- Drawing of Brahma, Vishnu, and Shiva
- Brahmi birch-bark script
- Statue of Jain saint Gomatesvara, South India
- Carving of Prince Siddhartha
- Stupa, Swat, Pakistan

BIG IDEAS IN UNIT 4

Religion and **social organization** are the big ideas presented in Unit 4. The unit presents the social classes and religious practices introduced in the Vedas. It expands on the elaboration of Vedic values in the great South Asian epics *Ramayana* and *Mahabharata,* including the *Bhagavad Gita,* and the way those ideas evolved into early humanism, as well as the new ideas of Buddhism and Jainism.

You may want to introduce these ideas by eliciting what students know about South Asian religion—gods, practices, and beliefs about reincarnation and social organization. Explain that at this time, South Asia did not share one single government and that the region's identity was largely determined by shared religious beliefs.

GEOGRAPHY CONNECTION

Have students refer to the map in their book on pages 12–13 as you discuss South Asia's size and topography. Ask: what would make travel difficult? (*mountain ranges, vast distances*) Before there were good roads and good communications, what are some ways the people of the subcontinent could be united? Elicit from students that common beliefs about the way society should be organized and people ought to behave—i.e., religion—could unify people in a way that a government could not.

TIMELINE

1900–1300 BCE	Indus cities decline
1600 BCE	*Rig Veda*, the oldest part of the Vedas, compiled
1500–1200 BCE	Earliest use of iron and horses in northern India
1500–1000 BCE	Vedic communities spread from Indus River valley to Ganges River valley
1300–700 BCE	Vedic era; the Vedas, a collection of hymns, mantras, and religious instructions, compiled
1000–600 BCE	Early Hindu epic poems, the *Mahabharata* and *Ramayana*, are composed
700–550 BCE	Brahmin influence, foundation of later Hinduism, spreads throughout northern subcontinent
600–500 BCE	Buddhism and Jainism (nonviolence) emerge
420–350 BCE	Buddha dies and attains Nirvana

UNIT PROJECTS

Drama

Divide the class into small groups to research stories from the *Ramayana* and the *Bhagavad Gita* and prepare skits to share with the class.

Meeting of the Minds

Have partners research religious figures, characters in the *Ramayana* and *Bhagavad Gita,* and/or members of different *varnas*. Distribute questions ahead of time and have them prepare their character's thoughts on such topics as *What is happiness?* or *What is the best way to live?* Have them hang a sign with the character's name around the neck and stage a meeting of the minds.

Research Report

Small groups of students can investigate subjects of their choice to bring more information back to the rest of the class. Possible subjects include Buddha and the Jataka Tales, Jainism and its influence on Gandhi, and social divisions in India today. Have students research sources to use from your school resource center. Groups can create a panel discussion or a visual display to explain the information to the class.

ADDITIONAL ASSESSMENT

For Unit 4, use any of these unit projects for additional assessment. To assess their work in Drama and Meeting of the Minds, note how the skits and staging show students' grasp of the significance of the teachings in the *Ramayana* and *Bhagavad Gita*. Use the scoring rubric at the back of this guide to assess group projects, and have students rate their own work with the self-assessment rubric. For the Research Report, be sure to distribute the library/media center research log (see rubric at the back of this guide) to help students evaluate their sources as they conduct their research.

LITERATURE CONNECTION

The best loved epic literary works of the ancient South Asian World are the *Mahabharata* and the *Ramayama*, which are read as often today as they were thousands of years ago. Full and abridged versions of both are available in translation from the library and on the web. An index to both great epics, as well as full text translations, is available online: *www.sacred-texts.com/hin/dutt/*.

UNIVERSAL ACCESS

The following strategies are designed to cover a range of learning styles and reading, language, and skill levels. You may find that any of your students will benefit from the various strategies presented.

Reading Strategies

- ▶ To facilitate reading, preview the artifacts in these chapters so that students will recognize the emphasis of this unit.
- ▶ Ask certain students to read aloud into a tape recorder, then play the tape back so they can hear themselves.
- ▶ Have partners read aloud to each other. When one partner has finished, the other can offer constructive criticism.

Writing Strategies

- ▶ Have students write their own episode in the *Ramayana*, a myth, or a Jataka Tale (a story about the Buddha in his previous lives). Have them illustrate their stories.
- ▶ Have students write dialogues about certain important events in this unit. For example, they might write a dialogue between a Brahmin and the Buddha explaining why each believes as he does. Students should include arguments for both sides.

Listening and Speaking

- ▶ To spark students' interest, read an excerpt from the chapter aloud before having students read the chapter. Use an expressive tone of voice for best effect.
- ▶ Help teams of students role-play events in the unit. Students should make and use basic masks and props.

UNIT VOCABULARY LIST

The following words that appear in Unit 4 are important for your students' understanding of the social studies content as well as for development of literacy. Use these words for vocabulary study or to reinforce language arts skills (e.g., synonyms, compound words, prefixes and suffixes, and related words). The words are listed below in the order in which they appear in the chapters.

Chapter 11	Chapter 12	Chapter 13	Chapter 14
subcontinent	intricately	deeds	luxury
dramatically	archery	clarified	abused
millet	confound	*mandalas*	celibacy
hymns	charioteer	guarantees	fordmaker
generation	fray	committed	pilgrimages
cosmic	*dharma*	charitable	lice
peasants	*chakra*	cascades	vermin
deserved	abundance	pervades	sandalwood
recite	magnificent	decay	vermilion
politician	tinkling	matted	disgusted
eventually	episode	fertility	enlightenment
butchered	exile	prosperity	nirvana
sacrifices	captured	obstacle	cremated
untouchable	triumph	embattled	stupas
initiation		lotus	snobby
plastered		detachment	converted
bacteria		represent	missionary
altar		latrines	
charred		encouraged	
purify		emphasized	
discriminated			

THE ANCIENT SOUTH ASIAN WORLD

CHAPTER 11

FIRE AND SACRIFICE: LIVING BY THE VEDAS

PAGES 77–81

FOR HOMEWORK
STUDENT STUDY GUIDE
pages 31–32

 **WRITING**

- **Interview** The story is told from the point of view of Ketu, a Brahmin boy who is mentioned in the Vedas. Have students pretend to interview his sister about what it was like to be a Brahmin girl during Vedic times. In what ways was her life similar to her brother's? In what ways was it different?

 **VOCABULARY**

Vedas early Hindu scriptures

mantra a word repeated during meditation or worship

CHAPTER SUMMARY

The Vedic era was characterized by a new social organization into four distinct *varna*, or classes: *Brahmin* (priests), *Kshatriya* (warriors and political leaders), *Vaisya* (merchants and artisans), and *Shudra* (peasants). The *Dasa* (non-Aryan people) were outside these four Vedic classes. Each *varna* had specific responsibilities that helped maintain society.

PERFORMANCE OBJECTIVES

▶ To understand the structure of Vedic society
▶ To describe Vedic rituals and appreciate the function of sacrifice
▶ To explain the distinct gender roles of Vedic times

BUILDING BACKGROUND

Elicit what students know about India's caste system. Emphasize that many cultures have thought of society as a body, with different parts doing different things but all working together for the good of the whole. Discuss with students the possible benefits and drawbacks of assigning different jobs to different segments of the population.

WORKING WITH PRIMARY SOURCES

Have a volunteer read the "Hymn to Agni" on page 80. Ask students if they can figure out what *oblation* means from its context in the sentence (*the offering of a gift to a deity*). Have students analyze the reference to a butter ladle. (*Butter was a common offering to Agni, perhaps because it burned so easily.*) You may also want to direct students' attention to the illustration of Agni on page 80. His two heads represent that he is both a god and the sacrificial fire itself.

GEOGRAPHY CONNECTION

Movement Remind students that the Khyber Pass is an important overland route into the South Asian subcontinent. Have students locate it on the map on page 110. Ask: If you were studying languages, would you expect to find remnants of pre-Aryan languages in the north or in the south? Why? (*in the south, because it is farther from where the Indo-Aryan language must have entered the subcontinent*)

READING COMPREHENSION QUESTIONS

1. What crops were introduced into the newly cleared land along the Ganga River? (*rice and millet*)
2. Why do we know so much more about South Asia during this period than during Harappan times? (*from the Vedas, religious hymns, prayers, and instructions composed during this period and passed on orally for a number of centuries before being written down*)

3. Who is Purusha? *(Purusha was the cosmic man from whom the four social classes, or varna, emerged. When he was sacrificed, the Brahmin came from his head, the Kshatriya from his arms, the Vaisya from his thighs, and the Shudra from his feet.)*
4. Who were the Dasa? *(the descendents of the Harappans who were despised by Indo-Aryan speakers)*

CRITICAL THINKING QUESTIONS

1. In Vedic India, people who were born into a higher *varna* had a different lifestyle from those born into a lower *varna*. How did South Asians explain this arrangement to each other? *(People's actions in their previous lives had qualified them for their placement in this one, just as their current behavior would determine their placement in their next life.)*
2. Brahmins kindled the sacred fire using a wooden drill that spun with the help of a cord. This device is called a bow drill, because the handle and cord that spin it resemble a bow. Ask: What is another way in which bow drills were used? *(to drill beads)*
3. What was the significance of the "sacred thread ceremony" for Brahmin boys? *(A priest draped a length of sacred thread over a boy's left shoulder to symbolize his second birth as a Brahmin student.)*

SOCIAL SCIENCES

Civics Have students make a two-column chart. In the left column, have them list the four *varnas* and the Dasas. On the right, they should list the responsibilities of each group.

READING AND LANGUAGE ARTS

Reading Nonfiction Elicit that the first paragraph of the chapter addresses the reader directly as *you*. Discuss the effect of this.

Using Language What word is used as a close synonym for *Brahmin* in this chapter? *(priest)* Have students distinguish shades of meaning between the synonyms.

SUPPORTING LEARNING

English Language Learners Have students use sticky notes to label those parts of the chapter that they understood, found exciting, didn't understand, or thought were important. As a group, develop symbols (smiley face, exclamation point, question mark, asterisk) to represent each thought.

Struggling Readers Have students use split-page note-taking. Have each student fold a sheet of paper down the middle, read a section silently, and jot down notes on the left side. Have students work in small groups to share their notes and invite other students to add notes on the right side of the paper.

EXTENDING LEARNING

Enrichment Distribute one copy of the Chapter 11 blackline master to partners. Have them cut it in half. Each partner should read one of the sections and then teach his or her companion about it.

Extension Have students create a skit based on Ketu's sacred thread ceremony as described in the chapter. Family members, including Ketu, can explain what ceremony means to them.

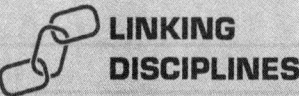

LINKING DISCIPLINES

Art Have students make posters of each of the Vedic gods, using online sources, such as *www.religionfacts.com/hinduism/beliefs/vedic_gods.htm* and *www.pantheon.org/articles/a/agni.html*, as well as suggestions from your media center.

THE ANCIENT SOUTH ASIAN WORLD

THE VEDAS

Directions
With a partner, read and discuss these two passages about the Vedas. Then, using information from the passages and from Chapter 11, answer the questions on a separate sheet of paper.

THE VEDAS: STUDYING AN UNWRITTEN LANGUAGE

Sanskrit, the language of the Vedas, was not written at first, but only spoken, so the Vedas were carefully memorized and passed from generation to generation. Young Brahmin boys had to learn the oral alphabet (like our alphabet song) of the sacred language of Sanskrit before they could begin to learn the hundreds of sacred texts. The alphabet was called the *varnamala*, or necklace of colors. Each sound had to be pronounced exactly right to bring the gods to the sacrifice.

To help students learn to speak with precision, teachers held their students' heads in a variety of postures. For a raised accent, the head was held facing forward. For a lowered accent, the head was held down. For the combined accent, the head was held back and to the side. Once the student learned the proper sounds, he had to recite them without moving his head. He also had to learn certain hand positions called *mudras*. These were used to help him remember the sequence of stanzas and repetitions of a mantra. Brahmin boys often studied for 12 years before mastering the four books of the Vedas.

THE FOUR BOOKS OF THE VEDAS

Rig Veda, the Veda of Praise, is the oldest collection of hymns, dating to about 1500 BCE. It includes around 1,028 hymns arranged into ten books, with an appendix containing further hymns.

Sama Veda, the Veda of Sacred Songs, is a collection of hymns drawn mainly from the Rig Veda and sung to melodies by a priest and his assistants during sacrifices.

Yajur Veda are the Vedas associated with *yajna*, or the performance of ritual.

Atharva Veda is the Veda of Atharvan, the priest who was first to kindle fire and worship it. The latest of all the Vedas, this is a collection of magical formulas both for protection from evil spirits and for inflicting injury on others.

1. What did young Brahmin boys have to learn to be able to recite the Vedas correctly?

2. Why did it take 12 years to master the four books of the Vedas?

3. Why was it so important to pass the information in the Vedas along word for word from generation to generation?

CHAPTER TEST 11

THE ANCIENT SOUTH ASIAN WORLD

A. MULTIPLE CHOICE

Circle the letter of the best answer for each question.

1. During Vedic times, villagers began to settle along the
    a. Indus River Valley.
    b. Saraswati River Valley.
    c. Ganga River Valley.
    d. Kabul River Valley.
2. New crops cultivated during Vedic times included
    a. wheat and barley.
    b. watermelon and cucumbers.
    c. plums and apricots.
    d. rice and millet.
3. Every day Brahmin boys like Ketu worshipped
    a. the sun god Surya and the fire god Indra.
    b. the sun god Surya and the fire god Agni.
    c. the sun god Indra and the fire god Yamuna.
    d. the sun god Indra and the fire god Agni.
4. According to the book, purification might include all the following **except**
    a. washing.
    b. touching a sacred person.
    c. plastering with cow dung.
    d. special prayers.
5. Students of the Vedas had to learn to pronounce the words exactly right so that
    a. the gods would know they were being called to a sacrifice.
    b. no one would mistake them for a Dasa.
    c. no one would forget their family's history.
    d. they wouldn't say anything to offend the gods.

B. SHORT ANSWER

Write a sentence or two to answer each question.

6. What did Vedic people believe about the *varna* a person was born into?

_____

_____

7. How did a Brahmin boy's life in Vedic times differ from his sister's?

_____

_____

C. ESSAY

Use the chart to compare and contrast Harappan and Vedic times. Then choose one topic to compare and contrast in an essay on a separate piece of paper.

	Harappan	Vedic
Most important river		
Social organization		
Importance of cleanliness		
Literature		

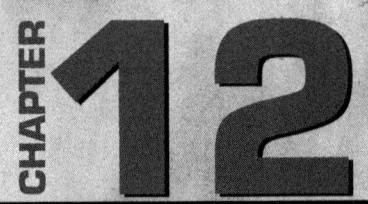

CHAPTER 12

TWO GREAT ADVENTURES: EPIC TRADITIONS

PAGES 82–87

FOR HOMEWORK

STUDENT STUDY GUIDE
pages 33–34

Arjuna (AHR-jun) legendary warrior prince who is the hero of the *Bhagavad Gita*

Bharata (BHAH-ruh-tuh) Rama's half brother

Draupadi (DRAOW-puh-dee) legendary wife of Arjuna and his four brothers

Hanuman (HUH-noo-mahn) monkey king in the *Ramayana* who helps Rama recover Sita; later worshipped as a god

Kaikeyi (kai-KAY-ee) Rama's stepmother and one of the villains of the *Ramayana*

Rama (RAHM-uh) hero of the *Ramayana*; believed to be a form of the god Vishnu

Ravana (RAH-vuh-nuh) evil 10-headed demon of the *Ramayana* who captures Sita

Sita (SEE-tah) Rama's wife, heroine of the *Ramayana*

Valmiki (vahl-MEE-kee) author of the most widely used version of the *Ramayana*

CHAPTER SUMMARY

The *Mahabharata*, including the episode known as the *Bhagavad Gita*, and the *Ramayana* are two of ancient India's greatest gifts to the world. The *Mahabharata* tells the story of Prince Arjuna. The *Bhagavad Gita* is the portion of the *Mahabharata* that addresses Prince Arjuna's reluctance to go to battle against his cousins. Lord Krishna convinces him that it is his *dharma*, or duty, to do so. The *Ramayana* tells the adventures of Prince Rama and his wife Sita, who endure many years of danger and separation before being reunited.

PERFORMANCE OBJECTIVES

▶ To summarize the *Ramayana* and *Bhagavad Gita*
▶ To analyze the stories for clues about their historical context
▶ To understand the limitations of reading literature as history

BUILDING BACKGROUND

Ask students if they have ever been in a situation where they had to make a difficult decision between what seemed to be two rights or two wrongs. Explain that philosophies and religions try to help people decide what the most important virtue is, so that they can depend on it in confused times. Each philosophy and religion chooses a slightly different virtue. As they read about the *Ramayana* and the *Bhagavad Gita*, tell students to look for the virtue that seems to have been most important to people during the Vedic era. (*duty*)

WORKING WITH PRIMARY SOURCES

Ask a volunteer to read the excerpt from the *Ramayana* in the sidebar on page 86 aloud and with expression. Explain that the technique of exaggerating or overstating something that is true is called hyperbole. What are some other examples of hyperbole in this chapter? (*Answers include Arjuna's ability to shoot the eye of the fish, Hanuman's mischief and the mountain, Ravana's multiple arms and heads.*)

GEOGRAPHY CONNECTION

Location Have students locate the cities of Mathura and Hastinapura, both mentioned in the *Bhagavad Gita*, on the map on page 85. (Hastinapura is now known as New Delhi and is India's capital.) What does their location suggest about new patterns of settlement during the Vedic era? (*that these were along the Ganga River basin*)

READING COMPREHENSION QUESTIONS

1. Who is Draupadi? (*a princess whose husband, Arjuna, won her by using a bow no one else could use to shoot out the eye of a golden fish spinning on a tall pole, all while looking at the reflection of a fish in a vat of boiling water*)
2. What is Arjuna's dilemma? (*whether to go to war against his cousins, the Kauravas*)

80 CHAPTER 12

3. Who is his charioteer? (*the god Krishna in disguise, who urges him to honor his dharma, or duty*)
4. Who are Ravana and Hanuman? (*a ten-headed demon who fights Rama and a monkey hero who helps Rama find Sita*)

CRITICAL THINKING QUESTIONS

1. What conclusions can you draw about the importance of military ability from these stories? (*Leaders like Arjuna and Rama were expected to be accomplished warriors who didn't hesitate to fight when necessary.*)
2. What conclusions can you draw about the relationships between men and women? (*A loving, loyal marriage was an important part of a well-lived life.*)
3. Distribute copies of the Chapter 12 blackline master and have students complete them to solidify their understanding of the characters of the *Ramayana* and *Bhagavad Gita*.

SOCIAL SCIENCES

Civics Ask: What problem do the poems suggest may have plagued South Asian governments? (*Both are about different members of a family fighting over who should be the next king; peaceful succession may have been a problem.*)

READING AND LANGUAGE ARTS

Reading Nonfiction Distribute copies of the main idea map organizer (see graphic organizers at the back of this book). Have students write *Items and Places in the Ramayana and the Bhagavad Gita* in the center circle. Direct students to turn to pages 84 and 85 in their books and use the information there to fill in as many examples of reliable historical information from the poems as they can.

Using Language The book describes "tinkling" bells. Explain to students that *tinkling* is an example of *onomatopoeia*, meaning a word that sounds like what it means. Other examples include the words *splat* and *buzz*. See how long a list of onomatopoetic words your class can generate.

SUPPORTING LEARNING

English Language Learners Make available old copies of magazines with photos of people. Instruct half the students to choose photographs to represent Arjuna, Lord Krishna, the Pandavas, and the Kauravas, while the others choose Sita, Rama, Ravana, and Hanuman. Have them cut out the pictures, mount them on construction paper or cardstock, and attach them to a craft stick as a handle. Then have them perform puppet shows of each story.

Struggling Readers Write key events from the two poems on index cards. Have students team up to put the shuffled events in order. Encourage students to prove the correctness of their ordering using the text.

EXTENDING LEARNING

Enrichment One way to teach the concept of *dharma* is by repeating a skit of a short scene from the *Ramayana*. After the initial performance, students are assigned to parts based on how well they stayed in character, that is, maintained *dharma*. The repeated performances of the skit are like *samsara*, the cycle of death and rebirth. You can find a lesson plan for this at www.askasia.org.

Extension Have a group of students select passages from the stories in the chapter and then read them aloud with expression.

THE ANCIENT SOUTH ASIAN WORLD

VOCABULARY

avatar the form a god or goddess assumes when appearing to mankind

WRITING

Narration Have students write a story about the adventures of Hanuman, who has come to your city during the 21st century as a result of your class discussing the *Ramayana*.

LINKING DISCIPLINES

Drama

Live performances of the *Ramayana* are regularly staged in virtually every corner of the globe. See if you can unearth one in your area. If not, consider showing students part of a video production.

CHAPTER 12 BLM
THE ANCIENT SOUTH ASIAN WORLD

NAME   **DATE**

WHAT ROLE DID THEY PLAY?

Directions
Use the chart to explain the role that each of the characters played in the *Ramayana* and the *Bhagavad Gita*.

Character	Role in the *Ramayana*
Rama	
Sita	
Ravana	
Hanuman	
Kaikeyi	
Bharata	
Kumbakarna	
Character	**Role in the *Bhagavad Gita***
Arjuna	
Lord Krishna	
Drapaudi	
Kauravas	
Pandavas	

CHAPTER TEST 12

THE ANCIENT SOUTH ASIAN WORLD

A. MULTIPLE CHOICE

Circle the letter of the best answer for each question.

1. The *Ramayana*
   a. was not based on an episode from the *Mahabharata*.
   b. tells the story of the war between the Pandavas and the Kauravas.
   c. explains how Bandar Poonch got its name.
   d. is the most famous episode of the *Mahabharata*.

2. Valmiki is the name of
   a. the king of the monkeys.
   b. Arjuna's charioteer.
   c. the author of the *Bhagavad Gita*.
   d. the author of the *Ramayana*.

3. The poems from this chapter tell historians that the people of the Vedic era did all of the following **except**
   a. go to war in chariots.
   b. use iron and horses.
   c. restore trade routes.
   d. know how to read and write.

4. What is the correct order of texts, from oldest to youngest?
   a. *Vedas, Mahabharata, Ramayana*
   b. *Ramayana, Mahabharata, Vedas*
   c. *Vedas, Ramayana, Bhagavad Gita*
   d. *Mahabharata, Ramayana, Bhagavad Gita*

5. The *Ramayana* is a poem whose message is that
   a. kings must fight for their thrones.
   b. queens are always in danger.
   c. good wins out over evil.
   d. monkeys are sacred animals.

B. SHORT ANSWER

Write a sentence or two to answer each question.

6. What have historians learned about the Vedic era from the *Mahabharata*?

7. What is the religious message of the *Ramayana*?

C. ESSAY

Write an essay on a separate piece of paper explaining the Vedic idea of *dharma*. Defend your ideas with specific examples from the chapter.

CHAPTER 13

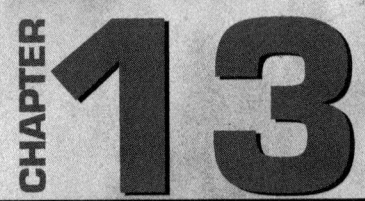

NEW GODS: FROM BRAHMANISM TO EARLY HINDUISM

PAGES 88–95

FOR HOMEWORK

STUDENT STUDY GUIDE
pages 35–36

 VOCABULARY

reincarnation the process of being reborn into a new body

Hindu a family of religious traditions that teaches reincarnation and worships gods like Vishnu, Shiva, and Devi

 **WRITING**

- **Picture Book** Have students obtain from the library/media center a variety of stories about Hindu gods and goddesses. Then ask small groups of students to examine the stories, choose one that appeals to them, and write and illustrate their own picture book based on that tale. Then read the stories to each other.

CHAPTER SUMMARY

The Vedic era made the transition to Early Hinduism with the addition of new gods and goddesses. The Hindu trinity became Brahma, the creator; Vishnu, the preserver; and Shiva, the lord of creation and destruction. Hinduism isn't so much a single unified religion as a family of religious traditions.

PERFORMANCE OBJECTIVES

▶ To understand the basic Hindu beliefs of *karma*, *dharma*, and reincarnation
▶ To describe the major Hindu gods and goddesses
▶ To comprehend the nature of these deities as changing manifestations of *brahman*, or ultimate reality

BUILDING BACKGROUND

As a class, construct a two-column chart listing Harappan religious beliefs and practices in one column and Vedic practices in the other. Explain that over time, old and new beliefs began to mix and resulted in a third distinct stage in South Asia's religious history that historians refer to as Early Hinduism.

WORKING WITH PRIMARY SOURCES

Have students preview the illustrations in the chapter. They will most likely have questions. Instruct them to make a K-W-L chart about the artwork and to complete it as they read the chapter.

GEOGRAPHY CONNECTION

Interaction Download the map of India's religions from *http://artworld.uea.ac.uk/teaching_modules/india/maps/indiareligion.html* and share it with students. Ask students to note the main religion of India today (*Hindu*). Ask if they notice a pattern to places in India where other religions are prominent. (*They tend to be near India's borders.*) Point out that borders are places where foreigners are likely to have an influence on local religious beliefs.)

READING COMPREHENSION QUESTIONS

1. What is *karma*? (*Karma refers to the consequences of one's behavior; good deeds result in good* karma, *while bad deeds result in bad* karma.)
2. What is the difference between *Brahma*, *Brahmin*, and *brahman*? (*Brahma: creator; Brahmin: the priestly varna; brahman: the Ultimate Supreme Being, with whom people will unite once they have achieved perfection*)
3. What is the significance of the Ganga River? (*It was believed to be a goddess capable of purifying those who bathed in it.*)
4. Who are the three great Early Hindu gods? (*Shiva: multi-armed god of fertility, creation, and destruction; Vishnu: god of preservation, who takes the form of Lord Krishna; Brahma: creator of the universe*)

5. Who are the five major manifestations of the Mother Goddess? (*Parvati—motherhood; Lakshmi—good luck; Saraswati—music and learning; Kali—fierce protectress and prosecutor of evil; Ganga—the river goddess*)

CRITICAL THINKING QUESTIONS

1. Why might Harappan practices like yoga and the use of conch-shell ladles for pouring butter on the altar and of conch-shell trumpets for calling the gods return to Vedic rituals? (*People may have been reluctant to give up religious practices that they had cherished.*)
2. What belief about the consequence of one's actions and attitudes in this life helped make the division of society into distinct *varnas* more acceptable? (*Where one was now was based on the decisions made in a previous life; good behavior in this life would be rewarded in the next, but if one complained in this life, there would be punishment in the next.*)
3. How can there be so many mother goddesses who are married to different gods? (*Hindus believe that all of us are constantly changing form until we are prepared to reunite with brahman; one god who was the same all the time simply didn't make sense.*)

SOCIAL SCIENCES

Economics Ask students to consider to what extent the social divisions of Vedic and Early Hindu times fulfilled economic as well as religious functions.

READING AND LANGUAGE ARTS

Reading Nonfiction The chapter divides easily into five sections: the Hindu doctrine of *karma* and reincarnation; Shiva; Vishnu; Brahma; and gender roles. Have students identify the main idea and details of each section.

Using Language The words *gods, goddesses, avatars, brahman,* and *deity* are all used in this chapter to refer to divine entities. Have students consult a dictionary or thesaurus as they attempt to define these words and distinguish between the shades of meaning.

SUPPORTING LEARNING

Struggling Readers Have a group of students write the names of the Hindu gods and goddesses on note cards, with a summary of their duties and characteristics. Discuss the idea that these gods and goddesses are changing manifestations of *brahman*, ultimate reality.

EXTENDING LEARNING

Enrichment The Smithsonian sponsors a superb online exhibit on *puja*, or Hindu worship, at www.asia.si.edu/education/pujaonline/puja/start.htm. Print out and distribute to each student the worksheet of objects associated with the major gods. Students can explore the site to find the answers. Or print out the posters and have students use them as a source.

Extension Distribute copies of the Chapter 13 blackline master to students and have them solve the crossword puzzle with the help of their books to help them solidify their understanding of the major Hindu gods and goddesses.

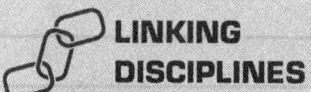

LINKING DISCIPLINES

Art The word *mandala* comes from the Sanskrit word for "circle." Mandalas are circular shapes that people look at to help them meditate. Have students draw or paint their own mandalas by drawing a small circle inside a larger one. Have students fill the small circle with symbols, colors, or objects that represent themselves. They should then divide the larger circle into quarters, and fill one quarter with symbols of their heroes or heroines, another with symbols of their goals, another with their hopes for the future, and the last with the things they love.

THEN and NOW

Today Hinduism is the third-largest religion in the world (after Christianity and Islam), with more than 750 million adherents.

THE ANCIENT SOUTH ASIAN WORLD

HINDU GODS AND GODDESSES

Directions
Complete the crossword puzzle about Hindu gods and goddesses.

Across
1. Elephant-headed god of luck and wisdom; son of Shiva and Parvati
5. Goddess of beauty, luck and wealth; Vishnu's partner
7. God of fertility, creation, destruction, and dance; often shown with many arms
8. Goddess of motherhood and mother of Ganesha
9. One of the oldest gods; sun god who rides in a chariot
10. Scary form of mother goddess who wears necklace of skulls

Down
2. River goddess; also goddess of wisdom and music
3. River goddess who rode a crocodile
4. "The Preserver"; appears on earth as Lord Krishna
6. Four-headed creator god who holds Vedas, prayer beads, conch shell, and water pot

CHAPTER TEST 13

THE ANCIENT SOUTH ASIAN WORLD

NAME _____ DATE _____

A. MULTIPLE CHOICE

Circle the letter of the best answer for each question.

1. When Vishnu says, "All creatures from Brahma to the small insect have to face the result of their deeds," he is explaining the Hindu idea of
   a. *karma*.
   b. sacrifice.
   c. reincarnation.
   d. mandala.

2. Brahmin responsibilities included all of the following **except**
   a. calling the gods to the sacrifices.
   b. making sacrifices for the whole community.
   c. protecting the laws of the community.
   d. kindling the sacred fire.

3. The three greatest Hindu gods include all of the following **except**
   a. Brahma.
   b. Vishnu.
   c. Indra.
   d. Shiva.

4. The holy river goddess who rides a crocodile and purifies all she touches is called
   a. Kali.
   b. Ganga.
   c. Lakshmi.
   d. Saraswati.

5. Many parts of women's worship
   a. are described in the Vedas.
   b. are the same as men's.
   c. are passed from mother to daughter.
   d. involve lighting the sacred fire.

B. SHORT ANSWER

Write a sentence or two to answer each question.

6. Explain how a person's karma affects his or her reincarnation.

_____

_____

7. Why is the Ganga River sacred to people of South Asia?

_____

_____

C. ESSAY

On a separate sheet of paper, use information from the chapter to write an essay answering this question: **Why do some people say that Hindus worship many gods, while others say they worship only one deity?** Provide a title for your essay.

CHAPTER 14
TWO GENTLE RELIGIONS: BUDDHISM AND JAINISM

PAGES 96–102

FOR HOMEWORK

STUDENT STUDY GUIDE
pages 37–38

VOCABULARY

Eightfold Path Buddhist teaching of eight behaviors that lead to enlightenment: right view, right resolve, right speech, right action, right living, right effort, right mindfulness, and right meditation

CAST OF CHARACTERS

Ashoka (ush-SHOK-uh) greatest of the Mauryan emperors; made Buddhism popular

Buddha (BOO-dhuh) born Prince Siddhartha Gautama in what is now Nepal; founder of Buddhism

Mahavira Vardamana (muh-hah-VEE-ruh vuhr-dah-MAH-nuh) founder of the Jain religion; taught the importance of living simply and practicing nonviolence

CHAPTER SUMMARY

Two of history's greatest religious figures, Vardamana (later known as Mahavira, the Great Hero) and Siddhartha Gautama (later known as Buddha, the Enlightened One), were both born into lives of privilege in South Asia in the 6th century BCE. Both sought peace and found it in practices that helped them leave the desires, distractions, and pain of the world behind them.

PERFORMANCE OBJECTIVES

▶ To understand the evolution of Jainism and the doctrine of *ahimsa*
▶ To describe the life of the Buddha, the Four Noble Truths, and the Eightfold Path
▶ To compare and contrast Jain and Buddhist beliefs with each other and with Early Hinduism

BUILDING BACKGROUND

Remind students of the Vedic and Early Hindu practices. What aspects of these religions might have been comforting to people? What might have frustrated some people? Tell them they will now read about two new attempts to put people in touch with the ultimate spirit.

WORKING WITH PRIMARY SOURCES

Ask a volunteer to read the instructions from Buddha on page 100. Point out that the Buddha uses two similes in only four short lines. Evaluate whether his listeners were likely to understand what he meant. (*Yes—these are homely and familiar images.*) Direct students to the excerpt from the Buddha's first sermon in *The World in Ancient Times Primary Sources and Reference Volume*.

GEOGRAPHY CONNECTION

Movement The founders of Jainism and Buddhism (Vardamana and Siddhartha Gautama, respectively) both began their lives as wealthy men from ruling families. They left their homes and traveled long distances to search for answers, and then to preach their wisdom. Have the class go through the chapter and identify all the places mentioned, using the map on pages 12–13. Talk about how far the two men traveled in the course of their lives. Ask: Why is it important to cover large distances when starting a new religion? (*because that is how more and more people will find out about a new belief system; they need to see and hear the religious founder for themselves to come to adopt his beliefs*)

READING COMPREHENSION QUESTIONS

1. What is *moksha*? (*release from the cycle of reincarnation*)
2. What did South Asian city-states do to safeguard themselves from attacks? (*They built defensive walls around their cities, trained their citizens to fight, built navies, maintained chariot forces, developed heavily armed units, and evolved the phalanx for warfare.*)

3. What are some of the things early Hindus did to purify themselves of sin? *(They bathed in sacred rivers, sang hymns to the gods and goddesses, gave alms to the poor and to charitable organizations, and took care of old and weak animals and people. They gave away all their wealth, devoted themselves to meditation, and made pilgrimages to sacred places.)*
4. Distribute copies of the blackline master for chapter 14 and have students complete it to reinforce their understanding of the basic tenets of Buddhism and Jainism.

CRITICAL THINKING QUESTIONS

1. Why did many Jains wait until old age to commit themselves fully to the principles of their religion? *(They wanted to have children; they wanted to be able to support their children.)*
2. Why might the Buddha have chosen to teach with simple examples in everyday language? *(He may have thought that the Brahmins made the Vedic religion too complicated for ordinary people to understand.)*
3. Have students use the main idea map graphic organizer (see graphic organizers at the back of this book) to analyze the Four Noble Truths. They might write *Buddhism and the Four Noble Truths* in the central circle and then describe one of the "truths" in each of the surrounding circles.

SOCIAL SCIENCES

Economics Jains can't engage in any occupation that would involve harming or killing animals, which includes agriculture. Elicit from students what occupations Jains could pursue, and where they would most likely live.

READING AND LANGUAGE ARTS

Reading Nonfiction Mahavira and the Buddha had very similar lives. Have students make charts comparing and contrasting the details of their biographies.

Using Language Point out that some Jain and Buddhist terms are translated into English (*ford-maker* and *enlightenment*), while others are not (*moksha, sangha, Nirvana*). Elicit why that might be. *(Some Jain and Buddhist ideas are common in the West, so we have words for them; others are not.)*

SUPPORTING LEARNING

English Language Learners Have students choose a sentence from the chapter that "speaks" to them. Tell them to practice reciting the sentence. Without interrupting, ask each student to recite the sentence one after the other (ghost-reading). Discuss the emotion and pictures the overall presentation provides.

Struggling Readers Have students paraphrase the definitions of *moksha* (page 97) and *Nirvana* (page 101).

EXTENDING LEARNING

Enrichment Have students investigate the Buddhist or Jain topic of their choice. Ask your librarian for help in assembling resources for them to use. Ask students to prepare a poster explaining the main points of what they have found and then make a presentation with the help of the poster to the rest of the class.

Extension Using their completed blackline masters and the information from the chapter, have students complete copies of the Venn diagram from the graphic organizers at the back of this book, comparing and contrasting Buddhist and Jain beliefs.

WRITING

Fable The Jataka tales are a series of fables about Buddha in his previous lives and stories to illustrate his Buddhist teachings. They are similar to the fables of Aesop. Choose a tale (see http://edsitement.neh.gov/view_lesson_plan.asp?id=600) and discuss it as a class. Then have students write their own tales.

TWO GREAT RELIGIONS

BUDDHISM AND THE WHEEL OF LAW

This is the Buddhist symbol of the wheel of law called the *Dharmachakra*. Although they are not usually a part of the *Dharmachakra*, this one has four outer circles to symbolize the Four Noble Truths. Write them in the outer four circles, and one of the eight ways to freedom from desire (the Eight-fold Path) on each of the inner spokes, which drive the wheel of life.

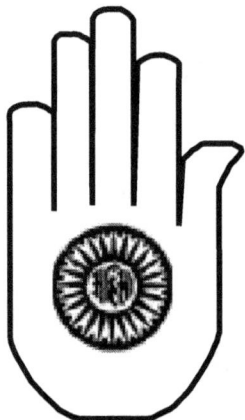

This emblem of Jainism represents *ahimsa*, or nonviolence. The symbol in the palm is the *samsara*, or wheel of reincarnation. The word in the center means *stop*, meaning that if you obey the five Jain tenets you can stop the wheel of reincarnation.

Write one of the Jain beliefs in each of the fingers of the hand.

CHAPTER TEST 14

THE ANCIENT SOUTH ASIAN WORLD

NAME _____ DATE _____

A. MULTIPLE CHOICE

Circle the letter of the best answer for each question.

1. Jains were taught to avoid all of the following **except**
   - a. violence.
   - b. marriage.
   - c. poverty.
   - d. meat.

2. *Mahavira* means
   - a. the Enlightened One.
   - b. Ford-maker.
   - c. Conqueror.
   - d. Great Hero.

3. Both Buddhism and Hinduism
   - a. emphasize the importance of observing *varna* to keep society organized.
   - b. believe in the importance of priestly sacrifices.
   - c. teach that yoga is a useful form of personal discipline.
   - d. believe spiritual matters should be discussed only in the sacred language of Sanskrit.

4. The Buddhist state of ultimate freedom is called
   - a. Nirvana.
   - b. *ahimsa*.
   - c. *jine*.
   - d. reincarnation.

5. The emperor Ashoka
   - a. built Buddhist *sanghas* for the monks.
   - b. achieved Nirvana before his death.
   - c. built Buddhist stupas to honor the Buddha.
   - d. published edicts in stone that told people they had to become Buddhist.

B. SHORT ANSWER

Write a sentence or two to answer each question.

6. Explain why archaeologists have found so few ancient South Asian documents.

7. What was the Buddha's message and how did he share it with others?

C. ESSAY

On a separate piece of paper write an essay in which you explain the relationship between the Four Noble Truths and the Eightfold Path.

UNIT 5: WAR AND EMPIRE

PAGES 103–125

Chapter 15	Word for Word: Early Historic Cities
Chapter 16	With Friends Like These, Who Needs Enemies? The Beginnings of the Mauryan Empire
Chapter 17	Nothing But a Zero: Science and Technology
Chapter 18	*Dharma, Artha, Kama,* and *Moksha:* War and Peace in the Time of Ashoka

UNIT OBJECTIVES

Unit 5 discusses the growing political sophistication of South Asia in the wake of Persian and Greek invasions as well as its remarkable mathematical, medical, and scientific legacy. In this unit your students will learn

- the significance of the Brahmi script.
- the circumstances and effect of the Persian and Greek invasions.
- about the discovery of zero and other advances in South Asian science and medicine.
- the brilliant careers of two of India's greatest leaders, Chandragupta and Ashoka.

PRIMARY SOURCES

Unit 5 includes excerpts from the following primary sources:

- the *Jataka Tales*
- Arrian, *Anabasis*
- Firdausi, *Shah Nama*
- Kautilya, *Arthashastra*
- Aryabhata, *Aryabhatiyam*
- *Charaka Samhita*
- Vishakadatta, *Mudrarakshasa*
- Ashoka

Pictures of South Asian artifacts can also be analyzed as primary sources. These include:

- Indo-Greek coin, Pakistan
- Brahmi inscription, India
- Punch-marked coins, Banaras, India
- Illustration of Sikander
- Carved war elephant
- Coin of Alexander
- Square coins
- Drawing of figurine of child with Brahmi tablet
- Lion capital
- Drawing of carving of Ashoka, South India
- Lion pillar
- Buddhist temple, Bodh Gaya, India

BIG IDEAS IN UNIT 5

Invasion, political centralization, and **science and technology** are the big ideas presented in Unit 5. The invasion of the Persians and the Greeks stimulated the adoption of the Brahmi alphabet, as well as growing political centralization, as exemplified by the careers of Chandragupta and Ashoka.

One way to introduce these ideas is to ask students to reflect on what commonalities unify the people of a country (*common spoken and written language; transportation system; communications; shared military; shared legal system, etc.*). List these on the board, and then ask students how much of this infrastructure was in place in South Asia in 600 BCE (*virtually none*). Make the point that although South Asia was unified economically and culturally, it had not yet been unified politically. Tell them to look for how this state of affairs changes as you work through the upcoming chapters.

GEOGRAPHY CONNECTION

Explain to students that in this unit they will learn the story of two different invading forces, those of Persia and those of Alexander the Great. Ask students to imagine that they are the generals of invading armies. What mountain ranges form natural barriers in the region? How can armies overcome these obstacles? Have students refer to the maps on pages 85 and 110.

TIMELINE

800–300 BCE	Brahmi script spreads throughout South Asia; cities established
558–529 BCE	Cyrus the Great of Persia invades
350 BCE	Buddha dies and attains Nirvana
327–325 BCE	Alexander the Great of Greece invades
326 BCE	Alexander and Porus wage battle, ending in a truce and friendship
325 BCE	Alexander and most of his army leave the Indus Valley and return to Babylon
322–298 BCE	Chandragupta Maurya reigns
302 BCE	Megesthenes, ambassador of Selukos, visits court of Chandragupta Maurya
About 275 BCE	Kautilya writes *Arthashastra*
269–232 BCE	Ashoka reigns
261 BCE	Ashoka embraces or promotes Buddhism
200 BCE–200 CE	Buddhist influence reaches its height
185 BCE	Mauryan dynasty ends
About 475 CE	Aryabhata active
595 CE	Earliest use of zero

UNIT PROJECTS

Dramatic Reading

Have a group of students write, rehearse, and perform a skit about one of the events in this unit, like James Prinsep's sad life or the battle between Alexander and Porus.

Chronology

Have a group of students research the actual or approximate birth and death dates of the personalities listed under the timeline above. Have them create their own timeline showing the life of each personality to see how their careers overlapped and how they influenced each other.

Book Report

Finding age-appropriate novels set in ancient India can be a challenge. Malcolm Bosse's *Tusk and Stone* is the happy exception. A historically accurate story of a young Brahmin boy who becomes part of a war-elephant corps and helps build a Hindu temple, this novel by the author of *The Examination* is a great supplement to many of this unit's themes. Have interested students read the book and then prepare an oral presentation about what they have learned about South Asian history.

Research Report

Have students investigate one of the figures or traditions mentioned in this unit, like Kautilya, Chandragupta, Ashoka, and Ayurvedic medicine, after you have ascertained that there is sufficient grade-level appropriate material on that particular topic. One age-appropriate resource is *Calliope* magazine, published by Cobblestone Publishing. Topics previously covered in the magazine include Buddhism and Ashoka. Check the *Calliope* online archive of back issues at www.cobblestonepub.com/pages/CalliopeArchives.html. Have them write reports, which they will then share with the class.

ADDITIONAL ASSESSMENT

Use any of these unit projects for additional assessment. For Unit 5, divide the class into groups and have all students take part in these projects. To assess their work in Dramatic Reading, note how the students' skits show their grasp of the significance of the Brahmi script and the invasions of the Greeks and Persians. For the Chronology, observe how well students understand Chandragupta and Ashoka. For the Book Report look for an understanding of how the book ties in with the unit's themes. Use the scoring rubric at the back of this guide to assess group projects, and have students rate their own work with the self-assessment rubric. For the Research Report, be sure to distribute the library/media center research log (see rubric at the back of this guide) to help students evaluate their sources as they conduct their research.

LITERATURE CONNECTION

The *Jakata Tales* (a collection of stories about the Buddha) provide some great stories about the growing empire. A guide to the Jakata Tales is available online: *http://watthai.net/talon/jataka/jataka.htm*.

UNIVERSAL ACCESS

The following strategies are designed to cover a range of learning styles and reading, language, and skill levels. You may find that any of your students will benefit from the various strategies presented.

Reading Strategies

- ▶ To spark interest in reading, first elicit what students know about Alexander the Great. According to most textbooks, Alexander never lost a battle. Tell students that that may have been true, but there was at least one that probably ended without a clear victory on either side.
- ▶ Have students read passages one-on-one with you to check their reading skills and comprehension.

▶ Have one student read a section of a chapter aloud to a partner, who will take notes. The students should then change roles.

Writing Strategies

▶ Have students imagine themselves as young assistants or apprentices to some of the personalities named in this unit. They should write journal entries describing a day in their life.

▶ Have students use a two-column chart to list the positive and negative aspects of the invasions of South Asia, both short and long term.

Listening and Speaking Strategies

▶ Have partners write a dialogue between a South Asian villager who was in the path of the Greeks or the Persians, and a historian, debating whether the invasions were good or bad for South Asia. Partners can present their dialogues to the class.

▶ To spark students' interest, read aloud the title and first paragraph of each chapter. Use the reading as a springboard for predicting what the chapter is about. Record and review students' predictions. When students have finished reading the chapter, ask whether their predictions were correct.

UNIT VOCABULARY LIST

The following words that appear in Unit 5 are important for your students' understanding of the social studies content as well as for development of literacy. Use these words for vocabulary study or to reinforce language arts skills (e.g., synonyms, compound words, prefixes and suffixes, and related words). The words are listed below in the order in which they appear in the chapters.

Chapter 15	Chapter 16	Chapter 17	Chapter 18
qualified	rumor	magnifying	satisfaction
coinage	messenger	gleaming	academy
enthusiasm	futile	surgery	lance
contagious	adjacent	arthritis	mace
decipher	impressive	celestial	centralized
documents	cavalry	manuscripts	established
delta	elite	smelting	edict
dense	turbans		pillars
assembling	exhausted		forbearance
profound	trampling		welfare
impact	traitor		coincidentally
administer	treacherous		
acquainted	plateau		
castes	inflicts		
	banyan trees		
	ministries		

THE ANCIENT SOUTH ASIAN WORLD

CHAPTER 15
WORD FOR WORD: EARLY HISTORIC CITIES

PAGES 103–108

FOR HOMEWORK
STUDENT STUDY GUIDE
pages 39–40

CAST OF CHARACTERS

Cyrus the Great Founder of the Achaemenid dynasty of Persia; conquered parts of Afghanistan and the Indus Valley

Darius I (DAHR-yuhs) Achaemenid emperor who extended his power to the Indus and set up his regional capital at the ancient Vedic city of Taxila

VOCABULARY

indigo a plant that is used to make blue dye

Three different cities were built over each other at Taxila, but the last one was abandoned almost 1,000 years ago. The location is still a strategic one, however, and Pakistan chose to build its capital of Islamabad only 20 miles away.

CHAPTER SUMMARY

The interpretation of the Brahmi script by the English numismatist James Prinsep in the late 1830s allowed historians to make connections between Greek and South Asian records of South Asia's history, including the Persian invasion and occupation of the Punjab.

PERFORMANCE OBJECTIVES

▶ To explain the significance of the Brahmi script to life in South Asia
▶ To investigate cause-and-effect relationships during the rise of South Asia's early historic cities
▶ To explore the significance of the great administrative and educational city of Taxila

BUILDING BACKGROUND

Tell students that everything they have learned about South Asia so far was discovered indirectly by historians examining objects and reading texts that were passed down orally for hundreds, sometimes thousands of years before being written down. Discuss with students the difference the availability of written records makes. (*greater precision and accuracy, especially with regard to dates*)

WORKING WITH PRIMARY SOURCES

Have a volunteer read the primary source excerpt about Taxila from the *Jataka Tales* on page 107. Say: Even though it was not the author's purpose, a careful reader can extract a lot of historical information from this excerpt. What can you conclude from it? (*Possible answers include sunshade and one-soled (thin) sandals as a status symbol, that life at the palace was probably pretty good, and that the living arrangements at the university were probably not very comfortable.*)

GEOGRAPHY CONNECTION

Place Help students locate Taxila on the map on page 106. (Modern-day Islamabad, Pakistan, is 22 miles to the south of the site of ancient Taxila.) Why might Cyrus, Alexander, and others have chosen this particular site for a major city? (*possible answers: equidistant from Indus and Jhelum Rivers; at the crossroads of east-west Mediterranean/China land route and trunk road heading south to India*)

READING COMPREHENSION QUESTIONS

1. Who was James Prinsep? (*A British architect who became interested in Indian coins while working at a mint in India; he was the first to decipher the Brahmi script.*)
2. Who was Cyrus the Great? (*He was the king who founded the Persian empire, conquered the northern portion of South Asia, and established a satrapy, or state, at Taxila.*)

96 | CHAPTER 15

3. What contributions did Persia make to South Asian life? (*coins, exposure to Mediterranean culture as soldiers in the army, wine, musical instruments, government*)
4. What are the traditional arts and sciences of South Asia? (*archery, swordsmanship, medicine, law, economics, astronomy, mathematics, and literature*)
5. What is *caste*? (*a subdivision of* varna *based on occupation*)

CRITICAL THINKING QUESTIONS

1. Is there a link between the development of castes and the growth of cities? (*probably, because there were now enough people in one place to sustain many castes, and because lots of castes provided order in the confusion of a city*)
2. Why do you think weights and measures didn't change when so much else had between Harappan and Early Historic times? (*possibly because they were used so often by so many people that it wasn't practical to change them*)

SOCIAL SCIENCES

Economics   Have a volunteer read the chapter title. Remind students that *historic* implies that the people in these cities were literate. Explore with students the relationship between urbanization and literacy. (*trade requires records, which requires literacy*)

READING AND LANGUAGE ARTS

Reading Nonfiction   As students read the chapter, have them identify turning points in the conflict and predict what will happen next.

Using Language   Have students find passages in the chapter that include figurative language. Have them copy one of these sentences and interpret its meaning. Students can draw the literal or alternate meaning of each expression.

SUPPORTING LEARNING

English Language Learners   Divide the class into groups of four. Have each group read a section of the chapter. One member should read the information, another should retell it, and a third should write down key information. When all the groups are finished, have the fourth member of each group make an oral presentation using the notes.

Struggling Readers   As a class, summarize the influence of Persia on South Asian life using the blackline master for Chapter 15. Have students quiz each other using the summary.

EXTENDING LEARNING

Enrichment   One of James Prinsep's enduring legacies is the *rupee*, still the currency of India. Have students go to *www.askasia.org/teachers/Instructional_ Resources/Lesson_Plans/India/LP_india_7.htm* for a lesson plan on what we can learn about India from the 10-rupee note.

Extension   Have students choose a sentence that highlights one of the contributions of the Greeks or Persians to South Asia and then create a visual display of the contribution, being certain to include the sentence from the chapter.

WRITING

Letter Ask students to imagine that they are the prince described in the excerpt from the *Jataka Tales*. Write a letter home to your family telling them about life in Taxila. Be sure to include specific sensory details—what does the city smell like? Look like? What do you miss about home?

LINKING DISCIPLINES

Music Although the Persians and Greeks introduced new instruments to South Asia, music and musical instruments, especially drums, had long been an important part of South Asia life. The goddess Saraswati, for example, is the goddess of music, and archaeologists have recently found a collection of musical rocks in Southern India that is thousands of years old. Find out more about it at *http://news.bbc.co.uk/2/hi/science/nature/3520384.stm*.

THE ANCIENT SOUTH ASIAN WORLD

CHAPTER 15 BLM
The Ancient South Asian World

NAME   **DATE**

PERSIA'S INFLUENCE ON SOUTH ASIA

Directions
Use the idea web to tell about how being part of the Persian Empire changed South Asia.

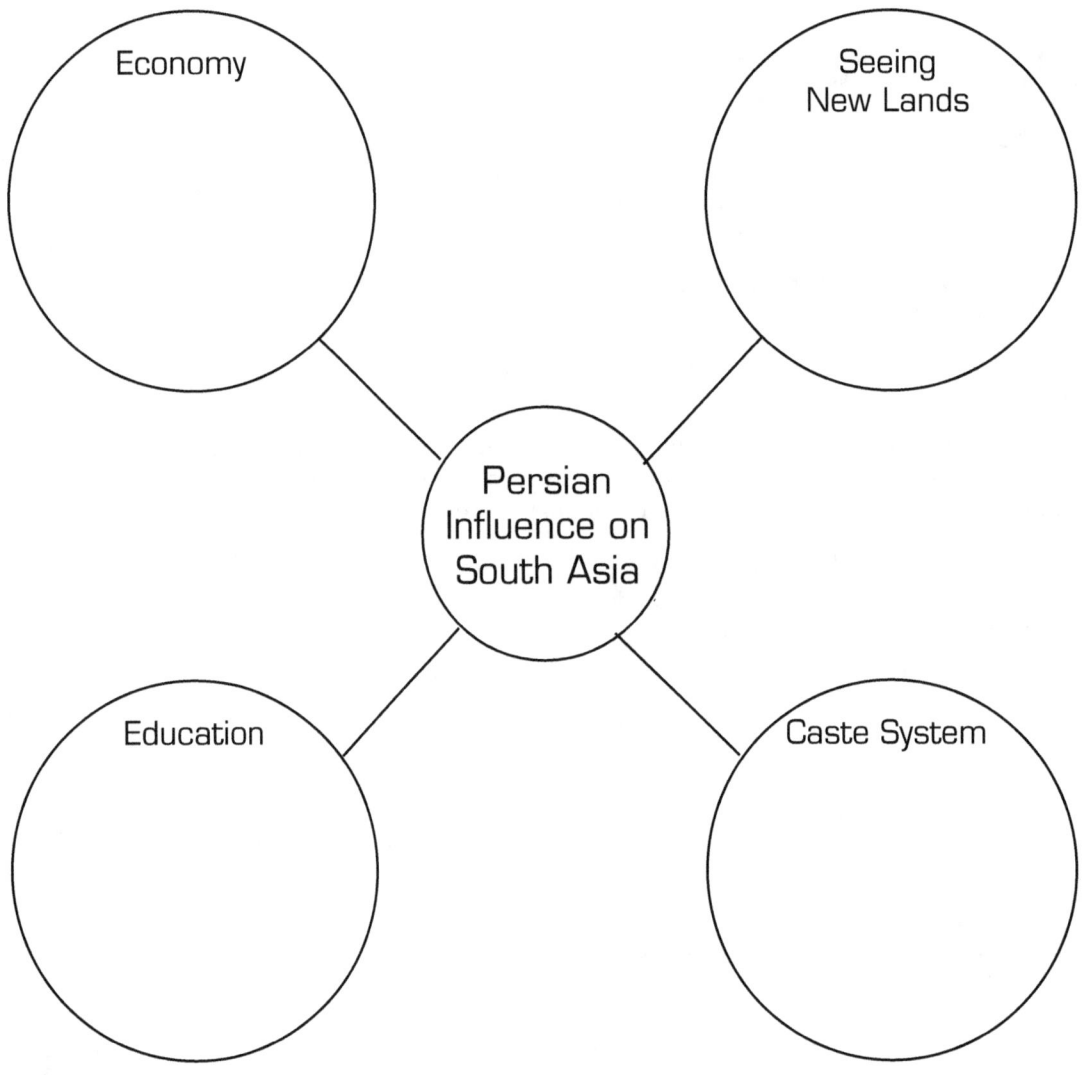

CHAPTER TEST 15

THE ANCIENT SOUTH ASIAN WORLD

A. MULTIPLE CHOICE

Circle the letter of the best answer for each question.

1. James Prinsep did all of the following **except**
   a. design buildings.
   b. decipher Brahmi.
   c. bring the first coin machine to India.
   d. invent the rupee.

2. Understanding Brahmi has helped historians
   a. match what was happening in South Asia to what was happening in other regions.
   b. understand the writing on Harappan seals and tablets.
   c. understand much more about life in Persia.
   d. reconstruct many buildings in Taxila.

3. Which of the following is **not** true about Taxila?
   a. It was the capital of a Persian satrapy.
   b. It was an important educational center.
   c. It was an important center for trade between Greece, Persia, China, and India.
   d. It helped break down social barriers between the castes.

4. Persian contributions to South Asian life included all of the following **except**
   a. coins.
   b. the weights they used.
   c. ideas about government.
   d. greater exposure to foreign products.

5. The growth of cities led to the
   a. use of the same currency (kind of money) in Greece, Persia, and India.
   b. use of the same language (Brahmi) in Greece, Persia, and India.
   c. increased demand for metals, especially steel.
   d. adoption of caste in Greece and Persia.

B. SHORT ANSWER

Write a sentence or two to answer each question.

6. What were some of the consequences of James Prinsep's interest in India's history?

7. Explain some of the ways in which the people of South Asia were affected by becoming part of the Persian Empire.

C. ESSAY

Write an essay in which you explain the changes in South Asia's economy between 800 and 300 BCE. Use a separate piece of paper.

CHAPTER 16

WITH FRIENDS LIKE THESE, WHO NEED ENEMIES? THE BEGINNINGS OF THE MAURYAN EMPIRE

PAGES 109–115

STUDENT STUDY GUIDE
pages 41–42

CAST OF CHARACTERS

Alexander the Great Macedonian Greek ruler who conquered Egypt, Persia, and northern India

Ambhi (AHM-bhi) king of Taxila, ally of Alexander the Great and opponent of King Porus

Chandragupta Maurya (CHUN-druh-GOOP-tuh MAOW-ryuh) one of India's great leaders; founder of the Mauryan dynasty

Firdausi (fir-DOW-see) Persian poet who compiled accounts of Alexander the Great

Kautilya (kaow-TIL-yuh) Chandragupta's great political adviser, author of the *Arthashastra*

Porus (POHR-us) king in the Punjab and opponent of Alexander the Great

CHAPTER SUMMARY

In 327 BCE, Alexander the Great invaded South Asia. After meeting a local king named Porus in an inconclusive battle, Alexander withdrew, but the men and institutions he left behind proved influential. Even more influential, however, was the rise of a young chieftain named Chandragupta, who with the help of his minister Kautilya, established the first empire uniting much of the subcontinent.

PERFORMANCE OBJECTIVES

▶ To understand the interaction between Alexander's Hellenistic empire and South Asia
▶ To comprehend the influence of Kautilya on South Asian notions of statecraft
▶ To identify Chandragupta's achievements

BUILDING BACKGROUND

Remind students that one of the reasons deciphering Brahmi was so useful was that it helped historians make connections between records about the same person using different names. Have students watch for two examples of unfamiliar names that actually refer to figures they have already met. (*Sikander is Alexander; Taxiles is Ambhi.*)

WORKING WITH PRIMARY SOURCES

Ask a volunteer to read the excerpt from Firdausi's poem on page 113. (Point out that King Porus's name is *Pauravi* in Sanskrit.) Ask students to describe Alexander's attitude toward Porus, and how they can tell what it was. (*Alexander's attitude was respectful; he addresses Porus as "Noble Man" and says they are both brave, young, intelligent heroes.*) Have students compare this excerpt with a Greek account of the meeting in *The World in Ancient Times Primary Sources and Reference Volume*. The *Reference Volume* also includes an excerpt from Kautilya's *Arthashastra*.

GEOGRAPHY CONNECTION

Interaction Have students look at the map on page 110. Why was Chandragupta able to control so much of the subcontinent when no one else had? (*advances in weaponry, communications, and bureaucratic organization*)

READING COMPREHENSION QUESTIONS

1. Who was in charge of Taxila in 327 BCE? (*A local king named Ambhi ruled; although the city was theoretically still part of the Persian Empire, the Persians no longer stationed troops there.*)
2. What was King Ambhi's dilemma? (*He faced attack by Alexander from the west and by Porus from the south.*)

3. Who was Kautilya? (*A very clever government official who wrote the* Arthashastra *and helped bring Chandragupta to power; he felt it was more important to govern with knowledge than force.*)
4. What is the Mauryan Empire? (*The Mauryan Empire was the kingdom founded by Chandragupta and ruled by him and his descendants. It lasted from 321–181 BCE.*)

CRITICAL THINKING QUESTIONS

1. Why might the Persian army have withdrawn from Taxila? (*They were needed at home to fight Alexander.*)
2. Why might Alexander have burned Taxila's neighboring city instead of making it part of his empire? (*Possible answers include that he had not enough men to secure it, or because he wanted to make an example of it.*)
3. Why do you think the chapter says that Chandragupta's roads were probably his most important innovation? (*Good roads would have made it much easier to unify and govern his kingdom, and they helped improve trade.*)
4. Distribute copies of the main idea organizer found with the graphic organizers at the back of this book. Have students write "Chandragupta's Accomplishments" in the center circle. Direct students to turn to pages 114 and 115 in their books and use the information there to fill in as many examples of his accomplishments as they can.

SOCIAL SCIENCES

Civics Kautilya believed that it was more effective to govern with knowledge than with force. Ask students if they agree. Which strategy might be more effective in the short term? In the long term?

READING AND LANGUAGE ARTS

Reading Nonfiction Have students preview the chapter by looking at the title, pictures, graphic aids, and sidebars. Help them formulate questions that they expect will be answered by the chapter. Have students write their questions in one column of a two-column chart and answer the questions with information from the text as they read.

Using Language Remind students that, in English, proper nouns such as the names of people, countries, wars, battles, rivers, and places are capitalized. Assign small groups a section of the chapter, and have them list the proper nouns they find and then sort them into categories.

SUPPORTING LEARNING

Struggling Readers Have students create a biographical dictionary of the people in the chapter. They should include the person's name, a phonetic respelling, birth and death dates and location (if known), and a summary of accomplishments.

EXTENDING LEARNING

Enrichment Distribute copies of the blackline master for Chapter 16 to students and have them complete it to explore some of the symbols of power important to South Asia. This can be a small group activity, helpful for ELL students

Extension Have a group of students stage an interview with Alexander the Great, asking the questions about his experiences in India (as described on pages 111–114).

LINKING DISCIPLINES

Math Have students figure out how many men and animals were involved in the battle between Alexander and Porus.

VOCABULARY

paladin knight

centralized government government in which an individual or a small group makes decisions for the country from the capital city

decentralized government government in which many people in many places have the authority to make decisions

WRITING

Journal Ask students to write two journal entries from the point of view of one of the people highlighted in the chapter.

THE ANCIENT SOUTH ASIAN WORLD

SIGNS AND SYMBOLS OF POWER

Directions
Study the coin and caption on page 115 of the book. This coin was used throughout the vast Mauryan Empire. Remember that Chandragupta introduced centralized rule, meaning he was a stranger to many of his subjects. The coin was designed to carry a message about the ruler. Complete the chart by writing a symbol from the list in the column next to its possible meanings. Then, on a separate sheet of paper, write a paragraph explaining what you think Chandragupta hoped this design would tell his people about his government.

Symbols on Coin

water tank   sun and moon   bull's head

fenced sacred tree   elephant   swastika

Symbol	Possible Meaning
1.	reminder of emperor's military power
2.	traditional symbol of sacred power
3.	ancient good luck symbol
4.	the emperor Chandragupta is higher than anyone on earth
5.	rest, protection from the sun, and immortality
6.	Chandragupta will nourish his people's basic needs

CHAPTER TEST 16
THE ANCIENT SOUTH ASIAN WORLD

NAME _____ DATE _____

A. MULTIPLE CHOICE

Circle the letter of the best answer for each question.

1. King Ambhi ruled
    a. Persia.
    b. Taxila.
    c. Greece.
    d. Macedonia.

2. The most feared South Asian weapon was the
    a. chariot.
    b. lance.
    c. war elephant.
    d. *chakra.*

3. In the end, who *really* won the battle between Alexander and Porus?
    a. Chandragupta
    b. Porus
    c. Alexander
    d. King Ambhi

4. *Arthashastra* means
    a. "the way of Enlightenment."
    b. "the book of war."
    c. "release from the cycle of rebirth."
    d. "the book of wealth and power."

5. The ministries in Chandragupta's government included all of the following **except**
    a. ocean mines.
    b. forests.
    c. metals.
    d. universities.

B. SHORT ANSWER

Write a sentence or two to answer each question.

6. For Alexander the Great, what were the short-term and long-term results of battling Porus?
   _____
   _____

7. How did Kautilya's ideas about how a king should rule affect Chandragupta Maurya?
   _____
   _____

C. ESSAY

Write a paragraph telling which of Chandragupta's accomplishments you think was most important. Be sure to give specific examples from the chapter.
   _____
   _____
   _____
   _____
   _____

CHAPTER 17
NOTHING BUT A ZERO: SCIENCE AND TECHNOLOGY

PAGES 116–120

FOR HOMEWORK

STUDENT STUDY GUIDE pages 43–44

CAST OF CHARACTERS

Aryabhata (AHR-yuah-BHUH-tuh) India's greatest ancient scientist and author of the *Aryabhatiyam*

 VOCABULARY

Ayurveda traditional South Asian medicine

rejuvenation the process of making something young again

 WRITING

Narration Choose a scientific or mathematical idea that you understand well and, like Aryabhata, write a story that explains it without numbers.

CHAPTER SUMMARY

Mathematics, science, and technology were particularly productive aspects of South Asian culture in antiquity. "Firsts" included an accurate calculation of π (pi), a heliocentric view of the solar system, large-scale production of steel, and the concept of zero.

PERFORMANCE OBJECTIVES

▶ To identify the ancient tradition of Ayurveda
▶ To explain South Asian advances in mathematics and astronomy
▶ To understand technological innovations in metallurgy and their implications for South Asian society

BUILDING BACKGROUND

Have students use what they already know about the climate of South Asia and the culture of its people to predict what kinds of scientific advances South Asians may have made during ancient times. Have them refer back to these predictions as you make your way through the material.

WORKING WITH PRIMARY SOURCES

Have a volunteer read the I've Got Your Nose sidebar on page 120. Discuss why people convicted of crimes might be particularly interested in disguising their punishment.

GEOGRAPHY CONNECTION

Location Have students locate the ancient city of Nalanda, site of Nalanda University on the online map at *www.ancientindia.co.uk/geography/explore/exp_set.html* (a website listed on the Websites page of the students' book). Ask students to zoom in to locate Nalanda and then describe how its location differed from the location of other ancient cities in the area. (*Nalanda was not close to a river.*)

READING COMPREHENSION QUESTIONS

1. What is Ayurveda, and what does it mean? (*traditional South Asian medicine that has been around for 5,000 years; "life-truth" or "the science of living"*)
2. What were rejuvenation clinics, and what do they tell us about South Asian medicine? (*They were clinics in the country for people with arthritis or other chronic diseases or who wanted to slow aging, like our spas; they tell us that South Asian medicine was geared toward prevention of as well as treating disease symptoms.*)
3. What are some of Aryabhata's accomplishments? (*Aryabhata discovered that the moon reflects the sun's light; he also discovered the accurate measurement of π (pi) and that the earth orbits the sun, as well as that the rising and setting of the sun, moon, and stars is the result of the daily revolution of the earth; in*

104   CHAPTER 17

addition, he developed an accurate calendar and wrote a book explaining all of this without using mathematical equations.)

4. What was ancient South Asia's greatest contribution to knowledge? *(the concept of zero, which allowed for greater ease and accuracy in calculations and record-keeping)*

CRITICAL THINKING QUESTIONS

1. Draw conclusions about what advances in smelting iron, steel, and other metals meant for the Mauryan Empire. *(These advances strengthened it; they helped in making weapons, coins for trade, accurate weights, and monuments and other buildings.)*
2. Why might Aryabhata, an astronomer, have found it necessary to calculate an accurate value for π (pi)? *(to help in calculating the orbits and revolutions of the planets)*
3. Distribute copies of the blackline master for Chapter 17 and have students write one thing they learned about South Asian science and technology in each of the leaves.

SOCIAL SCIENCES

Science, Technology, and Society Direct students' attention to the How Do You Spell Relief? sidebar on page 119. Discuss the branches as a class until you are sure that everyone grasps what they are. Then ask them whether they would choose the same categories today, and, if not, what categories they would select instead, and why.

READING AND LANGUAGE ARTS

Reading Nonfiction Have students categorize the information in the chapter. Categories could include medical, mathematical, and scientific advances. Have students include at least three details for each category.

Using Language Write this sentence on the board: "Aryabhata knew nothing about nothing." Then ask: Isn't that a double negative? Elicit the pun in the multiple meanings of *nothing*. Have students find other words in the chapter that have multiple meanings.

SUPPORTING LEARNING

Struggling Readers Assign small groups sections of the chapter to reread. Have students in each group identify the main idea and several details of their section. Ask groups to summarize their findings in an oral presentation.

EXTENDING LEARNING

Enrichment Have students research Ayurvedic practice today and present what they have learned to the class.

Extension Have each student write two questions that can be answered from the chapter. Collect the questions, and then divide the class into two groups, with yourself as host. Ask questions for the teams to answer. Each correct answer scores a point. The team with the most points at the end of the game receives a piece of celery.

LINKING DISCIPLINES

Health

Have students use the Internet or the school resource center to find out more about Ayurvedic medicine. If any of them practice it in their homes, ask them to tell the class about it. If not, invite an Ayurvedic practitioner to make a presentation to the class.

THEN and NOW

Ayurveda is very old; South Asians believe that Ayurveda was a gift from the god Brahma to mankind. Nonetheless, it remains extremely popular. In India alone, estimates are that people spent more than $800 million on Ayurvedic products in 2000.

THE ANCIENT SOUTH ASIAN WORLD

ANCIENT SOUTH ASIAN MEDICINE

Directions
Ancient South Asians made many discoveries in medicine, science, and math. Write one South Asian scientific discovery for each category in each relevant circle below.

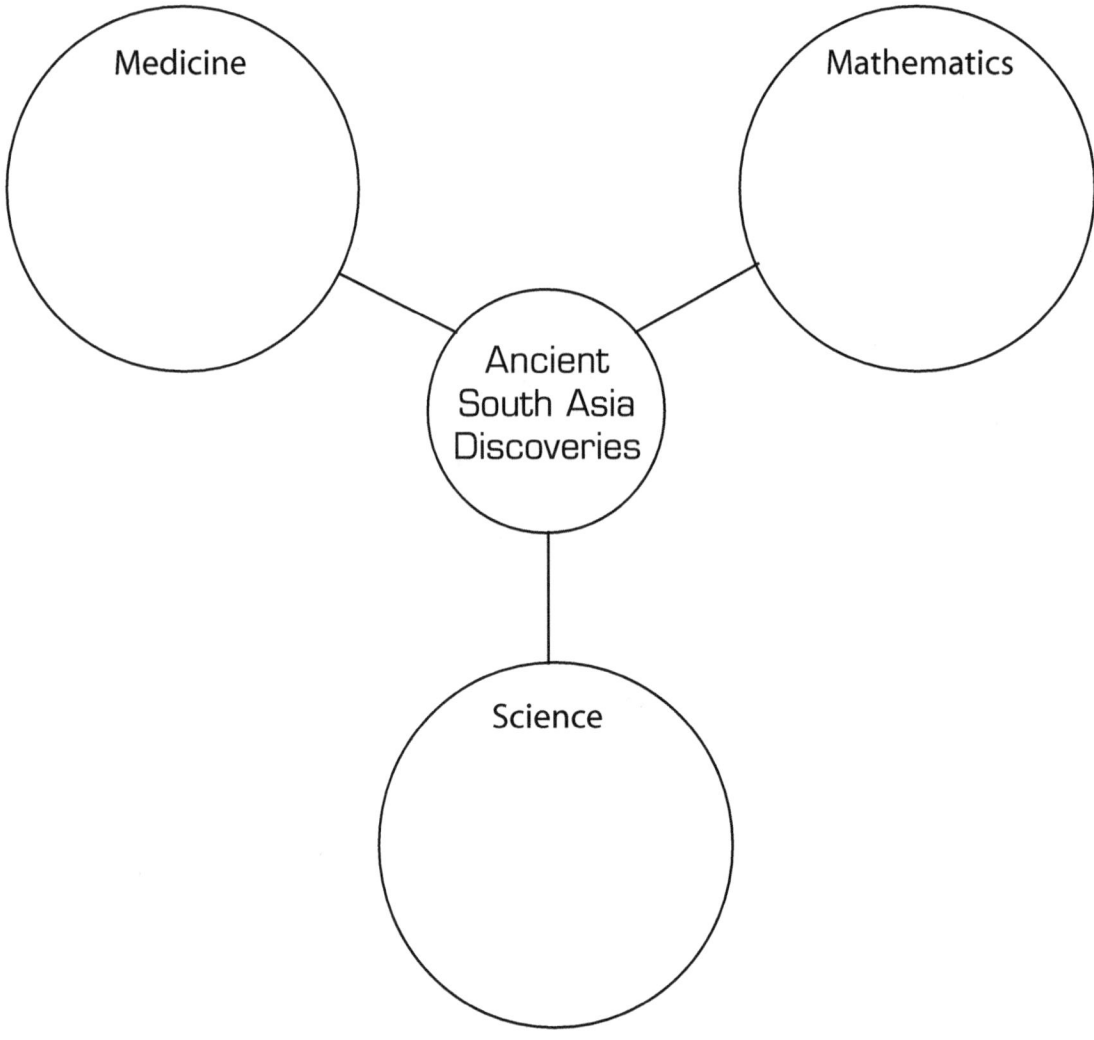

CHAPTER TEST 17

THE ANCIENT SOUTH ASIAN WORLD

NAME _____ DATE _____

A. MULTIPLE CHOICE

Circle the letter of the best answer for each question.

1. South Asian advances in the sciences discussed in this book included all of the following **except**
   a. lenses and telescopes.
   b. metallurgy (making metals).
   c. surgery.
   d. mathematics.

2. South Asian doctors sometimes used ants
   a. to stop bleeding.
   b. as an ingredient in medicine.
   c. to hold wounds together.
   d. as favorite foods.

3. Heating iron with carbon made
   a. iron ore.
   b. steel.
   c. charcoal.
   d. Ayurveda.

4. The most important ancient South Asian scientific invention was
   a. plastic surgery.
   b. calculating pi (π).
   c. an accurate calendar.
   d. zero.

5. South Asian scientists discovered all of the following more than a thousand years before scientists in the West **except**
   a. the fact that the earth goes around the sun.
   b. the importance of cleanliness during surgery.
   c. the value of pi (π).
   d. glassware.

B. SHORT ANSWER

Write a sentence or two to answer each question.

6. What do the authors mean when they say that "Ayurveda was more than medicine"?

_____

_____

7. Briefly describe the process of smelting iron and explain why it was important to the Mauryan emperor.

_____

_____

C. ESSAY

Write an essay on a separate sheet of paper in which you tell which South Asian invention or discovery described in this chapter is most interesting to you. Explain your reasons.

CHAPTER 18

DARMA, ARTHA, KAMA, AND MOKSHA: WAR AND PEACE IN THE TIME OF ASHOKA

PAGES 121–125

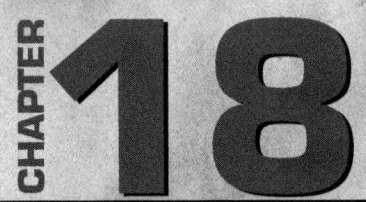

STUDENT STUDY GUIDE
pages 45–46

CAST OF CHARACTERS

Bindusara (BIN-doo-SAH-rah) Mauryan king; son of Chandragupta and father of Ashoka

dharma the path of virtue and goodness; duty

artha the path of success and riches

kama the path of beauty, peace, order, and pleasure in the world

moksha release from the cycle of life and rebirth

CHAPTER SUMMARY

One of South Asia's greatest leaders was the philosopher king Ashoka, grandson of Chandragupta. After winning a brutal victory against the Kalingans, Ashoka was shocked and dismayed by the destruction he had caused. Anxious that his people should not make the mistakes that he had, he erected a number of engraved stone pillars that exhorted his people to follow the gentle teachings of the Buddha.

PERFORMANCE OBJECTIVES

▶ To understand the role of the military at the time of the Mauryan Empire
▶ To explain the significance of the values of *dharma*, *artha*, and *kama* in achieving *moksha*
▶ To describe Ashoka's turning to Buddhist values
▶ To analyze Brahmin resistance to the Mauryan Empire

BUILDING BACKGROUND

Ask students to reflect on their personal goals. List their responses in two columns on the board. Put external goals such as professional success, wealth, and accomplishments on one side, and internal goals like kindness, honesty, being a good parent on the other. Discuss ways in which these two kinds of goals may conflict.

WORKING WITH PRIMARY SOURCES

Have students examine the drawing of the Ashoka sculpture on page 122. Ask: What similarities do you see to Harappan carvings like the one on page 61 or the Priest King on page 54? (*Both Ashoka and the god or leader in the Harappan seal are wearing bangles and a fancy headdress; both Ashoka and the Priest King have a robe/sacred thread over the left shoulder.*)

GEOGRAPHY CONNECTION

Regions Today Kalinga is known as Orissa. Distribute copies of the Chapter 18 blackline master to students and have them identify by color the various regions of South Asia in order to learn more about them.

READING COMPREHENSION QUESTIONS

1. What does the main title of the chapter mean? (*dharma: duty/honor; artha: money and success; kama: beauty; moksha: release from the cycle of rebirth*)
2. Why did Ashoka want to conquer Kalinga? (*He wanted to control the wealthy state that dominated trade with Southeast Asia; the principal north-south route went through it; possibly to reduce a military threat.*)
3. Was he successful? (*Yes, but the carnage was so great he turned away from conquest and toward Buddhism.*)

4. Why is it so hard for archaeologists to read some of Ashoka's edicts, even after the language and alphabet were deciphered? (*The stonemasons who were carving the edicts in stone probably couldn't read and were sometimes sloppy in copying the words.*)

CRITICAL THINKING QUESTIONS

1. Can you see any pattern to the weapons assigned to the various *varna*? (*Lower* varna *were assigned weapons used at close quarters; upper* varna *used longer-range weapons.*)
2. Do you think that Ashoka would have responded the same way to his victory at Orissa if his conquest of South Asia had not been complete? (*Answers will vary.*)
3. Instruct students to make a two-column chart of Ashoka's accomplishments, using one column for his military and political activities and the other for his ethical and moral activities.

SOCIAL SCIENCES

Civics Ashoka and his grandfather Chandragupta believed that the advantages of a unified state outweighed a loss of local power. Have students debate which system is better.

READING AND LANGUAGE ARTS

Reading Nonfiction Direct students' attention to the sentence on page 124 that begins, "He remembered the lessons . . ." Point out that the writer has used parallel organization to give the reader clues about the nature of *dharma, artha, kama,* and *moksha.* (Dharma *is honorable,* artha *is creative,* kama *is beautiful, and* moksha *is peaceful.*) Ask students to find a similar passage on page 121.

Using Language Direct students' attention to the beautiful description of Chandragupta's empire on page 122. Ask students to describe your community, state, province, or country in similar terms, "from the _____ (adjective phrase) to the _____ (adjective phrase)."

SUPPORTING LEARNING

English Language Learners Have students work individually or in small groups to make booklets of South Asian weapons. Using the information on pages 121–122, have them write the name of one weapon on each page. Help them to find information about that weapon, and then ask them to illustrate their book.

Struggling Readers Distribute copies of the main idea map organizer from the graphic organizers at the back of this book. Have students write *South Asian Beliefs* in the center circle and *Dharma, Kama, Artha,* and *Moksha* in the circles surrounding it. Define each of those concepts as a class. Have them write the definitions in each circle.

EXTENDING LEARNING

Enrichment Assign interested students to read all or part of Malcolm Bosse's *Tusk and Stone* and report back to the class what they have learned about life in ancient South Asia.

Extension Have students paraphrase Ashoka's edict about "conquest by dharma" (page 124).

WRITING

Persuasion Ask students to imagine that they are Ashoka. Write a letter to a local prince explaining why you want to unify the country. Then imagine you are the prince, and write a response.

LINKING DISCIPLINES

Math Assign pairs of students to investigate an Indian or Pakistani state or one of the other South Asian countries. Help the class, decide what kind of information to investigate—per capita income, life expectancy, percentage of population in agriculture or cities, etc. Assign students to find the information in encyclopedias or online at places like the *CIA World Fact Book*, at *www.cia.gov/cia/ publications/factbook/*. Once they gather the data have them produce comparative bar or pie graphs.

THE ANCIENT SOUTH ASIAN WORLD

SOUTH ASIAN GEOGRAPHY

Compare the map on page 123 with The Ancient South Asian World map on pages 12–13. Then complete the activity below:

1. You read on pages 121–122 about the military academy in Taxila. Find Taxila on the map on pp 121–13 and then mark it's location on the map below.
2. Taxila is at the base of which mountain range, and near which river?
3. The palace built by Chandragupta, Ashoka's grandfather, is in Pataliputra. Find Pataliputra on the map on page 123 and mark its location below.
4. Pataliputra is on the bank of which river?
5. Find and label the trade cities of Sopara and Tamralipti on the map.
6. What do you think is the best trade route from Pataliputra to Sopara? Mark it on the map.
7. An important geographic obstacle encouraged merchants along the Ganga River to sail around the Indian subcontinent to reach Sopara rather than travel over land. Mark it on the map.

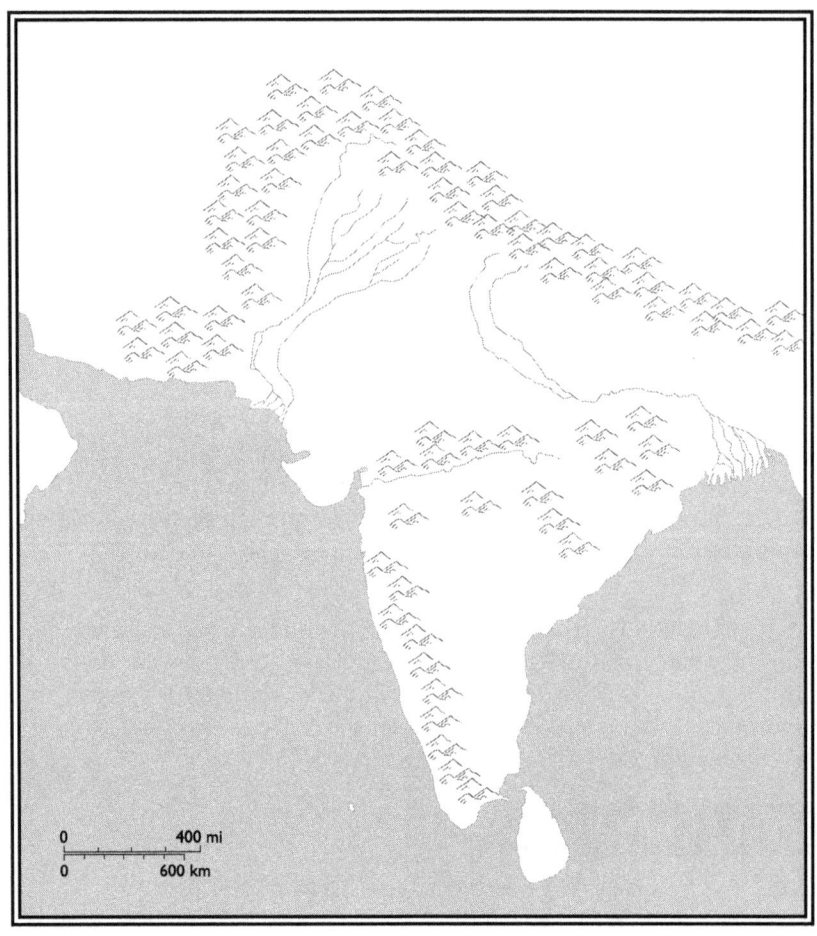

CHAPTER TEST 18

THE ANCIENT SOUTH ASIAN WORLD

NAME _____ DATE _____

A. MULTIPLE CHOICE

Circle the letter of the best answer for each question.

1. The major Mauryan emperors were, from first to last,
   a. Ashoka, Bindusara, Chandragupta.
   b. Chandragupta, Ashoka, Bindusara.
   c. Bindusara, Chandragupta, Ashoka.
   d. Chandragupta, Bindusara, Ashoka.

2. All of the following illustrate the importance of the military to South Asian life **except**
   a. Ashoka's rock edicts.
   b. armories in each city.
   c. military academies like the one at Taxila.
   d. Bindusara's nickname, "Slayer of Enemies."

3. A Brahmin soldier could have been taught how to use all of these weapons **except** for a
   a. war elephant.
   b. mace.
   c. bow and arrow.
   d. chakra, or flying disk.

4. Ashoka wanted to conquer Kalinga for all of the following reasons **except** its
   a. wealth, amassed by trade with Southeast Asia.
   b. Buddhist monuments.
   c. strategic position.
   d. military might.

5. The Mauryan Empire fell in part because
   a. poor roads and communication made it too difficult to govern.
   b. the Mauryans were defeated in a huge battle with Kalinga.
   c. all of Ashoka's children became Buddhist missionaries.
   d. Brahmins felt threatened by Ashoka's decree against sacrifice.

B. SHORT ANSWER

Write a sentence or two to answer each question.

6. Why did Ashoka turn to Buddhist values?

   _____

   _____

7. Describe Brahmin resistance to the Mauryan Empire.

   _____

   _____

C. ESSAY

On a separate piece of paper, write an essay in which you describe the values of *dharma*, *artha*, and *kama* and explain how they contribute to achieving *moksha*.

THE ANCIENT SOUTH ASIAN WORLD   CHAPTER 18 TEST

UNIT 6: LIFE IN ANCIENT SOUTH ASIA

PAGES 126–142

Chapter 19 Service and Study: The Cycle of Life
Chapter 20 Who's in Charge Here, Anyway? An Age of Religious and Political Confusion
Chapter 21 A Place for Everyone: Caste and Society

UNIT OBJECTIVES

Unit 6 discusses daily life in South Asia in an era of political confusion and unrest. In this unit your students will learn about

- the stages of life for men and women.
- changes in Buddhist and Hindu belief and practice.
- the reign of Kanishka.
- the use of the Code of Manu as a way of organizing society during a time of political uncertainty.

PRIMARY SOURCES

Unit 6 includes excerpts from the following primary sources:

- Ilango Adigal, "The Ankle Bracelet"
- Brahmanical Code of Conduct
- Yajurveda
- Code of Manu
- *Mahabharata*

Pictures of South Asian artifacts can also be analyzed as primary sources. These include:

- Illustration of initiation ceremony
- Terracotta figurine, Harappa
- Bride with wedding jewelry
- Yaksha statue, Barhut
- Cave painting of *bodhisattva*
- Carving of stupa
- Kanishka Kushana coin
- Stupa at Sanchi
- Buddhist cave, Ajanta
- Cave painting of life at court
- Scene from the *Ramayana*

BIG IDEAS IN UNIT 6

Class, family, and **society** are the big ideas presented in Unit 6. The unit begins with a presentation of daily life in ancient South Asia. It then reviews the chaotic period following the death of Ashoka, setting up a discussion of strategies the South Asians used to order society, especially the Code of Manu. One way to introduce these ideas is to discuss strategies that we use to order our society, including the rule of law. Then tell students to look for similarities and differences in the ideas of the ancient South Asians, particularly in a period without political stability.

GEOGRAPHY CONNECTION

Have students use the map on pages 12–13 of their book to trace the arrival in South Asia of the Kushana as described on page 135. Then ask them to describe in their own words the extent of the Kushana Empire referring to the scale and features shown on the map on page 132 of their book.

TIMELINE

327–325 BCE	Greeks invade under Alexander the Great
269–232 BCE	Reign of Ashoka
261 BCE	Ashoka promotes Buddhism as state religion
200 BCE–200 CE	Buddhist influence reaches its height
185 BCE	Mauryan dynasty ends
150 CE	Kushana invade; reign of Kanishka; Gandhara art; Buddhism splits into several sects
250 CE	Sanskrit literature develops; scribes write down *Mahabharata* and *Ramayana*
200–300 CE	Code of Manu emerges

UNIT PROJECTS

Dramatic Reading

Have a group of students write, rehearse, and perform a dramatic version of "The Ankle Bracelet." Caution: The original poem is long and difficult to read. You may wish to restrict students to the information in the book (without comment) or, if they want more, provide them with a summary like the one found online at *www.maddad.org/coll100.htm*.

Chronology

Have a group of students add the pertinent dates from this unit to the class timeline.

History of Costume

Have small groups research the history of Indian clothing. The website *www.globaled.org/nyworld/materials/india/worksheet2.html* is a wonderful coloring book that asks kids to make conclusions about the economy, clothing, and geography of various regions of the subcontinent. A brief history of South Asian clothing can also be found at *http://fga.freac.fsu.edu/misc/india.htm*.

Research Report

Have small groups learn more about the Central Asian kingdoms of Parthia, Bactria, and Scythia, or indigenous kingdoms like the Sungas, Kanvas, or Shatavahanas to better understand the historical context for the material in this chapter. Groups should summarize their findings and report them to the class.

ADDITIONAL ASSESSMENT

Use any of these unit projects for additional assessment. For Unit 6, divide the class into groups and have all students take part in these projects. To assess their work in Dramatic Reading students should demonstrate an understanding of ideas about the roles of men and women as well as the events of the story. For the History of Costume and Research Report, look for conclusions that show an understanding of how their findings illustrate the unit's themes. Use the scoring rubric at the back of this guide to assess group projects, and have students rate

THE ANCIENT SOUTH ASIAN WORLD

their own work with the self-assessment rubric. For the Research Report, be sure to distribute the library/media center research log (see rubric at the back of this guide) to help students evaluate their sources as they conduct their research.

LITERATURE CONNECTION

With people living in seven major countries—India, Pakistan, Afghanistan, Nepal, Bangladesh, Sri Lanka, and Bhutan—South Asia is a very diverse region of the world. As such, it has a rich cultural heritage, much of which has been passed down from ancient times through its religious and cultural traditions and folklore. Most collections of folktales available tend to be grouped by their region; examining these traditions as a whole offers a great opportunity for students to explore the great diversity among South Asian cultures. Look at these collections:

- ▶ Dasgupta, Sayantami, and Shamita Das Dasgupta. *The Demon Slayers and Other Stories: Bengali Folk Tales.* New York: Interlink Books, 1995. Folktales based on the regional languages and their dialects, specific traditions, local gods, and beliefs.
- ▶ Timpanelli, Gioia. *Tales from the Roof of the World: Folktales from Tibet.* New York: The Viking Press, 1984. Told in the manner of oral folktales, this collection is organized as a symbolic journey of the self toward spirituality.
- ▶ Beck, Brenda, et al. *Folktales of India.* Chicago: University of Chicago Press, 1999. A unique collection of stories newly collected from previously unrepresented tribal regions in India.
- ▶ Narayan, R.K. *Gods, Demons and Others.* Chicago: University of Chicago Press, 1993. Hindu myths and stories as freely adapted by Narayan, one of India's foremost writers. The collection includes from both the Ramayana and the Mahabarata. These tales are as wonderful to read as they are revealing of India's religious traditions.

There are also collections of Nepalese and Pakistani fairytales, all listed within Meena Khorana's very thorough *The Indian Subcontinent in Literature for Children and Young Adults: An Annotated Bibliography of English-Language Books* (New York, Westport, and London: Greenwood Press, 1991).

UNIVERSAL ACCESS

The following strategies are designed to cover a range of learning styles and reading, language, and skill levels. You may find that any of your students will benefit from the various strategies presented.

Reading Strategies

- ▶ Have the class read the chapters aloud. Stop the reading from time to time and lead students in taking notes about the text.
- ▶ Have students read the chapters in small groups. When they are done, one group member should act as the Questioner and ask questions about the text. Other group members should answer with details from the chapter.

Writing Strategies

- ▶ Have students imagine themselves to be a traditional South Asian woman as described in these chapters. Have them write journal entries explaining their goals and satisfactions.
- ▶ Have small groups write dialogues between a Theraveda and Mahayana Buddhist. Students can perform their dialogues for the class.

Listening and Speaking Strategies

▶ To spark students' interest, state examples of rules from these chapters that are diametrically opposed to students' life experiences. Have them read to understand the context of such statements. The following are some examples: *Don't eat after sunset* (page 127); *Wives eat in the kitchen, unless invited to join their husbands* (page 128); *Women must never try to live independently* (page 140); *Brahmins are not allowed to wear leather shoes* (page 142).

▶ Help teams of students prepare "debates" between types of people in these chapters. For instance, one student might be a Vaisya; the other, a Kshatriya. The two would debate the reasons for the Code of Manu. Or, one student might be a young woman; the other, an elderly hermit. The two could debate a woman's proper role in society.

UNIT VOCABULARY LIST

The following words that appear in Unit 6 are important for your students' understanding of the social studies content as well as for development of literacy. Use these words for vocabulary study or to reinforce language arts skills (e.g., synonyms, compound words, prefixes and suffixes, and related words). The words are listed below in the order in which they appear in the chapters.

Chapter 19	**Chapter 20**	**Chapter 21**
frail	vacuum	glance
inhabited	highlands	thread
pomegranates	rowdy	subgroup
sanctifies	squabbled	expenditure
revolved	continent	offspring
hermit	monuments	distinction
associate	conquest	pollute
sympathetic	overpower	clogs
renunciation		mode
pyre		

THE ANCIENT SOUTH ASIAN WORLD

CHAPTER 19

SERVICE AND STUDY: THE CYCLE OF LIFE

PAGES 126–131

FOR HOMEWORK

STUDENT STUDY GUIDE

pages 47–48

CAST OF CHARACTERS

Kannaki (KUH-nuh-kee) fictional wife in "The Ankle Bracelet"

Kovalan (KOH-vuh-luhn) fictional husband in "The Ankle Bracelet"

 WRITING

- **Narrative** Ask students to rewrite "The Ankle Bracelet" in the present. Have students use the plot, setting, characters mentioned, and what they already know about ancient South Asia to write an ending. Remind them to include tension and dialogue. Ask volunteers to read their stories to an audience.

CHAPTER SUMMARY

This chapter uses a famous poem from southern India, *Shilappadikaram*, or "The Ankle Bracelet" as a platform from which to discuss gender roles and the life cycle in ancient South Asia.

PERFORMANCE OBJECTIVES

▶ To draw conclusions from the traditional story of "The Ankle Bracelet" about social roles of the time
▶ To analyze the role of women in traditional South Asian society
▶ To understand the stages of the life cycle for both men and women

BUILDING BACKGROUND

Explain that sociologists (people who study the ways societies work) describe peoples' lives as a succession of stages, like infancy, childhood, etc. Brainstorm the life stages that are meaningful for your culture. Ask students to compare them to those you will discuss as you make your way through this chapter.

WORKING WITH PRIMARY SOURCES

Ask students to read the excerpt from the story on page 128. What does this suggest that women have to do in order to become divine? *(be a good wife)* What do men have to do? *(perform some incredible feat of daring or bravery)*

GEOGRAPHY CONNECTION

Place "The Ankle Bracelet" is a story from Kerala in southern India, a region that we have not yet said much about. An Edsitement lesson on Marco Polo includes activities for introducing students to southern India. Consult it online at *http://edsitement.neh.gov/view_lesson_plan.asp?id=494*.

READING COMPREHENSION QUESTIONS

1. What is the plot of "The Ankle Bracelet"? *(A man, Kovalan, irresponsibly loses his fortune. He and his loyal wife, Kannaki, travel to a city to sell her wedding jewelry, but he is murdered by a dishonest goldsmith. Despite his foolishness, she mourns him so sincerely that the gods make her a goddess.)*
2. What religion were Kovalan and Kannaki, and how did it affect their behavior? *(Jain; vegetarians who didn't eat after sunset)*
3. How did Kannaki show her love for her husband? *(washing his feet; purifying his eating place; preparing his dinner; giving him her ankle bracelet to sell; breaking her bangles and going into the wilderness to mourn him after his death)*
4. What was a man expected to do when his hair turned white? *(give his property to his oldest son, and retire to the forest to become a teacher)*

CRITICAL THINKING QUESTIONS

1. Can you find any references to *varna* in the story? (*Kannaki performs rituals proper to the merchant class—Vaisya; the cowgirls are expected to furnish brand new utensils for their guests' use.*)
2. According to the book, married women marked the parts of their hair with red, the color of fertility and power. Why was marriage seen as a source of power for women? (*They could have children; they could be sanctified by serving their husbands.*)
3. Distribute copies of the blackline master for Chapter 19 and have students complete it to reinforce their understanding of the events of "The Ankle Bracelet."

SOCIAL SCIENCES

Economics   As a class, consider the amount of time that was required to cook, clean, and provide clothing for a family in a time before electric light, running water, or machines of any kind, when even thread had to be grown, harvested, cleaned, and spun before being woven. Why did women devote all of their time to their family? (*because it took all of one person's time to provide food and clothing for a family*)

READING AND LANGUAGE ARTS

Reading Nonfiction   Have students create a character map for Kannaki. Have them divide a sheet of paper into four boxes with the labels *What Kannaki Says and Does*, *What Others Think About Kannaki*, *How Kannaki Feels About Others*, and *How I Feel About Kannaki*. Instruct students to fill in the boxes with information from the chapter and their own ideas about what they have read.

Using Language   According to the book, married women mark the part of their hair with red, which symbolizes blood, life, fertility, and power. Discuss the power of symbols—they associate qualities with someone or something, they don't require words to give meaning. Have students list modern symbols and discuss their meanings.

SUPPORTING LEARNING

English Language Learners   Review with students the ways that Kannaki shows her love for her husband (*washing his feet; purifying his eating place; preparing him dinner; giving him her ankle bracelet to sell; breaking her bangles and going into the wilderness to mourn him after his death*). Invite them to share ways in which family members serve each other in their country of origin.

Struggling Readers   Have students draw a comic strip summary of "The Ankle Bracelet."

EXTENDING LEARNING

Enrichment   Until the 19th century, most women spent a good part of every day spinning, weaving, and sewing. Have students research the textiles, costume, and needle arts common to ancient South Asia and report back to the class with illustrations.

Extension   Ask four students to explain the four stages of life for men and women, each taking responsibility for one of the stages.

LINKING DISCIPLINES

Music "The Ankle Bracelet" is traditionally performed with musical accompaniment. Help students rewrite the summary of the story in the chapter as a continuous narrative. Have volunteers take parts and read the story while other volunteers accompany them on rhythm instruments and cymbals.

THEN and NOW

Although many South Asian women today receive an excellent education and then pursue a profession, being a good wife and mother continues to be priority.

THE ANCIENT SOUTH ASIAN WORLD

THE ANKLE BRACELET

Directions
Read the list of events and then arrange them in the correct sequence on the chart to show the sequence in the story.

Kannaki marries Kovalan.
Evil goldsmith steals the bracelet and murders Kovalan.
Indra sprinkles Kannaki with flowers and takes her to heaven.
Kannaki and Kovalan set out to sell her ankle bracelet.
Kannaki breaks her bracelets and mourns Kovalan for 14 days.
Kannaki purifies the eating place.
Kannaki washes her husband's feet.
Kovalan loses the couple's money.
Kannaki is reunited with Kovalan.
The couple eats together, an emblem of their love.
The gods sing a hymn praising Kannaki.
They stop at the home of Madari and some cowmaids.

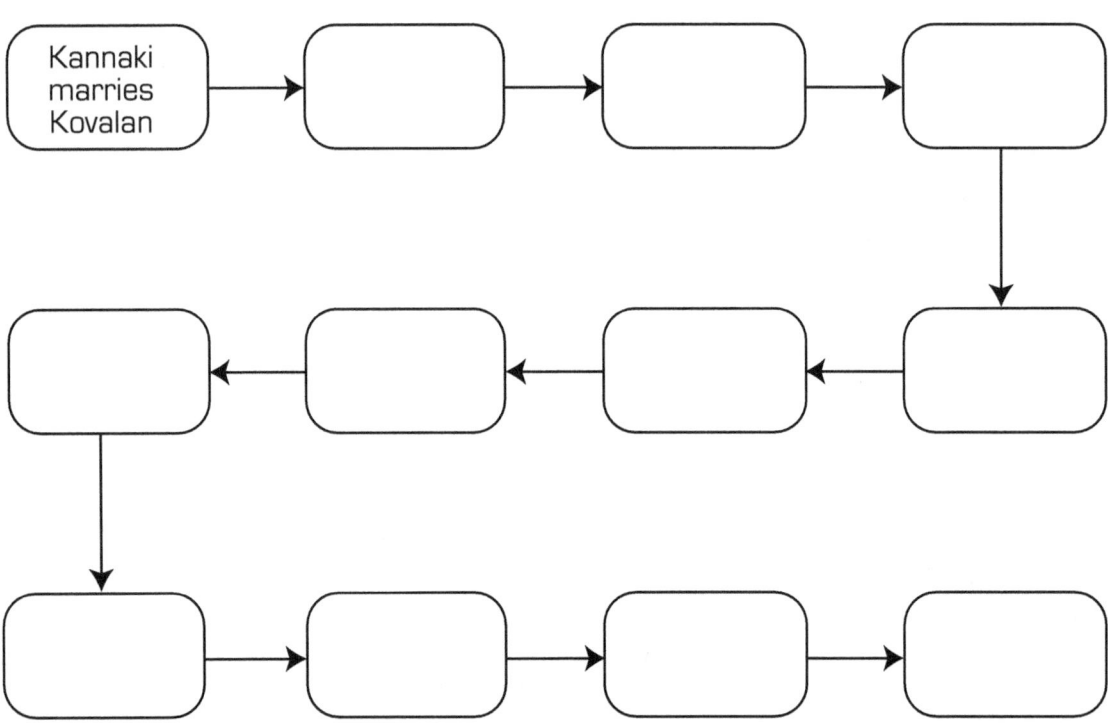

CHAPTER TEST 19

THE ANCIENT SOUTH ASIAN WORLD

A. MULTIPLE CHOICE

Circle the letter of the best answer for each question.

1. The cowgirls in the story "The Ankle Bracelet" are so poor that they
   a. don't need to be protected from men.
   b. wear bangles made of wood.
   c. are released from the obligations of caste.
   d. have no fruit or vegetables to eat.

2. A South Asian bride's wedding jewelry
   a. belongs to her husband, not to her.
   b. may be sold to pay for her education.
   c. is her insurance policy against hard times.
   d. is only worn by Brahmins.

3. Both *sati*, the practice of a woman's dying with her husband, and the practice of a man's retiring from public life and giving his property to his son when his hair turns white are examples of
   a. the importance of *varna*.
   b. acts from "The Ankle Bracelet."
   c. Jain beliefs.
   d. rituals with practical and religious purposes.

4. Boys were given unsewn robes during their initiation to
   a. help them learn more effectively.
   b. show off their weaving skills.
   c. prove that they were better than women.
   d. share with the poor.

5. Common marriage practices included all of the following **except**
   a. walking around the sacred fire.
   b. wearing the sacred thread.
   c. purification.
   d. multiple wives for wealthy men.

C. COMPARE AND CONTRAST

Use the Venn diagram to compare and contrast the life cycles of men and women in ancient South Asia.

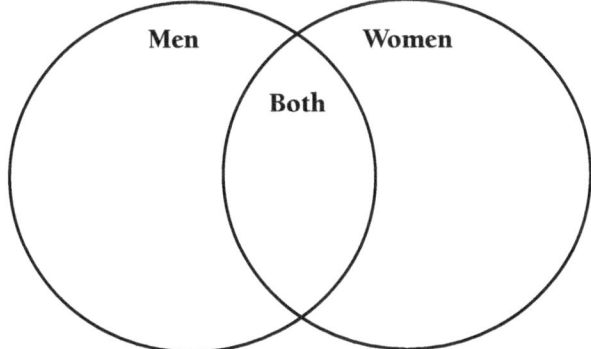

C. ESSAY

Write an essay on a separate piece of paper summarizing what "The Ankle Bracelet" says about the traditional roles of men and women at the time of the story.

CHAPTER 20

WHO'S IN CHARGE HERE, ANYWAY? AN AGE OF RELIGIOUS AND POLITICAL CONFUSION

PAGES 132–137

FOR HOMEWORK
STUDENT STUDY GUIDE
pages 49–50

CAST OF CHARACTERS

Kanishka (kuh-NISH-kuh) king of the Kushana who briefly united the northern subcontinent

VOCABULARY

bodhisattva a Buddhist saint; someone who delays achieving Nirvana to help others

- **Journal** Have students imagine being a dancer newly arrived from the countryside to be trained at a temple. Ask what they might notice and wonder about or be surprised by in their new home.

CHAPTER SUMMARY

The fall of the Mauryan Empire left the subcontinent politically divided and vulnerable to invasion. Under Kanishka's short-lived Kushan Empire, Mahayana Buddhism sought to make Buddhism more accessible to the people through monuments and the adoption of Buddhist saints called *bodhisattvas*.

PERFORMANCE OBJECTIVES

▶ To understand the dangers of a power vacuum
▶ To analyze the elaboration of Buddhist practice, including the adoption of *bodhisattvas*, in its historical context
▶ To describe the vigorous reign of Kanishka Kushana

BUILDING BACKGROUND

Ask students to imagine a world without adults. Are there times when it is useful to have a parent, teacher, or other authority figure around? Tell them that this chapter examines a time in South Asia's history when there was no clear authority figure, and the strategies people turned to in an effort to provide order and direction to their lives.

WORKING WITH PRIMARY SOURCES

Refer students to the photographs of the Kushana coin on page 135. Discuss Kanishka's policy of religious toleration. Why might he have thought it was a good idea to put a variety of gods on the back of his coins? (*Perhaps Kanishka thought this suggested he had the support of each of the gods.*)

GEOGRAPHY CONNECTION

Movement The text refers to the Bactrians, the Parthians, the Scythians (sometimes called the Shaka), and the Kushana. Locate Bactria (a Greek kingdom in what is now northwestern Afghanistan), Parthia (present-day Iran and Iraq), Scythia (the area between the Black and Caspian Seas), and Kush (probably from China along the Great Silk Road) on the map on page 132. Ask: in what direction did the Kushana move into Bactria? (*west*)

READING COMPREHENSION QUESTIONS

1. What is a power vacuum, and why is it dangerous? (*a time when no single political authority is in control; leads to fighting*)
2. Who are the Bactrians, Scythians, Parthians, and Kushana? (*invaders from Afghanistan, Iran, the Caucasus, and China, respectively, all of whom briefly ruled portions of the South Asian subcontinent after the fall of the Mauryan Empire*)
3. Why did the Kushanas invade South Asia? (*They were getting out of the way of Shi Huang Di, a Chinese leader who murdered millions of his own people.*)
4. What is Mahayana Buddhism? (*It means "the greater vehicle" and refers to reforms during Kanishka's rule that made Buddhism a more mainstream religion,*

including the invention of saints called bodhisattvas, *rituals, temples, and Buddhist representative art.*)

CRITICAL THINKING QUESTIONS

1. Why did Vedic sacrifices lose favor? (*A combination of Buddhist teaching and violent times had made people leery of blood sacrifice.*)
2. What do Kanishka's coin designs tell us about him? (*He was tolerant of other religions and wanted to appeal to as many people as possible.*)
3. What evidence do you see in the cave painting of the *bodhisattva* on page 133 that many South Asians had both Buddhist and Hindu beliefs? (*Even though he is a* bodhisattva, *a Buddhist saint, he is wearing the sacred thread of the twice-born over his left shoulder.*)
4. Why did Buddhist caves become banks? (*Possible answers: out-of-the-way, robbers would be less likely to rob holy men, stone caves hard to break into*)

SOCIAL SCIENCES

Civics Kanishka was religiously tolerant. What are the advantages of being tolerant? The disadvantages? (*possible advantages: everyone feels accepted; decreases religious strife; possible disadvantages: country less unified; some may be offended by inclusion of a group they find objectionable*)

READING AND LANGUAGE ARTS

Reading Nonfiction Direct students to the paragraph on page 135 that begins, "We don't know much about his personal life . . ." Have them find a generalization (*but we know he liked to try new things*) and the fact that supports it (*he struck coins modeled after the Romans and the Greeks*).

Using Language Discuss the symbols of the four stages of the Buddha's life in the Find the Buddha sidebar on page 135. What are some symbols students use in your school and community? (*team logos on a baseball cap, school mascot, etc.*) What effect do those symbols have? (*help create a shared sense of identity; remind people of certain qualities of a team or item*)

SUPPORTING LEARNING

English Language Learners Have students make a simple chart listing similarities between Ashoka and Kanishka.

Struggling Readers Have students use the outline graphic organizer from the graphic organizers at the back of this book to present the main ideas and details of the chapter.

EXTENDING LEARNING

Enrichment Distribute copies of the blackline master for Chapter 20 to students and have them complete it to learn more about Buddhist art. If a webquest is not practical, you may wish to assemble images for their use: *www.asia.si.edu/education/ArtofBuddhism.pdf* is an excellent source.

Extension Most ancient South Asians were illiterate. They relied on art to teach them. Have each student choose a different concept from the chapter to illustrate. Ask volunteers to compile the illustrations into a book. Show the pictures to the class and have the class figure out what each picture represents.

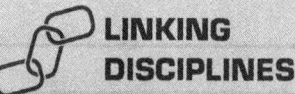

LINKING DISCIPLINES

Dance One of South Asia's most enduring cultural legacies is its classical dance, which originated as part of temple worship. Obtain a video recording of a performance, or consult websites like *www.webindia.com/artindia/cldance.htm* to learn more about the history of this remarkable art form.

LEARNING FROM THE BUDDHA: A WEBQUEST

Directions
Use the Internet to find pictures illustrating each of these ideas about Buddhist art. Print out the pictures and circle and label each item described below. As an alternative, you can draw a Buddha that matches this description on another sheet of paper.

▶ Drawing or carving a Buddha is different from drawing or carving a tree. People who make religious art are usually more interested in teaching people how to live beautiful lives than in making a beautiful object. Over time, artists invented a language to help people understand what they knew and loved about the Buddha. To show that he was enlightened, they added a bump to the Buddha's head that is called an *ushnisha*.

▶ To remind people that even the Buddha gave up riches to find peace, they gave him extra-long ears where he had once worn princely earrings, and short, tiny curls instead of the long hair he cut off when he left home.

▶ His face is shown with a peaceful expression. His eyes are partly closed, as if he were meditating. The dot on his forehead, called the *urna,* symbolizes his ability to see and understand all things.

▶ The Buddha wears a simple robe of unsewn cloth.

▶ The position of the Buddha's hands, called *mudras,* also have symbolic meanings. See if you can find examples of all four of these common *mudras*:

1. **Meditation.** The hands are held loosely on the lap, palms up, the right hand on top of the left. Sometimes they may be holding a small begging bowl.
2. **Calling the Earth to Witness.** At the moment of his Enlightenment, the Buddha touched the earth with his right hand to call it to witness his triumph. The left hand is left in the lap, palm up, as in the meditation pose.
3. **Fearlessness.** The right hand is raised and the left hand is lowered, with both palms facing outward. This is the Buddha's gesture of protection, telling his followers there is no need to fear.
4. **Teaching.** The hands are held as in the fearlessness position except that index fingers and thumbs form a circle, reminding the viewer of the Buddha's first sermon, when he set the *dharmachakra,* or wheel of law, in motion.

▶ Finally, the Buddha is often associated with the lotus flower. The lotus, which is a water lily, symbolizes enlightenment because it is something beautiful that emerges from muddy water. Look for lotus leaves on his throne or in the hands of people near him.

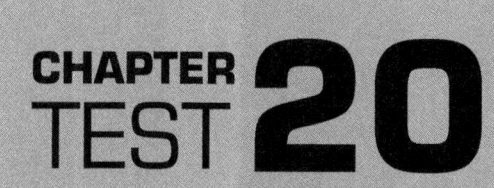

NAME   **DATE**

A. MULTIPLE CHOICE

Circle the letter of the best answer for each question.

1. *Bodhisattvas* are shown with crowns and jewels to remind people that
   a. only Brahmins could become *bodhisattvas*.
   b. they are returning to the world to help people, unlike the Buddha, who took off his jewelry because he was leaving worldly things behind him.
   c. they are not worthy enough to achieve nirvana.
   d. only kings had enough money to pay artists to make paintings and statues on Buddhist subjects.

2. Kanishka Kushana
   a. was a Bactrian Greek.
   b. felt it was wrong to reform Buddhism.
   c. grew up in present-day Iran.
   d. loved trying new things.

3. Kanishka's coins included pictures of all of the following **except**
   a. Ashoka.
   b. himself.
   c. Shiva.
   d. Greek and Persian gods.

4. Pictures and statues of the Buddha usually include all of the following **except**
   a. hand positions called *mudras*.
   b. a bump of enlightenment on his skull.
   c. extra arms.
   d. a peaceful face with half-closed eyes.

5. Mahayana Buddhism included all of these reforms **except**
   a. public festivals and rituals.
   b. "teachings of the elders"
   c. temples and devotional statues.
   d. *bodhisattvas*.

B. SHORT ANSWER

Write a sentence or two to answer each question.

6. What happened in South Asia during the "power vacuum" after Ashoka's death?
   _____
   _____

7. What were some of the reforms that made Buddhism more appealing to ordinary Indians?
   _____
   _____

C. ESSAY

Write an essay explaining the ways in which Ashoka and Kanishka were similar. Use a separate piece of paper.

A PLACE FOR EVERYONE: CASTE AND SOCIETY

PAGES 138–142

FOR HOMEWORK

STUDENT STUDY GUIDE
pages 51–52

CAST OF CHARACTERS

Manu (MUH-noo) mythical author of the Code of Manu

 WRITING

- **Explanation** Have students write their own Code of Manu (perhaps naming it after themselves) explaining how they think society should be organized.

CHAPTER SUMMARY

The most direct response to the political disorder of South Asia at the turn of the millennium was the emergence of the Code of Manu, an elaborate code of conduct based on divisions of *varna* and caste.

PERFORMANCE OBJECTIVES

▶ To understand *karma*
▶ To summarize the provisions of the Code of Manu
▶ To analyze its historical context

BUILDING BACKGROUND

Ask students if their behavior would change if the consequences of all their actions were immediate and obvious. For example, if a siren went off every time someone told a lie, might people tell fewer lies? Tell students that the people of ancient South Asia took the law of consequences—which they called *karma*—just that seriously.

WORKING WITH PRIMARY SOURCES

Direct students' attention to the Code of Manu, also known as the Law of Manu, in *The World in Ancient Times Primary Sources and Reference Volume*. Ask a volunteer to read aloud the section about proper behavior of students toward teachers. Have a debate about the possibility of adopting these guidelines for use in your classroom.

GEOGRAPHY CONNECTION

Movement Point out that around the year 1 CE there was increasing movement of peoples through South Asia as a result of trade along the Silk Road. How did this increase in the movement of people in the area affect the inhabitants of South Asia? (*Elicit that geography affected movement and movement affected society, leading to a desire for clear distinctions among people and eventually to the Code of Manu.*)

READING COMPREHENSION QUESTIONS

1. What is the difference between *varna* and caste? (*The* varna *were broad social classes; each* varna *was subdivided into a number of castes, which usually corresponded to professions.*)
2. What is *dharma*? How can you know what your *dharma* is? (Dharma *is your duty, your part in life; it is determined by your* varna *and is explained in the Vedas.*)
3. In the Code of Manu what was the connection between a person's actions and his or her *karma*? (*The result of making mistakes during your life was bad* karma *and a lower position when you were reincarnated. The result of good actions was an improvement your* karma *and a better life when reincarnated.*)
4. What is the difference between getting dirty and being ritually unclean?

(Getting your body dirty doesn't affect the worthiness of your soul; being ritually unclean, however, interferes with your ability to exercise the duties of your dharma.)

CRITICAL THINKING QUESTIONS

1. Have volunteers read the two excerpts from the Code of Manu that address women's position in society on pages 140 and 141. The first seems to imply that women are less capable than men, while the second seems to suggest they are almost divine. Does the Code of Manu contradict itself? *(Not necessarily; independence is so important to Western culture that it is hard for us to understand that women, while dependent, were also very powerful.)*
2. Was it likely that a Shudra who had long hair when he died would be reincarnated as a Brahmin in his next life? *(Probably not, since Shudra were supposed to shave their heads once a month.)*
3. Distribute copies of the blackline master for Chapter 21 to students and have them complete it to deepen their understanding of caste in modern India.

SOCIAL SCIENCES

Science, Technology, and Society Discuss the extent to which your school community has a code of expected behavior. What are its rules? How are people taught them? How are the rules enforced? Explain that for homework students are to discuss with their parents the code of expected behavior at home, in the community, and in the nation. Reports of home, community, and national codes of expected conduct can be shared orally or in writing in small groups, followed by a discussion with the whole class.

READING AND LANGUAGE ARTS

Reading Nonfiction As students read the text, have them copy words and phrases that show sequence. Then have them summarize the events in the chapter using these and other sequence words.

Using Language Relatively few South Asian words have found their way into the English language. Those that have include *bandana, calico, cashmere, chintz, dungarees, gingham,* and *shawl.* Have students look up the words. What do they have in common? Despite the Vedic prohibition on sewing, what does that suggest about South Asia's textiles? *(varied and frequently traded)*

SUPPORTING LEARNING

English Language Learners Write key words from the chapter (such as *dharma, karma, ritually unclean,* and so on) on note cards. Have students find the information in the chapter about these key words.

Struggling Readers Have students write an acrostic poem telling about the Code of Manu. Instruct students to refer to the chapter to be certain that their acrostics address all of the key ideas.

EXTENDING LEARNING

Enrichment Refer interested students to a translation of the Code of Manu online at www.19.5degs.com/ebook/laws-of-manu-hindu/852/read. While the text is difficult reading, students can get a sense of the length and level of detail involved in the Code. They can then report on their findings to the class.

Extension Ask students to act out certain scenes in the text. For example, a group can act out the description of purifying oneself according to *varna* while one student narrates.

THE ANCIENT SOUTH ASIAN WORLD

THEN and NOW

Despite efforts to end social division by *varna* and caste, differences still exist. The website http://news.nationalgeographic.com/news/2003/06/0602_030602_untouchables.html is a link to a June 2003 *National Geographic* article by Hillary Maxfield called "India's 'Untouchables' Face Violence, Discrimination" that students might find interesting.

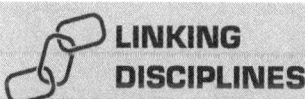

LINKING DISCIPLINES

World Health Some have argued that the Code of Manu was a strategy to regulate scarce resources among a growing population. The website www.askasia.org/teachers/Instructional_Resources/Lesson_Plans/India/LP_india_3.htm will take you to a great lesson that unforgettably illustrates the problem of scarce resources in the subcontinent.

CODE OF MANU

Directions:
Use the chart to organize information from the Code of Manu about the duties of each *varna* (and castes within each *varna*) as explained in the chapter. (If information isn't described in the chapter, leave the box blank.)

	Brahmin	**Kshatriya**	**Vaisya**	**Shudra**
Women				
Occupations				
Marriage				
Clothing/colors				
Purification				

CHAPTER TEST 21
THE ANCIENT SOUTH ASIAN WORLD

NAME   **DATE**

A. MULTIPLE CHOICE

Circle the letter of the best answer for each question.

1. *Dharma* is
    a. your social class.
    b. your mission in life.
    c. your profession.
    d. truth.

2. The Code of Manu taught that
    a. Shudras were not as important as Brahmins.
    b. Untouchables can't wear shoes.
    c. a good wife is like a goddess.
    d. men were better than women.

3. You could be born into a higher caste in the next life if you did all of the following **except**
    a. honored your *dharma*.
    b. made offerings to the gods.
    c. healed wounds of lower-caste people.
    d. purified yourself if you became unclean.

4. You could always tell a Shudra man by his
    a. white, unsewn robe and sacred thread.
    b. red clothing.
    c. yellow clothing.
    d. black clothing and short hair.

5. Hindus believed that the Code of Manu
    a. was made by Manu for Brahma.
    b. was made by Manu for humans.
    c. was made by Brahma for Manu.
    d. was a record of gods who appeared to be monkeys.

B. SHORT ANSWER

Write a sentence or two to answer each question.

6. What happens to someone who breaks the rules of their caste?

_____

_____

7. Describe what was happening in South India in the year 1 CE that made some people welcome a set of rules to live by?

_____

_____

C. ESSAY

Write a short paragraph explaining what the Code of Manu is, and why South Asians found it helpful.

_____

_____

_____

_____

UNIT 7: THE GUPTA ERA

PAGES 143–159

Chapter 22   South Asia's Golden Age: The Gupta Empire
Chapter 23   Gods and Caves: Literature and Art of the Gupta Era
Epilogue   The Legacy of Ancient South Asia

UNIT OBJECTIVES

Unit 7 discusses the formation of the Gupta Empire, South Asia's largest and most stable to that date. In this unit your students will learn

- how the Gupta family united South Asia.
- why the Guptas championed both religious toleration and greater attention to *varna*.
- the flowering of Gupta culture.
- the costs and benefits of the Great Silk Road—including the Hun invasion that ended the Gupta era.

PRIMARY SOURCES

Unit 7 includes excerpts from the following primary sources:

- Kalidasa, *Malavikagnimitram*
- Visakhadatta, *Devi-Chandraguptam*
- Xuanzang, *A Record of the Western Regions*
- Pillar inscription, Bhitari, India
- *Bhagavata Purana*
- Ramaprasad
- Kalidasa, *Shakuntala*

Pictures of South Asian artifacts can also be analyzed as primary sources. These include:

- Gupta coins
- Cave painting, Dunhuang
- Cave painting, Ajanta
- Chapel (*chaitya*) of a rock temple, Ajanta
- Figure of Durga
- Statue of musicians
- Terracotta tablet with sacrifice carving, Harappa

BIG IDEAS IN UNIT 7

Political unification, culture, and **diversity** are the big ideas presented in Unit 7. The unit opens by discussing how the Gupta dynasty brought much of South Asia under the control of one ruler, while allowing a measure of local autonomy and promoting religious toleration. Then it turns to a survey of the remarkable cultural achievements of the empire before it fell victim to repeated invasions by the Huns in the 6th century CE.

GEOGRAPHY CONNECTION

Refer students to the map of the Great Silk Road on page 150. Emphasize that, despite its name, it was a route between China and the Mediterranean rather than a physical road. What advantages might it offer South Asia? (*increased trade and contact with other civilizations like Rome and China*) What disadvantages might it offer? (*greater chance of invasion and crime*)

TIMELINE

320–550 CE	Gupta era; arts and sciences flourish and *Panchatantra* written
320–335 CE	Reign of Chandra Gupta I
335–376 CE	Reign of Samudra Gupta
376–415 CE	Reign of Chandra Gupta II
400 CE	Kalidasa, Sanskrit poet and writer, active
405–411 CE	Fa Hien visits India
414–455 CE	Reign of Kamura Gupta
454 CE	White Huns first invade and destroy religious centers and major cities
455–467 CE	Skanda Gupta defeats the first Hun invaders
475 CE	Astronomer Aryabhata active
495 CE	White Huns invade again, establish small kingdoms in the north
528 CE	Yashodharman, King of Malwa, expels Huns from northern India
550 CE	Gupta Empire ends
595 CE	Earliest use of zero
630_643 CE	Xuanzang visits India

UNIT PROJECTS

Great Silk Road Project

Have small groups research different locations along the Great Silk Road. Post a "Great Silk Road" along a wall and have each group put a poster up in their city's location. Two good online sources are *www.aasianst.org/EAA/silkroad.htm* and *www.silk-road.com*.

Chronology

Have a group of students add the pertinent dates from this unit to the class timeline.

South Asian Tales

Have students locate two of South Asia's greatest cultural treasures: the *Panchatantra*, source for both Rudyard Kipling's *Jungle Book* and the *Arabian Nights*, and the *Jataka Tales*. The *Panchatantra* can be found online at *www.pitt.edu/~dash/panchatantra.html*; the *Jataka Tales* at *watthai.net/talon/jataka/jataka.htm*. Have each student choose a different tale and write and illustrate his or her version of it.

Research Report

Have small groups learn more about the personalities mentioned in Chapters 22 and 23: Fa Hien, Kalidasa, Xuanzang, or any of the Gupta emperors. Groups should summarize their findings, and report them to the class.

ADDITIONAL ASSESSMENT

Use any of these unit projects for additional assessment. For Unit 7, divide the class into groups and have all students take part in these projects. To assess their work in the Great Silk Road Project, South Asian Tales, and Research Report, note how the content illustrates students' grasp of the importance of the Great Silk Road, literary treasures, the Gupta family, and Gupta culture. Use the scoring rubric at the back of this guide to assess group projects, and have students rate their own work with the self-assessment rubric. For the Research Report, be sure to distribute the library/media center research log (see rubric at the back of this guide) to help students evaluate their sources as they conduct their research.

LITERATURE CONNECTION

Stories for children were being told and written in South Asia in ancient times. Chapter 23 of *The Ancient South Asian World* describes much of the literature created in ancient South Asia. The Panchatantra tales are available on-line: *www.pitt.edu/~dash/panchatantra.html*.

Another useful online resource is *www.umakrishnaswami.com/southasia.html*, which discusses South Asia in children's literature and provides links to educational materials and publishers' websites specializing in South Asian literature and culture. This site is not limited to *ancient* South Asian Literature, but it may be useful for class activities.

UNIVERSAL ACCESS

The following strategies are designed to cover a range of learning styles and reading, language, and skill levels. You may find that any of your students will benefit from the various strategies presented.

Reading Strategies

- ▶ Chapters 22 and 23 are written in narrative style. You may want to list the personalities involved on the board, along with descriptions of who they are.
- ▶ Because the Epilogue is full of detail, have students read this chapter with partners. They can check each other's understanding of the facts.

Writing Strategies

- ▶ The Gupta era was a time of merging and changing culture in the Mediterranean and Central Asian region. Students should find material that they can compare and contrast not only with modern times, but with more ancient times, as well. Give students compare and contrast charts to use while reading.
- ▶ Have students write a postcard from Xuanzang in which he describes his experiences as a student at Nalanda.

Listening and Speaking Strategies

- ▶ Students can role-play the various personalities named in the text. Each student should state their person's name and an interesting fact or two about the person. Give students time to find new information about their personalities either online or in your resource center.
- ▶ Have partners read the chapters and then question each other on the personalities named.

UNIT VOCABULARY LIST

The following words that appear in Unit 7 are important for your students' understanding of the social studies content as well as for development of literacy. Use these words for vocabulary study or to reinforce language arts skills (e.g., synonyms, compound words, prefixes and suffixes, and related words). The words are listed below in the order in which they appear in the chapters.

Chapter 22
desirous
particles
princely
sensitive
ladies-in-waiting
infiltrated
outnumbered
unfurled
immaterial
reemphasizing
corpses
insignia
avatar

Chapter 23
grazing
barren
translations
desolate
adorned
turrets
congregated
medieval
cathedral
stained glass
lime
canvas
charcoal pencil
womb
spire
rafters
processions
garlands
devotee
incense
anointing
festive
broad
lotus
lavish

Epilogue
festivity
reborn
oasis
diverse
vegetarian
oil lamps
netherworld
buffalo
bamboo
coriander
cumin
turmeric
chutneys

CHAPTER 22

SOUTH ASIA'S GOLDEN AGE: THE GUPTA EMPIRE

PAGES 143–147

STUDENT STUDY GUIDE
pages 53–54

CAST OF CHARACTERS

Chandra Gupta (CHUN-druh GOOP-tuh) **I** founder of Gupta dynasty; father of Samudra Gupta and grandfather of Chandra Gupta II

Chandra Gupta (CHUN-druh GOOP-tuh) **II** greatest ruler of the Gupta era, a time when the arts flourished in India

Samudra Gupta (suh-Moo-drah GOOPT-ah) Gupta emperor and brilliant military leader

Skanda Gupta (SKUHN-dah GOOPT-ah) Gupta emperor who defeated the first Hun invaders

- **Newspaper Article** Have students write a newspaper article describing Skanda Gupta's victory over the Huns.

CHAPTER SUMMARY

The Gupta dynasty founded a South Asian empire that endured for more than 200 years, from 320 to 540 CE. Often compared to the Roman Empire and the Han Empire in China, the Gupta era was a time of unparalleled achievement in the arts and sciences.

PERFORMANCE OBJECTIVES

▶ To understand the formation of the Gupta dynasty
▶ To describe the renewed attention to caste
▶ To understand the roots of local rule by maharaja

BUILDING BACKGROUND

Tell students to imagine that they suddenly were named emperor of nearly the entire South Asian subcontinent in 350 CE. Ask: What strategies would you use to keep your kingdom together? Tell students to compare their solutions with those of the Gupta rulers as they read.

WORKING WITH PRIMARY SOURCES

One of the leading lights of Gupta culture was the brilliant playwright Kalidasa. Read the excerpt from his play *Shakuntala* in *The World in Ancient Times Primary Sources and Reference Volume*. Otherwise, find an appropriate excerpt online or in a collection of world literature in your media center. The *Reference Volume* also includes an expanded excerpt from Fa Hien, the Chinese Buddhist quoted in the sidebar on page 144.

GEOGRAPHY CONNECTION

Interaction Ask students to compare the extent of the Mauryan Empire (map on page 110) with that of the Gupta Empire (map on page 144). Discuss why Samudra Gupta's institution of local rule by maharajas proved to be such an effective strategy for ruling the country that it continued up to the 20th century. (*In a pre-modern world, it was simply impossible for a central power to determine local policies for such a large and diverse region.*)

READING COMPREHENSION QUESTIONS

1. What was South Asia's political structure at the beginning of the Gupta Empire? (*divided among more than 30 kingdoms and states*)
2. How did Samudra Gupta share power in his kingdom? (*He let local leaders, Maharajas, make decisions and take part in governing.*)
3. What religions were practiced or supported by the Guptas? (*The Guptas were Hindus but they supported Buddhist and Jain schools and temples.*)
4. What events led to the end of Gupta rule? (*Waves of people from Central Asia, the Huns, entered India, destroying temples and towns, and keeping Maharajas busy locally and therefore not serving the king.*)

5. Who are the Chandalas? *(the Untouchables—people without any caste who handled the dead and were forced to live outside the city gates)*

CRITICAL THINKING QUESTIONS

1. Why did the Gupta emporers support Buddhist and Jain institutions if they themselves followed Early Hindu teachings? *(Possible answers include that all of these traditions were flexible enough to combine ideas from many faiths and that they hoped to appeal to as many of their people as possible.)*
2. Chandra Gupta II believed that part of his *dharma* was establishing peace and wealth for his people. What are some examples of his policies to do so? *(greater attention to caste; forts; shared power with maharajas)*
3. Distribute copies of the blackline master for Chapter 22 to students and have them complete them to better organize their understanding of the Gupta emperors.

VOCABULARY

Maharaja South Asian king

SOCIAL SCIENCES

Science, Technology, and Society   Refer students to the Does Anybody Have the Time? sidebar on page 146. As a class, figure out how long an "hour" would be *(24 hours divided by 8 is 3 hours each)*. Then figure out how often the bowl was emptied *(4 times every 3 hours means once every 45 minutes)*.

READING AND LANGUAGE ARTS

Reading Nonfiction   Could a state in which each individual fills the role for which nature intended him or her exist today? Have students discuss whether there is a way to tell the role of education in helping one fulfill aspirations.

Using Language   Direct students' attention to Chandra Gupta II's quotation in the first paragraph of page 146. Have students rephrase the comment in straightforward English.

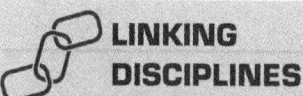

LINKING DISCIPLINES

Drama According to the Vedas, South Asian theater began when Brahma wanted to entertain the gods. Originally, South Asian drama was associated with religious rituals and harvest festivals like the one Sarang attends in Chapter 8. By the Gupta period, however, most drama was produced at court for the wealthy. Have students choose a scene in a play by Kalidasa to produce and present to the class.

SUPPORTING LEARNING

English Language Learners   Have students work in pairs taking turns reading a section of the chapter aloud and then retelling it in their own words.

Struggling Readers   Ask students to look at the painting of South Asian life at court on page 145 and read the caption. Discuss the picture's value as a primary source and elicit what information it provides about life the life of royal families in ancient South Asia.

EXTENDING LEARNING

Enrichment   Gupta coins are an important resource for historians. Have students research them using materials available in your media center or online at sites like *www.med.unc.edu/~nupam/Sgupta1.html*. Assign small groups an emperor and have each group design a coin that represents that particular emperor's accomplishments and values.

Extension   Following instructions available online, a small group of interested students can build and demonstrate a water clock. For directions (a lesson plan) go to *http://library.thinkquest.org/27691/wclp/dloads.htm*.

CHAPTER 22 BLM
THE ANCIENT SOUTH ASIAN WORLD

NAME   **DATE**

THE GUPTA EMPERORS

Directions
Using information from the book, summarize the highlights of each emperor's reign.

Emperor	Major Events and Policies of Reign
Chandra Gupta I	
Samudra Gupta	
Rama Gupta	
Chandra Gupta II	
Skanda Gupta	

NAME   **DATE**

A. MULTIPLE CHOICE

Circle the letter of the best answer for each question.

1. The Gupta era was the first time the subcontinent had been united
   a. in 500 years.
   b. ever.
   c. in 50 years.
   d. in 250 years.

2. _____ Gupta had a lot of nicknames, including "King of Poets."
   a. Chandra
   b. Samudra
   c. Rama
   d. Skanda

3. Chandra Gupta I
   a. lost land he had conquered.
   b. shared power with maharajas.
   c. invented the water clock.
   d. defeated the Huns.

4. Chandra Gupta II's efforts to create peace and prosperity for his people included all of the following **except**
   a. building forts.
   b. sharing power with Maharajas.
   c. reemphasis on maintaining caste.
   d. honoring his brother's claim to the throne.

5. The Huns
   a. married Kshatriya women.
   b. were defeated by Skanda Gupta.
   c. were good Buddhists.
   d. settled in southern India.

B. SHORT ANSWER

Answer each question in one or two sentences.

6. Describe the Guptas' religious practices.

_____

_____

7. What role in governing was played by the Maharajas?

_____

_____

C. ESSAY

On a separate sheet of paper write an essay describing how the caste system changed during the Gupta dynasty.

CHAPTER 23
GODS AND CAVES: LITERATURE AND ART OF THE GUPTA ERA
PAGES 148–154

EPILOGUE: THE LEGACY OF SOUTH ASIA

FOR HOMEWORK
STUDENT STUDY GUIDE
pages 55–56

CHAPTER SUMMARY

In the 7th century, a Chinese Buddhist named Xuanzang set out on an illegal, dangerous, solitary journey to South Asia in search of accurate translations of Buddhist scripture. Once in South Asia, after more than a year of traveling, he visited important examples of Gupta culture like the Buddhist University at Nalanda and the caves at Ajanta before returning home to China.

PERFORMANCE OBJECTIVES

- To understand the role of the Great Silk Road in fostering cross-cultural exchanges
- To explain the remarkable cultural flowering manifest in the University at Nalanda and the Ajanta caves
- To identify the major religious texts of South Asia during the classical period

CAST OF CHARACTERS

Muhammad (muh-HAH-mudh) Prophet of Islam; born in Arabia

Xuanzang (shwen-dzang) Chinese Buddhist monk who traveled to India and wrote *A Record of the Western Regions*

BUILDING BACKGROUND

Point out that although South Asia was a wealthy region, most people lived very simply. Ask students where they think the money came from that was used to build the University at Nalanda and temples and caves like those at Ajanta (*kings and wealthy people*). What effect would that have on Gupta culture? (*The culture tends to be sophisticated and fancy, rather than plain and realistic.*)

WORKING WITH PRIMARY SOURCES

One of South Asia's most enduring cultural treasures is the *Panchatantra*, a collection of stories, many of which may have been meant for children. Read "How to Get the Brahmin's Goat" in *The World in Ancient Times Primary Sources and Reference Volume*. Ask: What does the story tell us about Brahmins at the time this was written? (*that they worry about purity; that they believed in goblins*)

WRITING

- **Poem** Have students write a poem about life at a Hindu temple. Encourage them to include sensory images describing the smells, sights, sounds, and tastes they would find there.

GEOGRAPHY CONNECTION

Movement To get a sense of the extent of Xuanzang's journeys, have students calculate the following mileage: Beijing to Nalanda (100 miles east of Benares (Varanasi) and back to Beijing. Students can use an online map of Asia at *http://es.rice.edu/projects/Poli378/Maps/Korea/asia_regional.gif* along with the Silk Road map on page 150 to approximate Xuanzang's route. Then discuss how someone might travel the same route today.

READING COMPREHENSION QUESTIONS

1. Why had the Chinese emperor forbidden travel along the Great Silk Road? (*to minimize attacks by the Turks*)
2. Why did Xuanzang want to travel to South Asia? (*He wanted to find accurate Buddhist texts and study at the University of Nalanda.*)

3. What are the *Puranas, Tripitaka,* and *Panchatantra*? (*Mahayana Buddhist teachings, Buddhist teachings, and a collection of animal stories*)
4. What is the significance of the caves at Ajanta? (*beautifully painted Buddhist caves*)
5. Who plays the veena? (*the goddess Saraswati*)
6. What is Divali? (*the South Asian festival of lights whose various modes of celebration illustrate South Asia's diversity*)

CRITICAL THINKING QUESTIONS

1. What do the caves at Ajanta have in common with medieval European cathedrals? (*The cave walls are covered with paintings depicting sacred stories that teach about Buddha, much the way stained glass windows in medieval cathedrals conveyed Bible stories.*)
2. What might surprise a western visitor to a Hindu temple? (*noise, movement, visiting between people, smells of offerings, all the colorful statues*)

SOCIAL SCIENCES

Economics   Distribute copies of the blackline master for Chapter 23 and have students complete them to increase their understanding of the significance of Hindu temples to the economic life of their communities.

READING AND LANGUAGE ARTS

Reading Nonfiction   Have students draw a timeline of the major events of Xuanzang's journey mentioned in the chapter. Then have them summarize the events in their own words using time-order clues such as *next, then, the next year,* and so on.

Using Language   Direct students' attention to Xuanzang's description of the University of Nalanda on pages 148–149. Ask: What does Xuanzang's choice of language tell us about the way he feels about the university? (*Possibly that it is a magical, wondrous place.*)

SUPPORTING LEARNING

English Language Learners   Ask students to compare the festival of Divali with legends from their countries of origin. They can ask members of their families for information. Have them prepare a short oral report comparing the legends, to be presented to the class or a small group.

Struggling Readers   Have students complete the main idea map from the graphic organizers at the back of this book to illustrate Xuanzang's experiences. Have them write *Xuanzang's Journey* in the central circle, and in the outer circles, the possible stops along the way, and their importance (*Turfan, University of Nalanda, Ajanta, a Hindu temple,* and so on).

EXTENDING LEARNING

Enrichment   These chapters offer many potentially fascinating topics for research: the University at Nalanda; the caves at Ajanta, Ellora, and Elephanta; Hindu temples, Durga; and the festival of Divali, to name a few. Have students submit a word-processed report on the topic of their choice, complete with bibliography and illustrations.

Extension   Have students make a two column chart listing ways the different regions and populations of South Asia celebrate Divali.

THE ANCIENT SOUTH ASIAN WORLD | 137

LINKING DISCIPLINES

Architecture   Using a travel guide, art history book, or Internet resource, have students research a specific South Asian temple and build a model of it. Be sure that they include a written key explaining the significance of the various parts of the temple.

THEN and NOW

If students are curious about the diverging histories of the seven modern countries of South Asia, they can find a wealth of information at *www.asiasource.org/profiles/ap_mp_04.cfm*, which allows them to compare any two Asian countries on a wide range of geographic, demographic, and other statistical bases.

SOUTH ASIAN TEMPLES

Directions

Read the facts about ancient South Asian temples. Then, on a separate sheet of paper, write an essay explaining the impact these temples had on the economy of South Asia.

- ▶ Virtually all surviving ancient temples were built of stone. Building with stone was so expensive that only kings could afford it.
- ▶ All temples had to be designed by Brahmins. Brahmins also had to bless and purify the materials of the temple and supervise daily work on the temple when it was being built.
- ▶ Workers lived on-site. They were provided a dining hall, food, and shelter for themselves and their families.
- ▶ Brahmin boys were educated at temples.
- ▶ Temples often had schools of dance and music.
- ▶ Temples were centers for study in grammar and astrology.
- ▶ Temples often owned lots of land, which they rented out to tenant farmers.
- ▶ Temples were sacred and were left untouched during times of warfare.
- ▶ Temples provided food and housing for travelers and pilgrims, as well as health care for sick pilgrims.
- ▶ An average temple employed more than 600 people: dancing girls, dancing masters, singers, pipers, drummers, lute players, conch blowers, superintendents of temple women and female musicians, accountants, sacred parasol bearers, lamp lighters, sprinklers of water, potters, washermen, bearers, astrologers, tailors, jewel stitchers, brazier lighters, carpenters, and superintendents of goldsmiths.

THE ANCIENT SOUTH ASIAN WORLD

A. MULTIPLE CHOICE

Circle the letter of the best answer for each question.

1. By the 8th century,
   a. Buddhism had spread throughout east and southeast Asia.
   b. South Asia had once again lost its written language.
   c. China and South Asia were at war.
   d. the Great Silk Road had been paved.

2. All of the following statements about the University at Nalanda are true **except that**
   a. it was a Buddhist university.
   b. anyone could study there.
   c. it had an international student body.
   d. it was free for many of its students.

3. Hindus believe that "movable" statues
   a. are inhabited by gods part of the time.
   b. must be treated with reverence at all times.
   c. should never be painted or have anything hung on them.
   d. should not be disturbed by dance or music of any kind.

4. Divali, South Asia's festival of lights, is celebrated in all these ways **except**
   a. as Rama's birthday.
   b. as the anniversary of Chandra Gupta II's reign.
   c. as Durga's victory over the "Water Buffalo Demon of Ignorance."
   d. as the end of the monsoon.

B. SHORT ANSWER

Answer each question in one or two sentences.

5. What did Xuanzang bring back to China as a result of his 13 years in India?

   _____

   _____

6. What were two ways (and two places) a person could learn about Buddha and his previous lives?

   _____

   _____

C. ESSAY

On a separate piece of paper write an essay explaining how the Great Silk Road encouraged people from different cultures to share ideas. Give specific examples from the chapter.

WRAP-UP TEST

THE ANCIENT SOUTH ASIAN WORLD

NAME   **DATE**

Directions

On separate sheets of paper, answer each of the following questions.

1. Name four of the most important South Asian gods and their main functions. Then explain the relationship that the ancient South Asians had with their gods.
2. Write a short essay comparing life in Mehrgarh with life at Harappa. Which place would you rather have lived, and why?
3. Use a Venn diagram like this one to explain the similarities and differences between Buddhism, Hinduism, and Jainism.

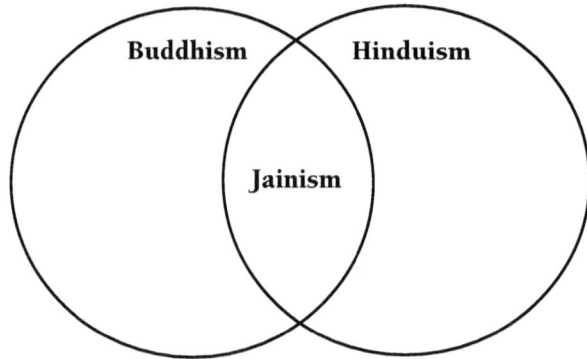

4. Write a paragraph in which you explain why no one knew about the civilizations of the Indus Valley before the 1920s. Tell how and why that changed.
5. In a short essay, explain the importance of trade to the people of Harappa, Mohenjo Daro, and Dholavira. Use the words Mesopotamia and Badakshan in your answer.
6. Write a paragraph explaining why the Vedas are so important, historically as well as religiously.
7. Write a paragraph explaining what Ayurveda is, and whether it is still practiced.
8. Write a paragraph explaining what important lessons we can learn about life from reading or watching a performance of a South Asian play like the *Ramayana*.
9. In an essay, tell who Ashoka was, what happened to him at Kalinga, and what James Prinsep did that helped us learn more about Ashoka and his times.
10. Write an essay explaining the difference that the Great Silk Road made to South Asian life, both positive and negative. Be sure to use specific examples in your answer.

GRAPHIC ORGANIZERS

GUIDELINES

Reproducibles of seven different graphic organizers are provided on the following pages. These give your students a variety of ways to sort and order all the information they are receiving in this course. Use the organizers for homework assignments, classroom activities, tests, small group projects, and as ways to help the students take notes as they read.

1. Determine which graphic organizers work best for the content you are teaching. Some are useful for identifying main ideas and details; others work better for making comparisons, and so on.

2. Graphic organizers help students focus on the central points of the lesson while leaving out irrelevant details.

3. Use graphic organizers to give a visual picture of the key ideas you are teaching.

4. Graphic organizers can help students recall important information. Suggest students use them to study for tests.

5. Graphic organizers provide a visual way to show the connections between different content areas.

6. Graphic organizers can enliven traditional lesson plans and encourage greater interactivity within the classroom.

7. Apply graphic organizers to give students a concise, visual way to break down complex ideas.

8. Encourage students to use graphic organizers to identify patterns and clarify their ideas.

9. Graphic organizers stimulate creative thinking in the classroom, in small groups, and for the individual student.

10. Help students determine which graphic organizers work best for their purposes, and encourage them to use graphic organizers collaboratively whenever they can.

11. Help students customize graphic organizers when necessary; e.g., make more or fewer boxes, lines, or blanks, if dictated by the exercise..

OUTLINE

MAIN IDEA: _____
_____
_____

    DETAIL: _____
    _____

    DETAIL: _____
    _____

    DETAIL: _____
    _____

MAIN IDEA: _____
_____
_____

    DETAIL: _____
    _____

    DETAIL: _____
    _____

    DETAIL: _____
    _____

Name _____ Date _____

MAIN IDEA MAP

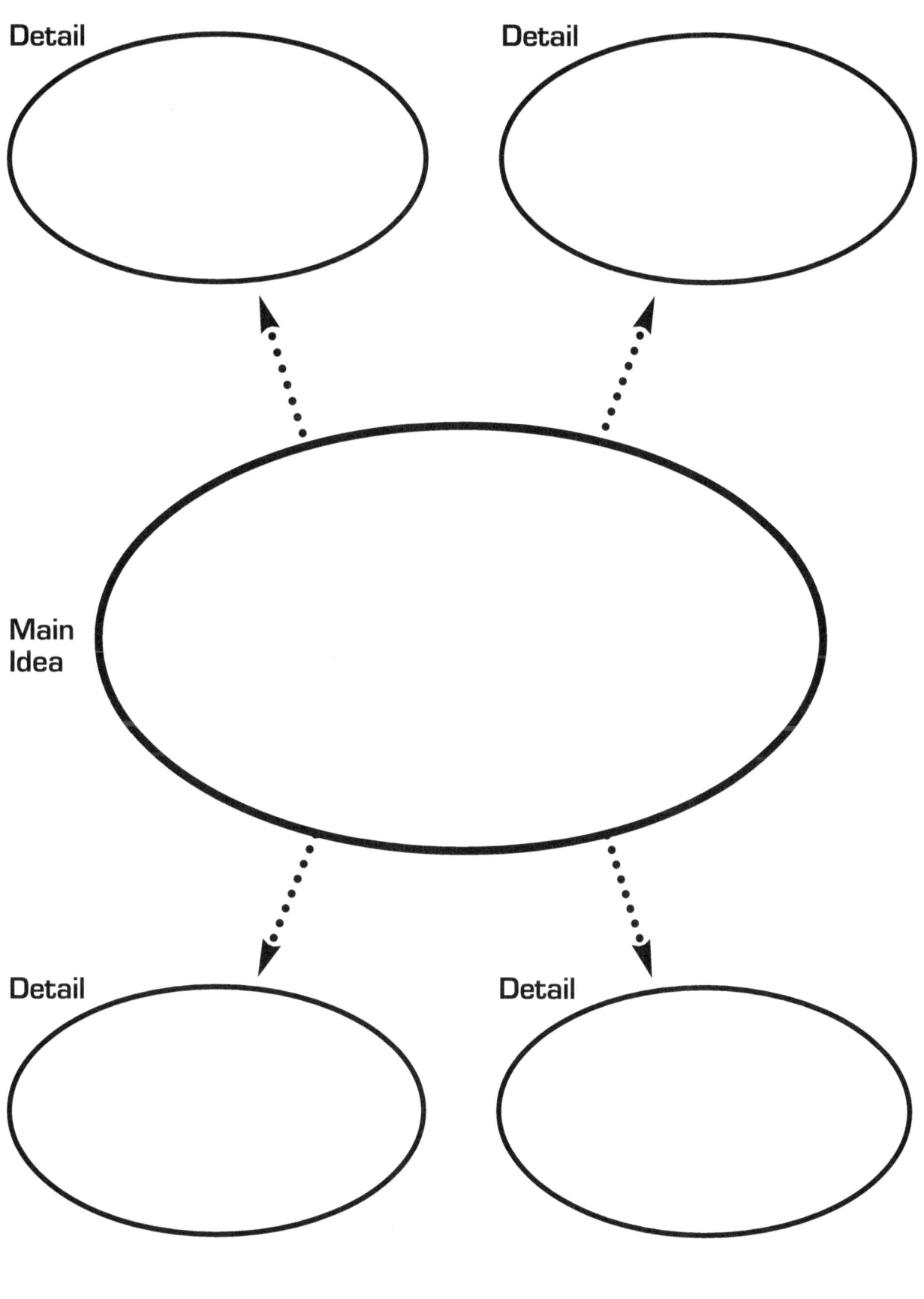

Name _____ Date _____

K-W-L CHART

K	W	L
What I Know	What I Want to Know	What I Learned

Name _____ Date _____

VENN DIAGRAM

Write differences in the circles. Write similarities where the circles overlap.

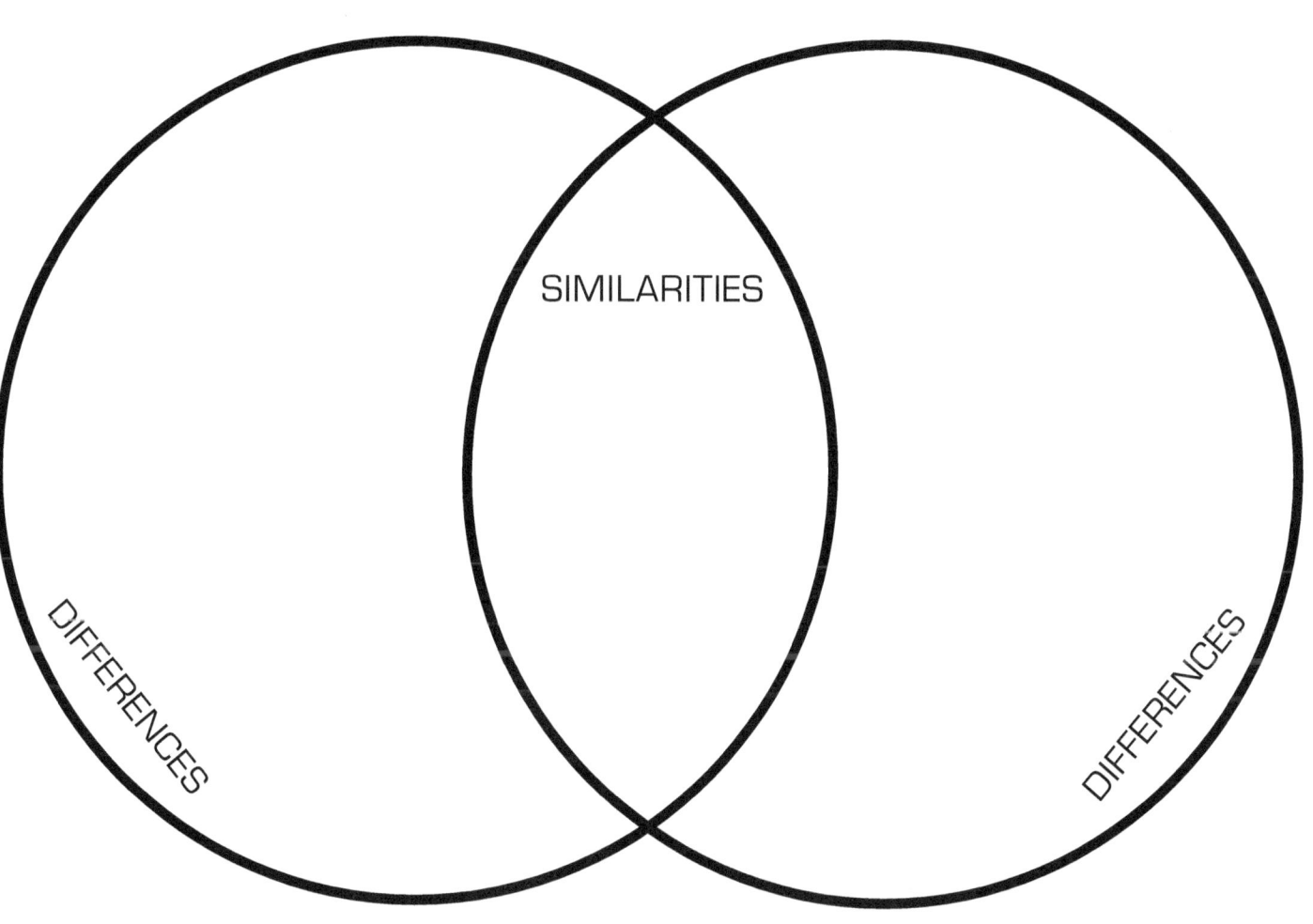

Name _____ Date _____

TIMELINE

DATE

EVENT Draw lines to connect the event to the correct year on the timeline.

Name _____ Date _____

SEQUENCE OF EVENTS CHART

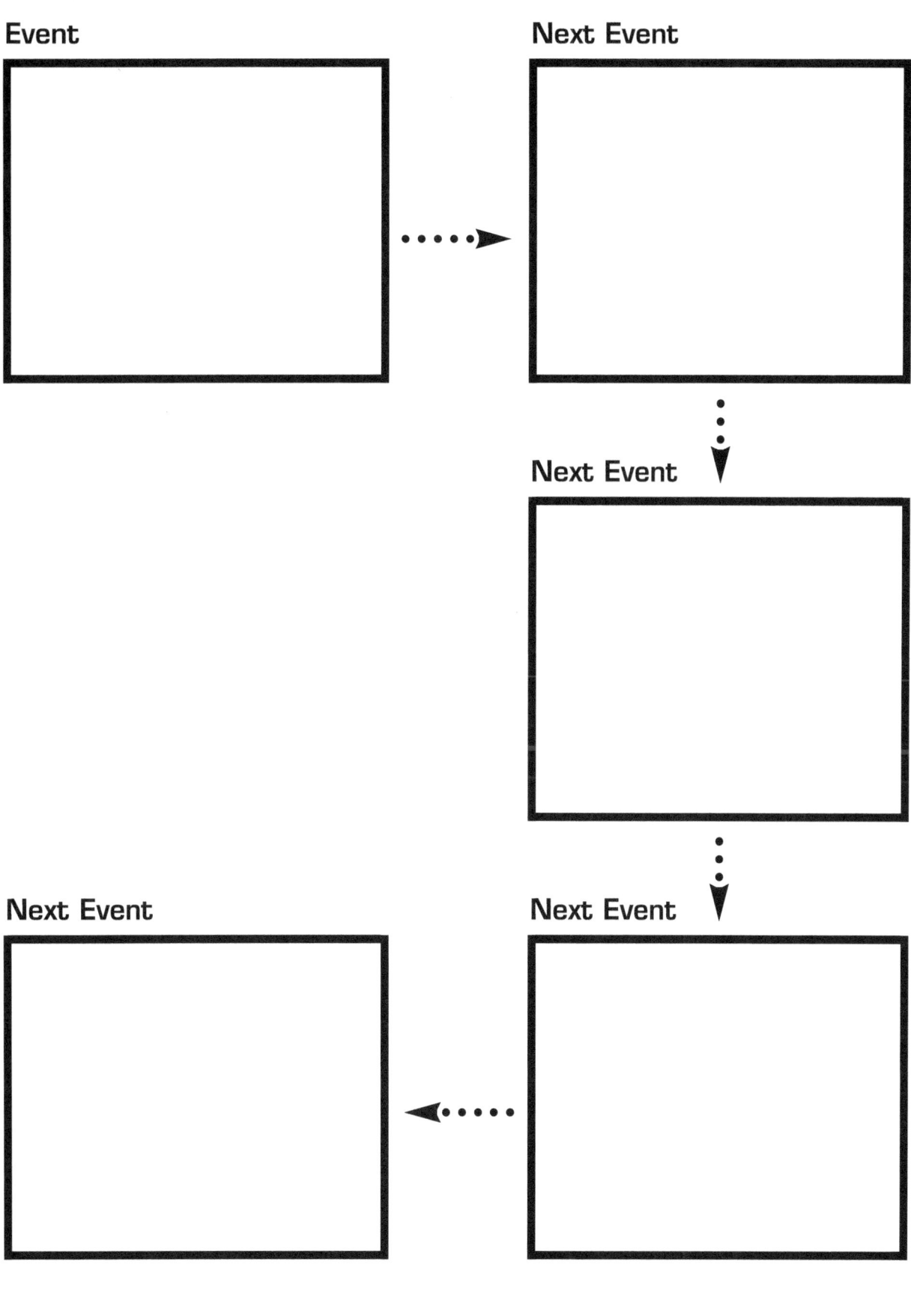

Name _____ Date _____

T-CHART

Cause	Effect

SCORING RUBRIC

The reproducibles on the following pages have been adapted from this rubric for use as handouts and a student self-scoring activity, with added focus on planning, cooperation, revision and presentation. You may wish to tailor the self-scoring activity—for example, asking students to comment on how low scores could be improved, or focusing only on specific rubric points. Use the Library/Media Center Research Log to help students focus and evaluate their research for projects and assignments.

As with any rubric, you should introduce and explain the rubric before students begin their assignments. The more thoroughly your students understand how they will be evaluated, the better prepared they will be to produce projects that fulfill your expectations.

	ORGANIZATION	CONTENT	ORAL/WRITTEN CONVENTIONS	GROUP PARTICIPATION
4	• Clearly addresses all parts of the writing task. • Demonstrates a clear understanding of purpose and audience. • Maintains a consistent point of view, focus, and organizational structure, including the effective use of transitions. • Includes a clearly presented central idea with relevant facts, details, and/or explanations.	• Demonstrates that the topic was well researched. • Uses only information that was essential and relevant to the topic. • Presents the topic thoroughly and accurately. • Reaches reasonable conclusions clearly based on evidence.	• Contains few, if any, errors in grammar, punctuation, capitalization, or spelling. • Uses a variety of sentence types. • Speaks clearly, using effective volume and intonation.	• Demonstrated high levels of participation and effective decision making. • Planned well and used time efficiently. • Demonstrated ability to negotiate opinions fairly and reach compromise when needed. • Utilized effective visual aids.
3	• Addresses all parts of the writing task. • Demonstrates a general understanding of purpose and audience. • Maintains a mostly consistent point of view, focus, and organizational structure, including the effective use of some transitions. • Presents a central idea with mostly relevant facts, details, and/or explanations.	• Demonstrates that the topic was sufficiently researched. • Uses mainly information that was essential and relevant to the topic. • Presents the topic accurately but leaves some aspects unexplored. • Reaches reasonable conclusions loosely related to evidence.	• Contains some errors in grammar, punctuation, capitalization, or spelling. • Uses a variety of sentence types. • Speaks somewhat clearly, using effective volume and intonation.	• Demonstrated good participation and decision making with few distractions. • Planning and used its time acceptably. • Demonstrated ability to negotiate opinions and compromise with little aggression or unfairness.
2	• Addresses only parts of the writing task. • Demonstrates little understanding of purpose and audience. • Maintains an inconsistent point of view, focus, and/or organizational structure, which may include ineffective or awkward transitions that do not unify important ideas. • Suggests a central idea with limited facts, details, and/or explanations.	• Demonstrates that the topic was minimally researched. • Uses a mix of relevant and irrelevant information. • Presents the topic with some factual errors and leaves some aspects unexplored. • Reaches conclusions that do not stem from evidence presented in the project.	• Contains several errors in grammar, punctuation, capitalization, or spelling. These errors may interfere with the reader's understanding of the writing. • Uses little variety in sentence types. • Speaks unclearly or too quickly. May interfere with the audience's understanding of the project.	• Demonstrated uneven participation or was often off-topic. Task distribution was lopsided. • Did not show a clear plan for the project, and did not use time well. • Allowed one or two opinions to dominate the activity, or had trouble reaching a fair consensus.
1	• Addresses only one part of the writing task. • Demonstrates no understanding of purpose and audience. • Lacks a point of view, focus, organizational structure, and transitions that unify important ideas. • Lacks a central idea but may contain marginally related facts, details, and/or explanations.	• Demonstrates that the topic was poorly researched. • Does not discriminate relevant from irrelevant information. • Presents the topic incompletely, with many factual errors. • Did not reach conclusions.	• Contains serious errors in grammar, punctuation, capitalization, or spelling. These errors interfere with the reader's understanding of the writing. • Uses no sentence variety. • Speaks unclearly. The audience must struggle to understand the project.	• Demonstrated poor participation by the majority of the group. Tasks were completed by a small minority. • Failed to show planning or effective use of time. • Was dominated by a single voice, or allowed hostility to derail the project.

NAME _____   **PROJECT** _____

DATE _____

ORGANIZATION & FOCUS	CONTENT	ORAL/WRITTEN CONVENTIONS	GROUP PARTICIPATION

COMMENTS AND SUGGESTIONS

UNDERSTANDING YOUR SCORE

Organization: Your project should be clear, focused on a main idea, and organized. You should use details and facts to support your main idea.

Content: You should use strong research skills. Your project should be thorough and accurate.

Oral/Written Conventions: For writing projects, you should use good composition, grammar, punctuation, and spelling, with a good variety of sentence types. For oral projects, you should engage the class using good public speaking skills.

Group Participation: Your group should cooperate fairly and use its time well to plan, assign and revise the tasks involved in the project.

NAME _____ GROUP MEMBERS _____

_____
_____
_____
_____

Use this worksheet to describe your project by finishing the sentences below.
For individual projects and writing assignments, use the "How I did" section.
For group projects, use both "How I did" and "How we did" sections.

The purpose of this project is to :

[   ]

Scoring Key =   **4** – extremely well
                3 – well
                2 – could have been better
                1 – not well at all

HOW I DID

I understood the purpose and requirements for this project…

I planned and organized my time and work…

This project showed clear organization that emphasized the central idea…

I supported my point with details and description…

I polished and revised this project…

I utilized correct grammar and good writing/speaking style…

Overall, this project met its purpose…

HOW WE DID

We divided up tasks…

We cooperated and listened to each other…

We talked through what we didn't understand…

We used all our time to make this project the best it could be…

Overall, as a group we worked together…

I contributed and cooperated with the team…

What I Need to **Find**

I need to use: ☐ primary sources.
☐ secondary

Places I **Know** to Look

Brainstorm: Other Sources and Places to Look

WHAT I FOUND

Title/Author/Location (call # or URL)

	Book/Periodical	Website	Other		Primary Source	Secondary Source		**How I Found it** Suggestion / Library Catalog / Browsing / Internet Search / Web link		**Rate each source** from 1 (low) to 4 (high) in the categories below — helpful / relevant
_____	☐	☐	☐		☐	☐		☐ ☐ ☐ ☐ ☐		___ ___
_____	☐	☐	☐		☐	☐		☐ ☐ ☐ ☐ ☐		___ ___
_____	☐	☐	☐		☐	☐		☐ ☐ ☐ ☐ ☐		___ ___
_____	☐	☐	☐		☐	☐		☐ ☐ ☐ ☐ ☐		___ ___
_____	☐	☐	☐		☐	☐		☐ ☐ ☐ ☐ ☐		___ ___
_____	☐	☐	☐		☐	☐		☐ ☐ ☐ ☐ ☐		___ ___

ANSWER KEY

CHAPTER 1

Blackline Master
(August) light, cool clothes that you wouldn't mind getting wet (January) something warm (April) something to keep you cool
4. and 5. Answers will vary but should indicate that monsoons are essential for South Asia's agrculture, but they can result in flooding and other related devastation to homes and crops.

Chapter Test
A. 1. c 2. d 3. c 4. d 5. c
B. 6. Where the Indian landmass crashed against the Eurasian plate millions of years ago, the lowest levels of the earth's crust were pushed up to form the Himalayas. 7. as mountains were formed, valuable metals and rocks came to the surface; Himalaya mountains are the source of Indus River; erosion of the mountains provided fertile soil;
C. Essay answers will vary but should explain not only the effects of the monsoon rains but also the effects of the period right before rains come.

CHAPTER 2

Blackline Master
1. carbon dating; because the material it was carved from was once alive; comparative; written or pictorial records 2. carbon dating 3. a. carbon dating; because the food was once alive b. comparative dating 4. Possible ways: thermoluminescence; comparative; written or pictorial records

Chapter Test
A. 1. d 2. c 3. b 4. a 5. d
B. 6. The hand axe discovery showed humans lived in parts of Asia earlier than previously thought; it was the same shape as tools found in parts of India and Africa from 400,000 BCE. 7. Nagas are legendary serpent-like beings living near lakes and springs who are supposed to have the power to make the land fertile and protect humans from evil spirits.
C. Answers will vary but should include details about the effects of earthquakes and warming climate on Kashmir

CHAPTER 3

Blackline Master
Animal bones near settlement with small horns; hoof prints in corrals; physical; domesticated animals. *The mountain climate is too cold in the winter for domesticated animals*; geographical; camped there only in the summer. *Mountain camps with stone tools similar to village tools*; analogy/physical; lived in both at the same time. *Deposits of bitumen tar in the mountain passes*; geographical; probable source of bitumen tar. *Modern nomad men and boys take the herds to the high mountains while women stay in camp and weave wool bags and willow baskets*; analogy; Neolithic peoples did the same. *Shell spinning weights*; physical; Neolithic peoples spun wool and wove woolen bags. *Woven baskets with bitumen tar*; physical; they made baskets and waterproofed them with tar. *Mud bricks with the impressions of wild wheat and barley*; physical; gathered wild wheat and barley even when living in village. *Chert blades in a row with bits of bitumen tar stuck to them*; physical/analogy; *They once formed a sickle.* Modern nomads load sheep, goats, and bullocks with saddlebags; analogy; so did Neolithic peoples.

Chapter Test
A. 1. b 2. d 3. b 4. d 5. a
B. 6. settled in one place; worth protecting accumulated goods 7. more dependable food supply meant that some people could specialize 8. banded together for markets and protection
C. Answers will vary but should include: bitumin-coated basket—bitumin (a natural tar) coating made basket waterproof for carrying food; ancient sickle—stone blade attached to wooden handle with bitumin glue used for cutting grasses. Artifacts provide evidence of planting crops and domesticating animals.

CHAPTER 4

Blackline Master
Students' essays may include reports of current reliance on fast foods and microwaving as evidence that family lifestyles have changed.

Chapter Test
A. 1. a 2. c 3. c 4. b 5. a
B. 6. Beads were symbols of wealth and power. 7. They wanted to live in protected trading centers.
C. Students' essays should show they understand that because materials used in different crafts were found in far flung places, trade developed as a way for people to obtain a variety of items.

CHAPTER 5

Blackline Master
Students' garbage pot contents and comments will vary but should be consistent with chapter content; their conclusions should be supported by a logical argument.

Chapter Test
A. 1. d 2. c 3. b 4. d 5. d
B. 6. Mohenjo Daro is disintegrating so all work has been stopped; no new excavations are being made. 7. Harappa's walls made it possible to control all goods entering and exiting the city for the purpose of inspecting, weighing, and taxing them.
C. Students' paragraphs will vary but should be supported by details from the chapter.

CHAPTER 6

Blackline Master
1. A calendar is useful for keeping track of the flood season. 2. Public works that benefit all (like an irrigation system) require specialized jobs and someone (or a small group) to make decisions for others to follow. 3. Workers on public works projects could be paid from taxes on those who benefit from the project, such as a tax used to pay workers to build and maintain an irrigation system. 4. Again, farmers would pay a tax in kind (food) to support the workers. 5. Traders need to keep track of supplies of trade goods, payments made and received in the course of trading. 6. Students' summaries in their essays will vary, but should be supported by a logical argument.

Chapter Test

A. 1. c 2. c 3. d 4. b 5. c

B. 6. writing, because it enables people to store knowledge and pass along information to others in different places and times 7. seals represented a person's wealth and as such had to be protected from theft

C. Students' explanations will vary but should be supported by a logical argument.

CHAPTER 7

Blackline Master

MD = Mohenjo Daro; Dh = Dholavira

Standard-sized mud bricks: MD; Standard-sized streets, doors, and windows: MD; Streets laid out north-south and east-west: MD; Great Hall: MD; City walls: MD, Dh; Walled neighborhoods organized by profession: MD; Sacred tree: MD; Great Bath: MD; City gates with sign: Dh; Nearby farms: MD; Nearby ports: Dh; Water tanks that covered one-third of city: Dh; Sandstone block buildings: Dh

Chapter Test

A. 1. d 2. a 3. c 4. a 5. c

B. 6. Fired, wedge-shaped bricks of a standard size 7. The Great Bath was used for public ceremonies and bathing rituals.

C. In their essays students should mention the cities' drainage systems; their standardized street orientation and building materials; the organization of neighborhoods by occupation; and city walls for protection and taxation purposes.

CHAPTER 8

Blackline Master

Walking with oxcart: animal smells, creaking of car; *Camping by road*: forest, other travelers, talk of bandits; *First sight of city*: light-colored buildings on horizon; *Passing furnaces and leather-working areas*: sparks of fires, people working, smells of dead animals and smoke, sounds of workers hammering copper; *Going through gates and having goods measured and weighed*: crowds of people, interesting items being weighed, smells of foods being brought in, shouts and grumbling as taxes were paid; *Wood-carver's shop*: chests and other items made of cedar and other woods, smell of wood, sounds of wood cutting; *Jeweler's shop*: gold and silver, precious stones and colorful beads, sounds of jewelers making beads, clinking bangles and belts on customers; *Pottery shop*: children sweeping, pots for sale, sounds of potters' wheels, and customers; *Harvest Festival*: crowds of people, possibly dancing and singing, or quiet and prayerful.

Chapter Test

A. 1. c 2. c 3. b 4. a 5. b

B. 6. a clan or community leader; in a position of worship, so not a king 7. valuable because time consuming to make. A bead maker would spend 480 days making a belt of 36 carnelian beads.

C. In their essays students should mention the Harvest Festival and desire to sell farm products as reasons for the trip; various city neighborhoods the family visited, things they bought, and other sights and sounds.

CHAPTER 9

Blackline Master

Dilmun (Bahrain): pearls; *Magan (Oman)*: heavy seashells, copper, pearls; *Dholavira*: cotton cloth, monkeys, peacocks, dogs; *Harappa*: carnelian, copper and lapis lazuli beads, wood furniture; *Ur*: embroidered woolen shawls and blankets, silver, gold bangles (from Egypt); *Afghanistan*: lapis lazuli, gold, tin

Chapter Test

A. 1. c 2. c 3. a 4. b 5. c

B. 6. carnelian, copper and lapis lazuli beads, wood furniture, seashells 7. people who had left the Indus Valley to settle there

C. In their essays students should mention the sea and river route to southern Mesopotamia with the dangers from submerged islands and the frustrating route north via riverboats and oxen to Badakshan. In both cases the goods traded made up for the dangers.

CHAPTER 10

Blackline Master

The Saraswati River dried up. Farmers moved to cities on Indus or Ravi Rivers or new farmland on Ganga Plain. Trade networks collapsed; government stopped keeping records. *Writing and long-distance trade stop.* No precious stones are coming by from trade. Jewelers begin to make imitation glass beads. People from the mountains of Central Asia moved into the Indus Valley. *Horses and camels introduced to the Indus Valley.* South Asians discovered how to make iron. *Iron tools and weapons appear.*

South Asians develop new type of kiln and new methods of working clay. *New pottery styles appear.* Religious ideas changed during difficult times or new burial practices were introduced by newcomers. *People are buried differently.* Students' opinions will vary, but should be supported by evidence from the chapter.

Chapter Test

A. 1. d 2. c 3. d 4. c 5. d

B. 6. Farmers had no water for crops so they crowded into cities. Long-distance trade stopped 7. The cave paintings in Central India show Indo-Aryan speakers using horses, chariots, and iron weapons against the local people.

C. Answers will vary but should be supported by a logical argument and specific information from the chapter.

CHAPTER 11

Blackline Master

1. The Vedas had to be pronounced correctly in order to bring the gods to the sacrifice. 2. It took that long to memorize and learn to correctly pronounce the thousands of hymns in the Vedas. 3. The Vedas had to be passed along orally because they were not written down. The only way for them to be known was through reciting them.

Chapter Test

A. 1. c 2. d 3. b 4. b 5. a

B. 6. People were born into the *varna* they deserved. By their actions during life they might be reborn into a higher or lower *varna*. 7. Brahmin boys were educated by learned priests and memorized the Vedas; girls worked at home with their mothers.

C. *Harappan times*—Indus; unknown or by profession or family; important (Great Bath and drains); could read and write, but no known literature; *Vedic times*—Ganga; by varna; important (purification); memorized Vedas. Students' essays will vary but should be supported by specific information from the chapter.

CHAPTER 12

Blackline Master

Ramayana—Rama: hero of Ramayana; believed to be a form of the god Vishnu; *Sita*: wife of Rama whose capture leads to events in the story; *Ravana*: evil 10-headed demon who captures Sita; *Hanuman*: monkey king who helps Rama reunite with Sita, later worshipped as a god; *Kaikeyi*: Rama's stepmother; one of the villains of the story; *Bharata*: Rama's half brother; *Kumbakarna*: Rama's brother whom Rama asks for help

Bhagavad Gita—Arjuna: Legendary warrior prince who is the hero of the *Bhagavad Gita*; *Lord Krishna*: a form of the god Vishnu who assists Arjuna; *Drapaudi*: Legendary wife of Arjuna; *Kauravas*: cousins of Arjuna and his four brothers; *Pandavas*: Five brothers who go to war with their cousins, the Kauravas.

Chapter Test

A. 1. c 2. d 3. d 4. a 5. b

B. 6. Vedic people had horses and knew how to work with iron and gold; traded with coastal people; setting indicates where India was being settled at the time. 7. the religious message of devotion and truth

C. Students' essays should include the Vedic idea expressed in the *Bhagavad Gita* that *dharma* (duty) is the only path to peace and salvation. Without it, people (such as Arjuna) are doomed to be reborn endlessly.

CHAPTER 13

Blackline Master

Across: 1. GANESHA   5. LAKSHMI   7. SHIVA   8. PARVATI   9. SURYA   10. KALI

Down: 2. SARASWATI   3. GANGA   4. VISHNU   6. BRAHMA

Chapter Test

A. 1. a 2. c 3. c 4. b 5. c

B. 6. *Karma* is the result of your actions while alive. If you have acted in a questionable way, you have bad *karma* and can be reincarnated in a non-human body. 7. The Ganga River is a goddess cascading from the head of the god Shiva, lord of creation and destruction.

C. Students' answers should mention Brahma, the oldest god and the Ultimate Supreme Being in Hinduism, as well as the other two important gods, Shiva and Vishnu.

CHAPTER 14

Blackline Master

Four Noble Truths of Buddhism: (1) humans experience pain (2) desire or wanting is what causes this pain (3) the only way to avoid suffering is to control desire (4) a person can be freed from desire and achieve Enlightenment by living with others and following the Eightfold Path. *Eightfold Path of Buddhism*: taking the right view, resolve, speech, action, living, effort, mindfulness, and meditation. *Five Jain Tenets*: telling the truth, never stealing, never owning anything, never hurting anything, remaining celibate.

Chapter Test

A. 1. c 2. d 3. c 4. a 5. c

B. 6. Most have not survived because they were written on fragile materials such as birch bark, cloth, or palm leaves. 7. He taught people about compassion and truth, traveling on foot from place to place, using simple, easily understood words in local languages to explain his message.

C. Students' answers should indicate that the Eightfold Path is the way to achieve the freedom from desire (the last of the Four Noble Truths) and the key to Enlightenment.

CHAPTER 15

Blackline Master

Persia's Influence on South Asia—Economy: throughout Empire standardized coins and weights and measures; trade made Taxila wealthy. *Seeing New Lands*: as part of Persian army young men traveled through Persian Empire and Greece and saw products (wine, musical instruments, gemstones) and processes new to them (organized athletics and clothing styles). *Education*: Taxila university became a center for study. *Caste System*: People of the four *varnas* lived in separate areas of cities and were subdivided further into job-based castes; travelers had to honor these divisions.

Chapter Test

A. 1. c 2. a 3. d 4. b 5. c

B. 6. He deciphered the Brahmi alphabet which enabled historians to read the records and inscriptions relating to the period 800–300 BCE. 7. exposed to new ideas, products, and ways of doing things; traded with Persian Empire and Greece; standardized weights and measures; caste system further entrenched in cities; Taxila became a great trading and education center

C. Students' answers should indicate movement of people into settled communities; new technologies; exploration by traders and merchants; Persian influence: standardized coins and weights and measures; trade made Taxila wealthy.

CHAPTER 16

Blackline Master

1. elephant, 2. bull's head, 3. swastika, 4. sun and moon, 5. fenced sacred tree, 6. water tank; Students' paragraphs will vary but should include the following information: Chandragupta respects the sacred traditions of South Asia; he is a powerful leader with a strong army; he cares for and protects his people, takes care of their needs, and will bring them good luck.

Chapter Test

A. 1. b 2. c 3. a 4. d 5. d

B. 6. short term: a truce; Alexander's army refuses to fight any longer; they leave for home; long-term: on return trip most of his army died 7. Chandragupta followed Kautilya's advice to rule "with knowledge and wisdom" and founded India's first centralized government. Citizens of his kingdom were better fed, wealthier, and better educated than ever before.

C. Students' essays will vary but should be supported by specific information from the chapter.

CHAPTER 17

Blackline Master

Answers will vary; students should include discoveries in the areas mentioned—medicine, science and math.

Chapter Test

A. 1. a 2. c 3. b 4. d 5. d

B. 6. Ayurveda went beyond describing treatments and taught habits that helped people stay healthy. 7. Iron, a mixture of rock and metal, was crushed and heated over a charcoal fire; carbon from the charcoal fused with the iron to make steel; steel was used in Mauryan government mints to stamp royal symbols on silver, creating coins.

C. Students' essays will vary but should be supported by specific information from the chapter.

CHAPTER 18

Blackline Master

1. Taxila is near top center of map, beneath mountain icons.
2. Karakoram Mountains, Indus Ruver 3. Pataliputra is approximately 300 mi upriver from mouth of Ganga. 4. Ganga River 5. Sopara is on the Arabian Sea coast, below Vindhya Mountains. Tamralipti is in the lower Ganga River delta.
6. Down the Ganga River to Tamralipti along coast of India east to Sopara. 7. Vindhya Mountains.

Chapter Test

A. 1. d 2. a 3. b 4. b 5. d

B. 6. After a bloody victory by his armies he remembered the lessons of *dharma, artha, kama,* and *moksha* and proclaimed his remorse at conquering the Kalingas. 7. Brahmins objected to Ashoka's ban on animal sacrifice so they convinced leaders of different regions to break away from Mauryan Empire after Ashoka's assassination by a Brahmin general.

C. *Dharma* means living with honor and justice; *artha* means the excitement of money and success; *kama* means contentment of enjoying world's beauties and pleasures. A life filled with these qualities would enable a person to reach *moksha*, the end of the cycle of death and rebirth.

CHAPTER 19

Blackline Master

Kannaki marries Kovalan. Kovalan loses the couple's money. Kannaki and Kovalan set out to sell her ankle bracelet. They stop at the home of Madari and some cowmaids. Kannaki purifies the eating place. Kannaki washes her husband's feet. The couple eats together, an emblem of their love. Evil goldsmith steals the bracelet and murders Kovalan. Kannaki breaks her bracelets and mourns Kovalan for 14 days. Indra sprinkles Kannaki with flowers and takes to her to heaven. The gods sing a hymn praising Kannaki. Kannaki is reunited with Kovalan.

Chapter Test

A. 1. b 2. c 3. d 4. a 5. b

B. *Both*: purification, study of Vedas (only for some); *Men*: student, parent, hermit, renouncer; *Women*: learning from mother, caring for husbands and children, dying with husbands

C. Students' essays will vary but should include a woman's devotion, respect, and service to husband and the man's role of protecting his wife and being financially responsible.

CHAPTER 20

Blackline Master

Internet searches and students' drawings will provide various responses.

Chapter Test

A. 1. b 2. d 3. a 4. c 5. b

B. 6. Power struggle among leaders within south and central India and wars with outsiders—Bactrian Greeks, Parthians, and Scythians. Leaders all wanted to become the next Ashoka and unite the continent. 7. statues, festivals, saints (bodhisattvas), temples, and rituals

C. Essays should include the following similarities: learned from Buddhism and wanted to find ways to spread its message; tolerated other religions; ambitious; loved fighting and learning new things; ran well-organized empire that grew quickly and became wealthy from trade but did not last long.

CHAPTER 21

Blackline Master

Women—All: women are subject to father, husband, or son; women work at home, always cheerful, careful, frugal. *Occupations—Brahmin*: intellectuals who did the thinking; *Kshatriya*: warriors and kings *Vaisya*: merchants, gold workers; *Shudra*: exist to serve other *varnas*. *Marriage—All*: only people of same caste can marry. *Clothing/colors—Brahmin*: clothing could be wrapped but not stitched; could not wear leather; wore white with sacred thread over left shoulder; *Kshatriya*: red clothing; *Vaisya*: yellow; *Shudra* black. *Purification—All except women and Shudra*: three sips of water and wipe mouth with water three times; *Shudra*: sips and wipes mouth with water once; shaves head once a month, eats leftover food of twice-born (Brahmin) persons

Chapter Test

A. 1. b 2. c 3. c 4. d 5. c

B. 6. They become "polluted" and have to follow ritual to clean themselves; they acquire bad *karma* and are reincarnated in a lower *varna*. 7. New languages, new gods, and new people from other parts of the world came into South Asia and disrupted the traditional social organization based on *varnas*.

C. Students' paragraphs should include details from the chapter about disrupted social organization and what the Code of Manu contained.

CHAPTER 22

Blackline Master

Chandra Gupta I: through marriage and conquests united northern and central India for the first time in 500 years; *Samudra Gupta*: conquered new lands and reclaimed land conquered by his father; required poet-announcers to sing his praises throughout the day; developed new form of government in which he shared governing and decision-making with local leaders (maharajas); *Rama Gupta*: coward in battle; *Chandra Gupta II*: brother of Rama, killed enemy Rama had fled from; believed his dharma was to make peace and wealth for his people; built forts to defend his conquests; reemphasized caste system to bring order to society; *Skanda Gupta*: defeated invasion of White Huns, nomad people from Central Asia but could not hold Gupta Empire

Chapter Test

A. 1. a 2. b 3. a 4. d 5. a

B. 6. worshiped Vishnu, Shiva, the Goddess; offered milk and rice to gods; tolerant of other religions; strengthened caste system 7. The Maharajas were local leaders who were allowed to govern and make decisions affecting their local areas.

C. Students' essays should include details about how and why the caste system was reemphasized under Chandra Gupta II and about rules affecting the Chandalas (untouchables).

CHAPTER 23/EPILOGUE

Blackline Master

Essays should include the following impacts on South Asian economy: provided employment for 600 people (average temple); temples rented some of their land to farmers; kings' money went into building temples instead of for other purposes;

Chapter Test
A. 1. a 2. b 3. a 4. c

B. 5. He carried with him the knowledge he had gained as well as 657 Buddhist texts written on palm leaves and paper, which he translated from Sanskrit into Chinese. 6. By reading sacred texts at Nalanda University and by visiting caves at Ajanta to see images of sacred Buddhist stories painted on the walls.

C. Students should show an understanding of the variety of places and travelers sharing the Silk Road; the difficulty of the journey; and oases where people stopped and shared information.

WRAP-UP TEST
1. Agni, Brahma, Indra, Surya. Gods were called to sacrifices, could take the form of avatars and descend to earth to help people, inhabited clay figurines and statues.

2. Life in the village of Mehrgarh centered on agriculture; homes of mud brick had to rebuilt after monsoons and floods; Harappa was a city with a drainage system, neighborhoods of craftsmen, animal markets, and merchants, with walls to protect inhabitants, houses of brick and stone, and a bustling economy. Students will probably choose Harappa because it would have been an interesting place to live.

3. *All:* believe in *karma*, worship in temples; practice yoga or meditation, go on pilgrimages, believe one can break cycle of birth, death, and rebirth, have temples and religious statues; *Buddhism & Hinduism:* religion is spelled out in famous sacred texts; *Buddhism & Jainism:* believe all things are connected, strive for freedom from desire as a way to enlightenment, monks and nuns, non-violence against living things; *Buddhism:* stupas house Buddha's ashes, send out missionaries; *Jainism:* original tenets included celibacy; *Hinduism:* family of religious traditions, worship gods and goddesses, animal sacrifice (changed to flowers and fruits), strict social divisions.

4. Students should mention the fact that no one could read the documents or inscriptions regarding that time period until James Prinsep deciphered the Brahmi alphabet.

5. Harappa and Mohenjo Daro traded carnelian, copper and lapis lazuli beads, wood furniture through traders who sailed from Dholavira. Ships stopped at Magan (Oman) for heavy seashells, copper, pearls; on the way to cities like Ur in southern Mesopotamia. From Ur traders received embroidered woolen shawls and blankets, silver, and gold bangles (from Egypt) to bring back to India. Harappan traders who went up the Indus and Kabul Rivers to Badakshan received lapis lazuli, gold, tin in exchange for beads furniture, shell bangles, and fine cloth.

6. Historically the Vedas give insights into life and customs and culture of the people in Yamuna and Ganga River valleys who composed the Vedas orally and passed them down by memorization and recitation. Religiously, the Vedas are important as hymns, stories, and religious instruction in Sanskrit.

7. Students should define Ayurveda as a traditional form of Indian medicine and refer to specific Ayurvedic treatments. They should explain that Ayurveda goes beyond treating ailments and teaches people how to stay healthy. It is practiced today.

8. The *Ramayana*'s hero, Rama, believed to be a form of the god Vishnu, inspires viewers and readers with his devotion to his wife Sita. Rama's steadfastness and devotion are rewarded and he is reunited with Sita after vanquishing enemies. Hanuman, the monkey who helps Rama, is regarded as sacred because of the connection.

9. Ashoka was a prince who was influenced by Vedic scriptures and pursued the life of a warrior. At Kalinga, after a bloody victory in which tens of thousands of people were deported and killed, he decided to give up fighting and pursue "inner worthiness" and devotion to *dharma*. James Prinsep deciphered the Brahmi alphabet, which made it possible to read inscriptions and texts related to Ashoka and his times.

10. *Positive:* provided access to new people, ideas, products, trading partners; *Negative:* allowed invaders access to South India.

ANSWERS FOR THE STUDENT STUDY GUIDE

CHAPTER 1
Cast of Characters
Valmiki wrote the *Ramayana* in the 7th century BCE.
What Happened When?
In July and August, the monsoon rains come.
The Indus civilization began around 2600 BCE.
January 26 is the anniversary of India's independence from Great Britain.
On January 26, 2001, an earthquake struck, leaving 20,000 dead and 600,000 homeless.
Word Bank 1. Paleolithic 2. monsoons 3. millet, sorghum 4. basalt
Sequence of Events The Indian landmass crashed against the Eurasian plate millions of years ago. The lowest levels of the earth's crust were pushed up to form the Himalayas. Deeply buried layers of the crust, with metals and valuable rocks, were brought to the earth's surface. Molten rocks called lava escaped through cracks in the crust. The lava cooled. Mineral gases collected and slowly hardened to form chalcedony. Over millions of years the softer rock around the chalcedony wore away. Lumps of chalcedony were washed down the mountains and collected in the valleys.

CHAPTER 2
Cast of Characters
Hasmukh Sankalia: found evidence of human habitation in India in 400,000 BCE
What Happened When?
1969: Hasmuch Sankalia finds evidence of 400,000-year-old human habitation in Kashmir
about 1100 CE: epic of *Nilmatha Purana* written.
Do the Math: 3069 years
Word Bank Nagas
Timeline 4,000,000 years ago: A huge lake formed when the Indian subcontinent crashed into Asia. 400,000 years ago: Earthquakes tilted up one side of the valley, moving the lake and exposing new land. 200,000 years ago: Earthquakes cracked the mountain ranges and water escaped the lake, forming the Jhelum River. 10,000 BCE: The climate warmed, and humans could live on the land all year long. Ancient people in the Nagin Lake region lived there only in the summer because winters in this valley were too harsh for humans to survive.
Primary Source 1. a 2. d 3. b 4. a
Making Inferences 1. Their ancestors may have handed down that knowledge. 2. Answers will vary.

CHAPTER 3

What Happened When?
9,000 7000 5500

Word Bank 1. analogies 2. domestication 3. Neolithic

Critical Thinking Smaller animal bones were found, SO we know that people made their living by herding sheep, cattle, and goats. Archaeologists found evidence of the same kinds of tools used in both mountain camps and villages, SO it is possible that the same people lived in both places. Houses, tools, weapons, and garbage were left behind by the ancient South Asians, SO historians are able to figure out a lot about their daily lives. Neolithic South Asians couldn't write, SO we don't have any written records of their lives.

Outline Students' outlines will vary, but should include details from the chapter.

Drawing Conclusions 1. People needed to develop agriculture to have enough food to be able to stay in one place. 2. Benefits of living in one place include having a dependable food source, building durable structures, developing many different crafts. 3. The development of agriculture is called the Agricultural Revolution because it changed people's lives so much. 4. They did not understand the effects of the changes they were making because they were just a part of their everyday lives.

CHAPTER 4

What Happened When?
about 5500 BCE: villagers of Mehrgarh begin to make pottery
about 3500–3300 BCE: potters were using potter's wheel and "throwing" pots
about 2800 BCE: trading centers grow into South Asia's first cities

Go Figure 2800 BCE came after 5500 BCE.

Word Bank 1. ore 2. bangles

Word Play 1. Italian 2. baked earth 3. brown and orange

Sequence of Events The potter shaped the clay on the wheel into a pot. The potter sliced the pot off the wheel with a tightly held piece of thread. An artisan coated the inside or outside of the pot with slip. The artisan decorated the pot with red, brown, black, or white slip. The pot was fired in a kiln.

Drawing Conclusions 1. Before kilns, pots were fired by being put in bonfires covered with brush. 2. To make a pot especially beautiful, the potter could paint it with paints made with lapis lazuli or malachite. 3. Potters also made small figures for praying to gods as well as children's toys. 4. Archaeologists believe women may have made the first coiled pots because they needed them for cooking, and because they made the baskets that came before the pots and they have similar designs. 5. Men began making pots after the potter's wheel was developed, because it takes more strength and training that cannot be achieved between other tasks.

Write About It Students' ads will vary but should be based on details from the chapter. South Asian craftspeople wanted to live in larger towns because there were more people to buy their crafts and the town walls would protect their workshops.

CHAPTER 5

Cast of Characters
1. Alexander Cunningham was a British archaeologist who was digging in the area that the British army was building a railroad in the Punjab in the 1850s. 2. He was hoping to find evidence of Buddhist times, about 500 BCE. 3. He found a stone seal that had a picture of a unicorn and some writing carved on it. This was the first artifact found of the Indus civilization that was 5,000 years old.

What Happened When?
about 2600 BCE: Harappa had two major walled sections; baked-brick houses filled the city
about 1900 BCE: Harappa begins to decline
about 500 BCE: Buddhist times in Punjab
early 1850s: Cunningham excavates at Harappa, finds carved stone seal
1893: Cunningham dies
early 1920s: scientists begin to realize what is at Harappa

Word Bank caravanserai

Word Play Students' words, definitions, and sentences will vary.

Critical Thinking Things that would be found in Harappa: gateways, offices, markets, craft workshops, drainage systems

With a Parent or Partner Have students read their essays to the class. 1.–2. Students' answers will vary.

CHAPTER 6

What Happened When?
about 4500 BCE: early potter's marks on pottery at Mehrgarh and Baluchistan
about 4000 BCE: early graffiti on pottery
about 3300 BCE: earliest examples of graffiti on pottery from Harappa
about 2800–2600 BCE: writing spreading rapidly throughout Indus Valley

Word Bank 1. graffiti 2. steatite 3. faience

Word Play Students should write definition and sentence for *shards*.

Compare and Contrast Indus script: 2,000 examples found, not related to any known writing system, written from right to left, sometimes written in boustrophedon style, used about 450 symbols, used both symbols and letters; Urdu: written from right to left; Sumerian: first used more than 700 symbols, number of symbols later dropped to fewer than 50

Fact or Opinion 1. Fact 2. Fact 3. Opinion 4. Fact 5. Opinion 6. Fact 7. Opinion 8. Fact 9. Fact 10. Fact

CHAPTER 7

Cast of Characters
Heather M.-L. Miller specializes in pyrotechnics and medieval trade routes.

What Happened When?
The Great Bath was built at Mohenjo Daro about 2000 BCE.

Word Bank orientation

Word Play 1. Pyr means "fire." 2. Definitions will vary. 3. Examples will vary but may include fireworks displays.

Critical Thinking Students' outlines will vary but should include ideas and details from the chapter. Students' paragraphs will vary.

Comprehension 1. Miller wanted to avoid bugs, snakes, and diseases. 2. a 3. c 4. c 5. For Miller, the most important thing about archaeology is that it connects people to the past.

CHAPTER 8

What Happened When?
Sarang's fictional trip takes place about 2100 BCE.
Hinduism's roots go back to 2600–1900 BCE.

Word Bank 1. inlay 2. yoga

Word Play 1. Possible answer: ornament allowed to hang free 2. Possible answer: an electrical fixture hanging from the ceiling 3. Possible answers: Middle English, Middle French, Latin

Critical Thinking Coppersmiths and potters worked on the southern edge of Harappa SO that the sparks from their furnaces would be blown away from the crowded city streets. It took several days to drill a hole in one long bead, SO it would have taken one worker more than 480 working days to complete a belt of 36 beads. The flat clay disks used to cover pots have been found to have child-sized hand- and footprints pressed into them, SO archaeologists believe that children helped make them. People traveling to the city from the country with their goods would have set up camp with other travelers SO that their goods would be protected from bandits who hid in the forest.

With a Parent or Partner Have volunteers tell about their experiences with yoga.

CHAPTER 9

Cast of Characters
Queen Puabi of Ur: Mesopotamian queen whose burial tomb had extravagant materials
King Sargon: Mesopotamian king
What Happened When?
The Indus Valley civilization was discovered in the 1920s.
Word Bank 1. landing place where boats can load or unload cargo 2. two: *kee* and *kway* 3. key
Comprehension Order of sailing: The ship sailed west from Dholavira across the delta of the Indus River. The coast became dangerously rocky and the waters filled with sea snakes. The captain could sail across the Arabian Sea to Oman, or sail directly north through the Persian Gulf to Mesopotamia. The ship arrived at the delta of the Tigris and Euphrates Rivers. A local fisherman was hired to help guide the ship through the channels of the Tigris and Euphrates Delta. The ship arrived in Ur. 1. b 2. c 3. c
All Over the Map 1.–2. Have students show their work. 3. Traders would have to cross mountains and rivers. 4. about 1,500 miles 5. over 2,000 miles

CHAPTER 10

What Happened When?
about 1900 BCE: Saraswati River began to dry up.
about 1500–600 BCE: Indo-Aryan invaders gained power in Ganges Valley.
about 1200–600 BCE: Iron came into common use in Indus Valley.
Do the Math 1,300 years
Word Bank 1. Aryans 2. Intrepidly 3. Indo-Aryan
Critical Thinking Students' outlines will vary, but should include ideas and details from the chapter.
Comprehension 1. b 2. b 3. *Arya* referred to a person who spoke the ancient Sanskrit language. 4. The *Rig Veda* is a collection of Sanskrit chants and hymns sung to the gods and goddesses. 5. c

CHAPTER 11

Cast of Characters
God of war and rain: Indra
Sun god: Surya
God of fire and sacrifice: Agni
River goddesses: Saraswati, Ganga
Creator and sustainer of the universe: Brahma
What Happened When?
Around 2000 BCE, the Saraswati began to dry up, older cities were abandoned, and new farming areas were carved out of the jungle.
Word Bank 1. mantras 2. Vedas

Critical Thinking A person lived a good life, SO he or she would be born into a higher class. A person did not live a good life, SO he or she would be born into a lower class. Ketu was born in to a priestly Brahmin family, SO everyone believed that he had followed the rules of the Vedas in his last life. A person lived a perfect life, SO he or she would be united with the universe. The work that Shudras did was considered unclean, SO they were not allowed to learn mantras.

Sequence of Events Ketu's father and the priests brought out a wood plank and a wooden drill to kindle the sacred fire. Ketu's father pulled back and forth on the cord wrapped around the wooden drill, so that the drill pressed into the wood plank. After a few turns, the stick started to smoke and the charred wood powder began to glow. A priest blew on the glowing embers and added kindling soaked in butter. Agni sprang to life.

Write About It 1. The kitchen was located in the northeastern part of the house because that was the purest and most holy part of the home. 2. During Vedic times, people from different varnas could not marry, but that practice was later discouraged and then banned. 3. The sacred thread was a symbol of the boys' second birth as Brahmin students. 4. The Vedic people discriminated against the Dasa because they did not speak Sanskrit, they had darker skin, and the Vedics believed they were barbarians. 5. The ancestors of the Dasa were the Harappans.

CHAPTER 12

Access
Prince Arjuna: M; hero of *Mahabharata*
Princess Draupadi: M; wife of Arjuna
the Pandavas: M; brothers of Arjuna
the Kauravas: M; cousins and enemies of Arjuna and Pandavas
Lord Krishna: M; god who preserves life
Prince Rama: R; hero of *Ramayana*
Sita: R; wife of Rama
Kaikeyi: R; Rama's step-mother who sends Rama into exile for 14 years
Bharata: R; son of Kaikeyi, becomes crown prince when Rama is in exile
Lakshmana: R; younger brother of Rama
Ravana: R; ten-headed demon that captures Sita
Hanuman: R; brave monkey who helps Rama find Sita
Kumbakarna: brother of Ravana
What Happened When?
9th century BCE: *Mahabharata*
7th century BCE: *Ramayana*
Go Figure The *Mahabharata* was written first, about 200 years before the *Ramayana*.
Word Bank avatar
Word Play 1. A cudgel is a short, heavy club. 2. To cudgel someone means to hit them repeatedly. 3. Possible answer: I would not like to be cudgeled awake because it would hurt.
Critical Thinking Students' outlines will vary but should contain ideas and details from the chapter. 1. The *Ramayana* was written by Valmiki. 2. The three heroes of the *Ramayana* are Prince Rama, Laksmana, and Hanuman. 3. Monkeys are considered sacred because of the help they gave Rama and Sita.
All Over the Map 1. Conch shell markers should appear along the western coast of South Asia. 2. The major battle site should be identified as Kurukshatra. 3. The Yamuna and Ganga rivers should be labeled. 4. The Saraswati River, which dried up, should be labeled. 5. The people had to travel more than 1,000 miles to collect conch shells (up the Yamuna River, and then down the Indus River to the coast).

CHAPTER 13

Cast of Characters
Arjuna: hero of *Mahabharata*
Mahavira: founded religion of Jainism
Siddharta Gautama: founded religion of Buddhism

What Happened When?
Shiva joined Brahma and Vishnu as one of the three major Hindu gods about 1000 BCE. By the 6th century BCE, Mahavira and Siddhartha Gautama were trying to find gentler, more peaceful ways of finding God.

Word Bank Hindus; *karma*; reincarnated

Critical Thinking Brahmin acts of purification: bathe in sacred rivers, sing hymns to gods and goddesses, give alms to the poor and charitable organizations, take care of old and weak animals and people, give away all their money, devote themselves to meditation, and make pilgrimages to sacred places.

Compare and Contrast Shiva: Has 3 eyes, Holds a trident, Holds a conch shell, Has a masculine and a feminine side, Is sometimes completely female, Known as the Mother Goddess, "The Destroyer" Vishnu: Also appears as Krishna, Has four heads, Holds a conch shell, Holds a lotus, Can be destructive, or loving and gentle, "The Protector" Brahma: Holds prayer beads, Rides a swan or goose, Holds a conch shell, "The Creator"

CHAPTER 14

Cast of Characters
Vardamana (Mahavira): prince born in 6th century BCE whose ideas developed into Jainism
Prashavanatha: holy man who lived about 800 BCE whose teachings Mahavira followed
Ashoka: ruler of the Mauryan Empire who made Buddhism the state religion

What Happened When?
sometime during the sixth century BCE: Vardamana was born.
about 800 BCE: Prashavanatha taught about how to live a pure life.
about 261 BCE: Emperor Ashoka converted to Buddhism and made Buddhism the state religion.
about 2500 BCE: earliest images of people meditating

Word Bank Eightfold Path sangha

Critical Thinking Students' outlines will vary but should include ideas and details from the chapter. 1. *Moksha* means "release from the cycle of rebirth." 2. *Jina* is another word for the five senses, and means "conquerors."

Drawing Conclusions Humans experience pain. Desire or wanting is what causes this pain. The only way to control suffering is to control desire. A person can be freed from desire and achieve Enlightenment by living with others and following the Eightfold Path. Eightfold Path: The eight ways to freedom of desire are taking the right view, resolve, speech, action, living, effort, mindfulness, and meditation.

CHAPTER 15

Access
1. to fight the Greeks; 2. new products such as wine, musical instruments, gemstones, and new practices such as athletics and different ways of dress; 3. coins with pictures of gods and rulers on them

Cast of Characters
John Prinsep: English tradesman who brought coin-making machinery to India and made copper coins for use in Indian trade
James Princep: son of John; studied ancient Indian coins and deciphered Brahmi alphabet
Cyrus the Great of Persia: founder of the Achaemenid dynasty of Persia; conquered parts of Afghanistan and the Indus Valley

Challenge: Achaemenid dynasty

What Happened When?
1819: James Prinsep sets sail for India, where he will study ancient coins and decipher the Brahmi alphabet
1780: John Prinsep brings the first coin-making machinery to India
800–300 BCE: People move to settled communities in South Asia and start trading with Sri Lanka, Southeast Asia, Arabia, and northern Africa.
558–529 BCE: Cyrus the Great rules Persia.

Do the Math 2,348 years

Word Bank mint indigo satrap

Comprehension 1. d 2. c 3. *varnas* were priests, castes were job-based groups 4. b

Write About It Taxila was a wealthy center of trade, so there were many opportunities to make money. It was also a center of learning and religious thought, and was a very beautiful and prosperous city, where people from all over came together.

All Over the Map Check students' maps against map on page 106 of the Student Edition.

CHAPTER 16

Cast of Characters
King Ambhi: king of Taxila and ally of Alexander the Great
King Porus: king in the Punjab and opponent of Alexander the Great
Sikander: Indian name of Alexander the Great, the Macedonian ruler who conquered Egypt, Persia, and northern India
Arrian: diplomat travelling with Alexander the Great
Firdausi: Persian poet who compiled accounts of Alexander the Great
Chandragupta: founder of India's Mauryan dynasty
Kautilya: adviser to Chandragupta

What Happened When?
327 BCE: Alexander the Great marches into Taxila and the Punjab
317 BCE: Chandragupta controls much of the Indian subcontinent

Word Bank paladins centralized

Word Play 1. Latin *futilis*, meaning leaky 2. one meaning is useless, unsuccessful; the other meaning is frivolous 3. sentences will vary

Critical Thinking
Sequence of Events 5. Alexander and his men attacked Porus's army during a heavy rainstorm. 6. The battle lasted for more than eight hours. 3. Alexander sent small bands of men out at night to trick Porus. 7. Thousands of warriors and their horses and elephants were killed. 9. Both armies were exhausted, and Alexander called a truce. 2. Porus refused to surrender. 1. Alexander demanded that Porus surrender at once. 8. Porus was wounded, but he led the charge against Alexander's forces. 4. Porus sent troops out to meet Alexander, but no one was there.

Outline
Under Topic I: rule by knowledge and wisdom instead of by force; spy on people to know what they are doing; assassinate enemies. Under Topic II: built highway system and installed guards to protect travelers against bandits; set up ministries to strengthen and centralize power and protect wealth. Under Topic III: superintendent of mines; superintendent of trade of goods from the sea; superintendent of metals; superintendent of forests.

CHAPTER 17

Cast of Characters
1. Aryabhata 2. *Arhabhatiyam* 3. The poem explains the movement of the sun and planets. 4. People memorized the poem and recited it. 5. The original paper it was written on might have gotten destroyed, and we would have lost the poem forever.

What Happened When?
476 CE: Aryabhata is born

Word Bank rejuvenation Ayurveda

Fact or Opinion? Ayurveda has been around for 5,000 years (F). A lot of people still use Ayurveda. (F) Many Indian mothers massage their babies with oils.(O) They believe the massages help soothe their children and prevent stomach pains.(O) Western doctors used leeches until the beginning of the 20th century.(F) Ayurvedic surgeons knew that patients and surgical instruments had to be clean to stop infections.(F) Ayurvedic nursing homes were probably located outside the cities. (O)

Making Inferences 1. herbal medicines, massage, surgery, yoga, meditation. 2. It taught good habits to help people stay healthy as well as making ill people well again.

Think About It Modern medicine usually addresses illness directly, and focuses on painful symptoms. It doesn't focus as much on preventing illness.

Main Idea and Supporting Details 1. Cross out (c) 2. Cross out (b) and (d) 3. Cross out (d)

Write About It Zero allows people to write numbers in columns so they can add, subtract, multiply, and divide numbers. It also helps them keep track of numbers on a counting board.

CHAPTER 18

Access Brahmins: bows and arrows; Kshatriya: swords; Vaisya: lance; Shudra: mace

Cast of Characters
Ashoka: greatest of Mauryan emperors who popularized Buddhism
Bindusara: Mauryan king; son of Chandragupta and father of Ashoka
Chandragupta: founder of Mauyran dynasty

What Happened When?
269 BCE: Death of Bindusara, Ashoka's father
265 BCE: Ashoka defeats all his rivals and becomes king of northern subcontinent
185 BCE: The last Mauryan ruler is assassinated

Word Bank Sentences will vary; note definitions: *dharma*: living with honor and justice; *artha*: the excitement of money and success; *kama*: contentment of enjoying beauty and pleasures; *moksha*: the end of the cycle of life, death, and rebirth.

Outline Topic I: Kalinga was a rich and powerful state from trade with Southeast Asia, and its highways connected north and south India; Topic II: a quarter of the Kalingans were killed or wounded, others were taken prisoner, and Kalingan homes and fields were destroyed. Topic III: He regretted all the destruction and decided to rule by dharma rather than by force, and to promote the teachings of Buddha

Primary Sources
1. dharma is living with honor and justice; 2. Ashoka hated to see the destruction he had caused by defeating the Kalingans, and he wanted to rule in a new way, promoting peace and justice instead of ruling by force.

All Over the Map Check answers against map on page 123; 4. About 2,000 miles, using the coastal route

CHAPTER 19

Cast of Characters
Ilango Adigal: author of "The Ankle Bracelet"

What Happened When?
200 BCE–200 CE height of Buddhist influence
1500–500 BCE Vedic communities spread from Indus to Ganga River valley

Word Bank 1. vegetarian 2. cremation 3. sanctify

Word Play 1. cinnabar 2. bright red 3. blood, life, fertility, and power

Primary Sources
3. The cowgirls helped Kannaki prepare a vegetarian meal for Kovalan. 4. Kannaki washed her husband's feet. 7. Kannaki gave Kovalan one of her bracelets to sell. 1. Kovalan wasted all their money, so he and Kannaki decided to move and begin a new life. 9. Kannaki lay on the sacred mountain for 14 days, grieving. 2. They arrived at the house of some poor cowherds. 10. The god Indra took Kannaki to heaven as a goddess, where she was reunited with Kovalan. 8. Kovalan was killed, and the bracelet stolen. 5. Kannaki sprinkled water on the ground and beat the soil with her palms. 6. She served him the food, and they ate their dinner together.

Drawing Conclusions
1. so they don't accidentally swallow and kill insects drawn by lamplight; 2. washing each other's feet, touching the ground near their feet, putting both hands together and bowing the head; 3. no because it was considered improper; 4. The people of ancient South Asia believed it was improper to write about women in historical accounts, which are written by men and are mainly about the deeds and activities of men.

Outline Stage I: learned at home, then started school. Depending on caste attended school to learn Vedic scriptures. Onto university in Taxila. Stage II: Marriage and children. Stage III: Give up wealth to oldest son and retire to community of older men and teach a new generation of boys. Stage IV: after birth of first grandson, renounce all needs and become a wandering beggar, or live at a temple until ready for death and rebirth.

CHAPTER 20

Cast of Characters
Kanishka: briefly united the northern subcontinent, first century BC

What Happened When?
1. 232 BCE: Death of Ashoka
2. end of 3rd century BCE: fighting between Bactrian Greeks and Parthians in northern Indus Valley
3. 2nd century BCE: Kushana tribe moves into northern Afghanistan and spread Greek and Persian culture to South Asia
4. about 200 CE: Buddhist temples become more elaborate

Word Bank c. being of perfect knowledge who unselfishly helps others to become like him/her.

Word Play tolerance: a willingness or ability to tolerate; forbearance

Critical Thinking Ashoka and Kanishka overlap in similarities:
1. Ambitious 2. Loved fighting 3. Loved learning new things 4. Wanted to share Buddhism with his people

Primary Sources 1. He modeled the weight and value of his gold and silver coins after the Romans and the Greeks 2. "King of Kings Kanishka Kushana" 3. Shiva and the Greek gods Hephaestus and Helios to the Persian goddess of fortune.

CHAPTER 21

Access 1. d 2. a 3. f 4. c 5. b 6. e

Cast of Characters

Manu: mythical author of the Laws of Manu

What Happened When?

Code of Manu

Word Bank purify: cleanse or make pure

Critical Thinking A person made a lot of mistakes in his last life resulting in bad *karma*, SO he became ritually unclean. The "clacking" noise of wooden shoes was heard coming down the street, SO Brahmins were not allowed to use leather, even for their shoes. By 1 CE, society was beginning to fall apart, SO the Brahmins introduced the Code of Manu to help organize society. Leather could not be purified by fire, SO Brahmins were not allowed to use leather even for their shoes. A person behaved well in his current life, SO that his good *karma* would help make his next life better. A person did not follow the actions or rituals of his caste, SO he was born a Shudra, the lowest *varna* in the next life.

CHAPTER 22

Cast of Characters

Chandra Gupta I: greatest ruler of the Gupta era, 376–415 CE. Fa Hein: Chinese pilgrim who visited India to collect Buddhist scriptures in 405–411 CE. Kalidasa: great poet and writer of Gupta era, 5th and 6th centuries. Rama Gupta: cowardly son of Samudra Gupta, reigned 376 CE. Xuanzang: Chinese Buddhist monk, 602–648 CE. Samudra Gupta: Gupta emperor, reigned 335–376 CE. Kautilya: Chandragupta Maurya's great political adviser, 4th century BCE. Chandra Gupta II: greatest ruler of the Gupta era, reigned 376–415 CE. Skanda Gupta: Gupta emperor who defeats the first Hun invaders, reigned 455–467 CE.

What Happened When?

320 CE: Indian prince married an Indian princess. 376 CE: Rama Gupta succeeded Samudra Gupta. 5th century CE: tribes of White Huns began raiding northern India.

Word Bank Maharajas

All Over the Map

1.–4. Check students' work against map on page 54. 5. a) about 1,300 miles b) about 900 miles

CHAPTER 23/EPILOGUE

Cast of Characters

Xuanzang: Chinese Buddhist monk. 1. Traveled to India. 2. Wrote *A Record of the Western Regions*. 3. Crossed the desert that lay between China and India.

What Happened When?

627 CE: Xuanzang crossed the desert that lay between China and India.

Word Bank 1. mudras 2. oasis

Comprehension Hindu myths for ordinary people: g. Puranas Buddhist sermons: b. Tripitaka. Explains what a *bodhisattva* is: h. Sutras. Stories for children about animals: e. Panchatantra. Stories about Buddha that explain what *karma* is: h. Sutras. The oldest Hindu scriptures, including the Rig Veda: c. Vedas. Poem about Prince Arjuna: a. Mahabharata. Story of Prince Rama and his wife Sita: d. Ramayana.

Fact or Opinion? Fact: It was against the law for Xuanzang to leave China and cross the desert. Fact: Xuanzang stayed in India for 13 years. Opinion: Xuanzang probably would have said that his time at the University of Nalanda was the most important part of his trip. Opinion: Xuanzang may have visited the Ajanata caves at some point in his studies. Opinion: If Xuanzang visited the caves today, he probably would not be studying Buddhism, but life at the Gupta court. Fact: Xuanzang took 657 Buddhist text back to China with him. Fact: Xuanzang translated the texts from Sanskrit into Chinese.